VOLUME 535

SEPTEMBER 1994

THE ANNALS

of The American Academy *of* Political
and Social Science

RICHARD D. LAMBERT, *Editor*
ALAN W. HESTON, *Associate Editor*

THE ARMS TRADE:
PROBLEMS AND PROSPECTS
IN THE POST-COLD WAR WORLD

Special Editors of this Volume

ROBERT E. HARKAVY   STEPHANIE G. NEUMAN

Pennsylvania State University   *Columbia University*
University Park   *New York City*

 SAGE Periodicals Press *THOUSAND OAKS LONDON NEW DELHI*

THE ANNALS

© 1994 *by* The American Academy *of* Political *and* Social Science

Editorial Office: 3937 Chestnut Street, Philadelphia, PA 19104.

For information about membership (individuals only) and subscriptions (institutions), address:*

SAGE PUBLICATIONS, INC.
2455 Teller Road
Thousand Oaks, CA 91320

From India and South Asia, *write to:*	*From the UK, Europe, the Middle East and Africa, write to:*
SAGE PUBLICATIONS INDIA Pvt. Ltd.	SAGE PUBLICATIONS LTD
P.O. Box 4215	6 Bonhill Street
New Delhi 110 048	London EC2A 4PU
INDIA	UNITED KINGDOM

SAGE Production Staff: ERIC L. LAW, LIANN LECH, DORIS HUS, and JANELLE LeMASTER
Please note that members of The Academy receive THE ANNALS with their membership.
Library of Congress Catalog Card Number 93-85878
International Standard Serial Number ISSN 0002-7162
International Standard Book Number ISBN 0-8039-5593-6 (Vol. 535, 1994 paper)
International Standard Book Number ISBN 0-8039-5592-8 (Vol. 535, 1994 cloth)
Manufactured in the United States of America. First printing, September 1994.

The articles appearing in THE ANNALS are indexed in *Academic Index, Book Review Index, Combined Retrospective Index Sets, Current Contents, General Periodicals Index, Public Affairs Information Service Bulletin, Pro-Views,* and *Social Sciences Index.* They are also abstracted and indexed in *ABC Pol Sci, America: History and Life, Automatic Subject Citation Alert, Book Review Digest, Family Resources Database, Higher Education Abstracts, Historical Abstracts, Human Resources Abstracts, International Political Science Abstracts, Managing Abstracts, Periodica Islamica, Sage Urban Studies Abstracts, Social Planning / Policy & Development Abstracts, Social Sciences Citation Index, Social Work Research & Abstracts, Sociological Abstracts, United States Political Science Documents,* and/or *Work Related Abstracts,* and are available on microfilm from University Microfilms, Ann Arbor, Michigan.

Information about membership rates, institutional subscriptions, and back issue prices may be found on the facing page.

Advertising. Current rates and specifications may be obtained by writing to THE ANNALS Advertising and Promotion Manager at the Thousand Oaks office (address above).

Claims. Claims for undelivered copies must be made no later than three months following month of publication. The publisher will supply missing copies when losses have been sustained in transit and when the reserve stock will permit.

Change of Address. Six weeks' advance notice must be given when notifying of change of address to ensure proper identification. Please specify name of journal. Send address changes to: THE ANNALS, c/o Sage Publications, Inc., 2455 Teller Road, Thousand Oaks, CA 91320.

Origin and Purpose. The Academy was organized December 14, 1889, to promote the progress of political and social science, especially through publications and meetings. The Academy does not take sides in controverted questions, but seeks to gather and present reliable information to assist the public in forming an intelligent and accurate judgment.

Meetings. The Academy occasionally holds a meeting in the spring extending over two days.

Publications. THE ANNALS is the bimonthly publication of The Academy. Each issue contains articles on some prominent social or political problem, written at the invitation of the editors. Also, monographs are published from time to time, numbers of which are distributed to pertinent professional organizations. These volumes constitute important reference works on the topics with which they deal, and they are extensively cited by authorities throughout the United States and abroad. The papers presented at the meetings of The Academy are included in THE ANNALS.

Membership. Each member of The Academy receives THE ANNALS and may attend the meetings of The Academy. Membership is open only to individuals. Annual dues: $49.00 for the regular paperbound edition (clothbound, $72.00). Add $12.00 per year for membership outside the U.S.A. Members may also purchase single issues of THE ANNALS for $14.00 each (clothbound, $19.00). Add $2.00 for shipping and handling on all prepaid orders.

Subscriptions. THE ANNALS (ISSN 0002-7162) is published six times annually—in January, March, May, July, September, and November. Institutions may subscribe to THE ANNALS at the annual rate: $168.00 (clothbound, $196.00). Add $12.00 per year for subscriptions outside the U.S.A. Institutional rates for single issues: $28.00 each (clothbound, $33.00).

Second class postage paid at Thousand Oaks, California, and additional offices.

Single issues of THE ANNALS may be obtained by individuals who are not members of The Academy for $14.00 each (clothbound, $19.00). Add $2.00 for shipping and handling on all prepaid orders. Single issues of THE ANNALS have proven to be excellent supplementary texts for classroom use. Direct inquiries regarding adoptions to THE ANNALS c/o Sage Publications (address below).

All correspondence concerning membership in The Academy, dues renewals, inquiries about membership status, and/or purchase of single issues of THE ANNALS should be sent to THE ANNALS c/o Sage Publications, Inc., 2455 Teller Road, Thousand Oaks, CA 91320. Telephone: (805) 499-0721; FAX/Order line: (805) 499-0871. *Please note that orders under $30 must be prepaid.* Sage affiliates in London and India will assist institutional subscribers abroad with regard to orders, claims, and inquiries for both subscriptions and single issues.

Printed on recycled, acid-free paper

95 0308

THE ANNALS

of The American Academy *of* Political *and* Social Science

RICHARD D. LAMBERT, *Editor*
ALAN W. HESTON, *Associate Editor*

―――――――――――― **FORTHCOMING** ――――――――――――

EMPLOYEE DISMISSAL: JUSTICE AT WORK
Special Editor: Stuart Henry

Volume 536   November 1994

ETHICS IN AMERICAN PUBLIC SERVICE
Special Editor: Harry W. Reynolds, Jr.

Volume 537   January 1995

BEING AND BECOMING CANADA
Special Editors: Charles F. Doran and Ellen Reisman Babby

Volume 538   March 1995

See page 3 for information on Academy membership and
purchase of single volumes of **The Annals.**

CONTENTS

BOOK DEPARTMENT CONTENTS

INTERNATIONAL RELATIONS AND POLITICS

AFRICA, ASIA, AND LATIN AMERICA

EUROPE

UNITED STATES

SOCIOLOGY

ECONOMICS

PREFACE

The rather sudden and unexpected ending of the Cold War has resulted in fundamental changes in the international system and in the conduct of global diplomacy. Likewise, and as an obvious correlate, there have been significant changes in the workings of the international arms trade, which, as has often been observed, is a key indicator of the state of international affairs, policy writ large.

Some 15 years ago, the special editors of this volume coedited a general work on arms transfers, *Arms Transfers in the Modern World*.[1] In light of the massive recent upheavals in international affairs, we thought this an appropriate juncture to publish a new collection of articles on this subject, which would examine the prospects for the arms trade in the emerging new world order of the 1990s.

The contributions presented here will, we hope, provide a panoramic perspective on most of the important aspects of arms transfers. Some, such as those on supplier markets or on arms control, represent the latest thinking and information on subjects that have long been the focus of attention in the arms trade literature. Others, such as the contributions on financing and intelligence, represent initial attempts at opening up new areas of inquiry.

The article by Robert Harkavy compares patterns of the arms trade in the interwar, postwar (Cold War), and emerging post-Cold War periods, raising the question of whether some currently emerging trends are reminiscent of the 1930s, before the age of superpower bipolarity. That by Ian Anthony reviews the different types of available data on the arms trade and uses currently available aggregate data to assess current trends and to offer a speculative projection of macro trends over the medium term. The article by Elisabeth Sköns and Herbert Wulf discusses the ongoing internationalization of arms production and trade, focusing on multinational production programs not only within Europe or on a transatlantic basis but now also involving cooperative projects between firms in the West and in Russia.

Michael Brzoska and Frederic Pearson provide a comparative analysis of the arms production and trade policies—and the opportunities and motives—of each of the major supplier nations, namely, the United States, Russia, the major European countries, China, and also third-tier countries. The article by Keith Krause focuses on the recipient side and on arms transfers to the crucial Middle Eastern region. It actually shifts the focus somewhat away from arms transfers toward overall changes in weapons arsenals and the relationship between weapons and armed forces. That by Stephanie Neuman reexamines the debate over the relationship between arms transfers, military industrial production, and economic development, long a staple conceptual

1. New York: Praeger, 1979.

8

issue in the academic literature and a contentious one. She argues that as the Cold War has receded, the debate on this issue has become less heated. Emerging today is a tentative consensus between old antagonists that the relationship between the military sector and development—if there is one—is more complex than originally believed.

In an emerging global situation that witnesses the increasing commercialization and partial depoliticization of the arms trade, Joel Johnson focuses on the financing of that trade. He shows that with the end of the Cold War, and the sharp decline in military assistance formerly available from the superpowers, the issue of how arms sales are financed will become more important for purchasers and vendors. The article by David Silverberg indicates how, as the demand for defense goods declines in the post-Cold War era, the major arms-producing nations are attempting to convert their defense industries to civilian production, albeit in all cases—the United States, Western Europe, Russia—with little success.

Michael Moodie's contribution examines whether the new features of the post-Cold War security landscape create an environment more conducive or more hostile to control of the arms trade, focusing on what he perceives as a widening North-South split on this issue. Geoffrey Kemp's article provides some historical perspective on U.S. arms transfer policies, in which he points out that the global impact of arms transfers has increased over the past sixty years and that American foreign policy has been greatly influenced by decisions to transfer, or not to transfer, weapons. He reviews the tensions between idealist and realist tendencies in U.S. arms transfer policies.

Henry Sokolski provides an analysis of U.S. intelligence capabilities and policies in connection with the emerging arms trade of the 1990s, an important aspect of this subject for which there was heretofore almost no academic literature. Seth Carus, meanwhile, examines the forthcoming impact on the arms trade of the now vaunted Military Technical Revolution, that is, of the new revolutionary military technologies demonstrated by the United States in Desert Storm. He sees the Military Technical Revolution as potentially producing a fundamental change in the arms trade. The contribution by Aaron Karp directs attention to the dark underside of the arms trade, the black and gray trades involving covert, clandestine transfers either with or without knowledge or involvement by supplier state governments. Once thought virtually a historical anachronism, the clandestine private trade has made a comeback in the Iraq-Iran war and in other situations where combatants or isolated states have been embargoed. Finally, Christian Catrina provides an outline of past and present areas of research focuses in the arms trade literature and some suggestions for future needed lines of research.

The special editors wish to acknowledge a number of institutions and individuals that have provided financial and administrative support for this project. The John D. and Catherine T. MacArthur Foundation funded a workshop at Columbia University in November 1993 that allowed the contributors to this volume to present initial drafts of their work and to have them critiqued and discussed. That workshop was administered by Columbia's Institute for War and Peace Studies. Our thanks to the director, David Baldwin, for his support and to the institute's administrative staff, which handled the many organizational details and helped to make the workshop a success. Additional support was provided by the Institute for Policy Research and Evaluation, the director of which is Irwin Feller, and the Political Science Department at the Pennsylvania State University. We also acknowledge the contributions of the many arms trade experts who attended the workshop and offered valuable suggestions to the authors. In addition to the authors, workshop participants were Richard K. Betts* (Columbia University), Steve Chan* (University of Colorado), Joseph J. Collins* (U.S. Military Academy), Dan Dennison (Department of Defense), Ingemar Dörfer (Foreign Ministry of Sweden), Carol Evans (Central Intelligence Agency), Lee Feinstein (Arms Control Association), Richard F. Grimmett* (Library of Congress), Carlo Grunow (U.S. Army), Priscilla Hayner (Joyce Mertz-Gilmore Foundation), David Isenberg (Center for Defense Information), Charles J. Jefferson (Department of State), Ethan B. Kapstein* (Harvard University), Efraim Karsh* (King's College London), Michael Klare* (Hampshire College), Edward A. Kolodziej* (University of Illinois), Edward J. Laurance (Monterey Institute of International Studies), Dan McMahon (Department of Defense), Morton Miller (consultant), Michael D. Morin (Department of State), Alden F. Mullins, Jr.* (Department of State), Andrew J. Pierre* (Carnegie Endowment for International Peace), Andrew L. Ross (U.S. Naval War College), Peter Schoettle (Department of State), John Thomas Tyler (Department of Defense), Dov S. Zakheim* (SPC International Corporation), and John Zavales (consultant).[2]

The special editors believe that the quality of this volume has been immeasurably improved by the generous support it received.

ROBERT E. HARKAVY
STEPHANIE G. NEUMAN

2. An asterisk denotes a workshop discussant.

ANNALS, *AAPSS*, **535**, September 1994

The Changing International System and the Arms Trade

By ROBERT E. HARKAVY

ABSTRACT: This article examines the impact of the changing structure of the international system on various aspects of the arms trade. The passing of the Cold War allows for comparative analysis of three distinct international systems: the interwar, the postwar or Cold War, and the emerging post-Cold War period. This involves gauging the impact of changing system structure (bipolarity, multipolarity), the degree of ideological conflict at the big-power level, alliance patterns, rates of military technological change, and so forth on such aspects of the arms trade as supplier markets, patterns of supplier-recipient relations, transfer modes, and levels of arms dependency by recipients. The emerging post-Cold War period already appears to evidence some trends in arms transfer patterns reminiscent of the interwar period, specifically those involving the depoliticization and denationalization of that trade. The impact of the Military Technical Revolution in an era of contracting global arms transfers is viewed as crucial to the emerging arms trade.

Robert E. Harkavy is a professor of political science at Pennsylvania State University, specializing in national security studies and international relations. His publications include The Arms Trade and International Systems *and* Bases Abroad. *He has served with the U.S. Arms Control and Disarmament Agency and as consultant to the Department of Defense. He has recently had Fulbright and Humboldt fellowships in Sweden and Germany, respectively, and was a visiting professor at the U.S. Army War College.*

T HE cataclysmic events of the years 1989-91 ended the Cold War and heralded the advent of an entirely new and unpredictable epoch of world affairs. Amid these massive changes there was also the American technological tour de force of Desert Storm, which, according to some military analysts, appeared to herald a military technological revolution (now commonly referred to as "MTR" in the Pentagon). These telescoped events have raised profound questions about their coming impact on the international arms trade.

Almost 20 years ago, I published a doctoral dissertation that, at the time, was an initial halting effort at assessing the impact of broad systemic factors on the arms trade.[1] More specifically, it involved a comparison of the patterns of the arms trade for the interwar period (but focusing more on the 1930s) with those of the postwar period up to 1968. Since then, there have been a few efforts at extending this type of analysis,[2] though for the most part, what commonly is meant by "international systems analysis" has fallen into theoretical disuse or, rather, has been folded into a broader set of theoretical issues under the banner of "structural realism."[3]

At any rate, the end of the Cold War and the initial glimmerings of a

new system provide a golden opportunity to revisit the impact of comparative international systems on the arms trade. But, indeed, such an effort may, at present, be a bit premature. The emerging data on arms transfers provided by the major year-to-year sources—the U.S. Arms Control and Disarmament Agency, the Congressional Research Service, the Stockholm International Peace Research Institute (SIPRI)—bring us up only to 1991-92.[4] That is a slim basis for comparison with the lengthy postwar period (or various slices of it) or with the 20-year-long interregnum between the two great wars. We have only a very dim picture of the emerging post-Cold War era, one from which an analyst would extrapolate only at great risk. This article will, therefore, necessarily be devoted to guesses and speculations, both about an emerging arms trade and a comparison of it to the patterns of the past. The end of the Cold War and the emergence of a wholly new epoch provides the timely if tentative basis for a comparison of the arms trade

1. Robert E. Harkavy, *The Arms Trade and International Systems* (Cambridge, MA: Ballinger, 1975).

2. Keith Krause, *Arms and the State: Patterns of Military Production and Trade* (New York: Cambridge University Press, 1992); Edward J. Laurance, *The International Arms Trade* (New York: Lexington Books, 1992).

3. The related and often interchangeably used concepts of neo-realism and structural realism are discussed in Robert Keohane, *Neorealism and Its Critics* (New York: Columbia University Press, 1986); Joseph Nye, "Neo- realism and Neoliberalism," *World Politics*, 40: 235-57 (Jan. 1988); Kenneth Waltz, *Theory of International Politics* (Reading, MA: Addison-Wesley, 1979); Randall Schweller, "Tripolarity and the Second World War," *International Studies Quarterly*, 37(1): 73-103 (Mar. 1993).

4. U.S., Arms Control and Disarmament Agency, *World Military Expenditures and Arms Transfers* (Washington, DC: Government Printing Office, annually); Richard Grimmett, *Conventional Arms Transfers to the Third World* (Washington, DC: Congressional Research Service, 1992); Stockholm International Peace Research Institute, *World Armaments Yearbook* (New York: Oxford University Press, annually), chap. on arms transfers.

across three distinct periods: the interwar, the postwar, and the (nascent) post-Cold War.

COMPARING INTERNATIONAL SYSTEMS

Beginning with Morton Kaplan's seminal, pathbreaking work, *System and Process in International Politics*, international systems analysis came to be thought of as one of the most promising avenues toward a general theory of international relations.[5] Kaplan's work provided an avowedly deductive basis for such a theory, laying out some 10 "ideal-type" international systems, under such headings as "balance of power," "loose bipolar," "tight bipolar," "universal," "hierarchical," and "unit veto" systems, plus a number of hybrids, only a few of which had ever been approximated in the real world. Richard Rosecrance, proceeding more inductively, produced a set of common variables or criteria for any system, which he then proceeded to apply to some nine epochs, starting with the eighteenth-century system from 1740 to 1789 and ending with the postwar period from 1945 to 1960.[6]

Later, as noted, Kenneth Waltz and others were to meld some of the basic tenets of classical realism—emphasis on power, balance of power, national interest, and so on—to this newer focus on systems structure, producing a new dominant paradigm under the banner of "structural realism." Mostly, systems analysis came to be utilized merely to describe one or another historical era. But otherwise, it inspired arguments about which kind of systems, relatively speaking, was more likely to produce stability or equilibrium or peace (most such hypothetical arguments went back and forth between claims on behalf of bipolar and multipolar systems). In the process, these analyses may at least have pointed the way to a form of analysis whereby types of systems structure can be used as independent variables, and some important issues of world politics, such as the arms trade, as dependent variables.

Much of the theoretical literature on systems analysis seems tangled in a complex, almost unreadable mode of analysis. Because our purposes here are not so much theoretical in a broader sense but rather to shed some light on the historical evolvement of the arms trade, it may be appropriate to reduce what is involved to a simpler language.

Simply stated, such an analysis has to do with arranging history by slices of time, divided by appropriate watersheds or major historical events such as hegemonic wars or other upheavals that have substantially transformed the patterns of world politics. Along with that, such analyses may provide checklists of relevant variables or factors that can form the basis for comparison between periods. Alternatively, one might list a variety of key features for each period in question, aggregating to an overall portrait of an era, so that comparisons might then be made of periods as a whole rather than variable by variable.

5. Morton Kaplan, *System and Process in International Politics* (New York: John Wiley, 1957).

6. Richard Rosecrance, *Action and Reaction in World Politics: International Systems in Perspective* (Boston: Little, Brown, 1963).

There is little problem in dealing with watersheds or boundaries between periods in this particular case. World War II and the end of the Cold War have provided clear watersheds between the interwar, postwar, and post-Cold War periods, even if some observers might further choose to subdivide the interwar period in the early 1930s—the rise of Nazism, the onset of Japanese aggression, the depression, and so on—and to subdivide the postwar period as well with a variety of possible watersheds, such as the early 1970s with the Organization of Petroleum Exporting Countries (OPEC) phenomenon, the Strategic Arms Limitation Talks I and détente, and the end of the Bretton Woods economic system.

There are even more widespread disagreements about characterizing or defining periods of history in the imagery of systems structure. The interwar period, for instance, has been characterized by various theorists either as unipolar, bipolar, tripolar, or pentapolar. Retrospective analyses now argue about the long-assumed bipolar structure of the postwar Cold War period. And, nowadays, pundits vie for labels to be placed on the emerging post-Cold War system. The Gulf war produced flurries of attribution of a "unipolar moment" for the United States, even as declinist theorists were insisting on the basic reality of power diffusion. Looking forward, some analysts see the emergence of a three-way economic rivalry between a U.S.-led Americas bloc, a German-led European bloc (perhaps to include Russia), and a Japan-led East Asian bloc.[7] They and others speculate whether this economic rivalry must, inevitably, turn into a security rivalry, particularly if trade competition should result in escalating beggar-thy-neighbor trade policies.

COMPONENTS OF THE
ARMS TRADE: BROAD BASES
FOR COMPARISON ACROSS ERAS

What, then, are the major aspects or components of the arms trade that can serve as a basis for comparison between different systems or eras? Essentially, they come down to four areas of concern, with numerous subdivisions within them. They are the supplier markets and supplier behavior; supplier-recipient acquisition patterns, that is, who sells to whom; transaction modes, or the way arms are transferred; and a continuum of dependency to autarky, the latter constituting somewhat the obverse of the supplier category.

On the supplier side, there are the fundamental questions of the makeup of the market, somewhat analogous to markets in commodities such as computers or automobiles. How many active suppliers exist for each major weapons system? How much market share is held by each, translating into an analysis of levels of oligopoly, that is, what percentage of the market is held by the first two, three, or four largest suppliers? How do these statistics vary over time?

7. Jeffrey Garten, *A Cold Peace* (New York: Random House, 1992); Walter Russell Mead, "On the Road to Ruin," in *The Future of American Foreign Policy*, ed. C. Kegley and E. Wittkopf (New York: St. Martin's Press, 1992), pp. 332-39.

Then there is the question of the motivations of suppliers, which makes this aspect of the arms markets wholly distinct from that for automobiles and other commercial products, where there are rarely any motivations other than money. But historically, at least for some suppliers, arms have been sold or given away or sold at discounts for a variety of motives, habitually broken down into economic and political motives. In the former category are business profits (or government "profits"), employment, balance of payments, amortization of research and development costs, and maintaining a warm base for cyclical arms industries dependent on high levels of external threat. In the latter category are a plethora of factors involving the cementing of alliances, ties between military officers' corps, maintenance of regional balances of power, base acquisitions, the forestalling of nuclear proliferation, political leverage or influence, and so on.

Regarding supplier-acquisition patterns or styles, one may resort to the somewhat arbitrary typology developed long ago by Amelia Leiss, whereby recipients can be divided by sole acquisition styles, in which all arms are received from one supplier; a predominant style, where 60 percent or more are from one supplier; and a multiple-source acquisition style, where less than 60 percent are from any given supplier.[8] In the latter

8. Amelia C. Leiss et al., *Arms Transfers to Less Developed Countries* (Cambridge: Massachusetts Institute of Technology, Center for International Studies, 1970).

two categories, the bipolar nature of the Cold War produced a further important distinction between those recipients that acquired weapons wholly from one bloc, east or west, and those that distributed their acquisitions across the ideological bloc divide. However, once China was no longer part of the Soviet bloc—even though it continued almost entirely to license-produce or copy Soviet-bloc weapons—such an analysis became much more complex, requiring either the assumption of a third, albeit smaller, bloc in effect or the assumption that China was still effectively, for purposes of measuring arms transfers, a member of the Soviet bloc. Generally speaking, however, this aspect of the arms trade raises fundamental questions about the extent to which arms acquisition patterns are explicable on the basis of the known facts of political alignment or, inversely, enmity.

Under "transaction modes" are a host of more or less related questions about how arms are transferred. There is the division of aid and trade, with gradations in between. There are a host of issues involving coproduction, licensing, codevelopment, transnational ventures, the role of multinational entities, barter, offsets, buy-ins, and what have you.

Most nations, most of the time, have been dependent on others for weapons; few have been wholly autarkic. But here too there have been some important historical variations, and as we shall see, these can be linked, for instance, to the nature of alliance relationships among the first- and second-tier powers.

THE INTERWAR ARMS TRADE: BASIS FOR A CURRENT SENSE OF DÉJÀ VU?

The interwar "system" is not easily characterized according to any common checklist of variables or attributes, not least because of the great divide in the early 1930s wrought by the Great Depression and because of the rise of the radical nationalist regimes that later were to constitute the Axis, in turn accompanied by trade wars and escalating arms races. For those and other reasons, the arms trade of the interwar period also underwent somewhat of a transformation as the period progressed, though it also remained very distinct from what would follow after World War II.

Different analysts have proffered various labels to describe the structure of the interwar international system. Though seemingly contradictory, these contrasting efforts may rather be complementary in that each may highlight a different aspect of what was a complex reality. Russett's work, for instance, would imply a degree of unipolarity in the 1920s and 1930s, solely on the basis of what was already a huge U.S. preponderance in gross national product, the facts of American isolationism and its essentially disarmed state notwithstanding.[9] Rosecrance, meanwhile, sees a basic bipolarity emerging in the 1930s, involving a face-off between a radical nationalist bloc (Germany, Japan, Italy) and a Western liberal-democratic bloc, hinged on the United States, France,

and Britain.[10] He ignores the role of the USSR, assumes the United States to have been, at least implicitly, a member of a nascent Western bloc, and also ignores the fact that right up until the eve of the war, Italy and Japan were considering alternatives to alliance with Nazi Germany. Randall Schweller characterizes the late interwar period as tripolar—Moscow is granted the status of a pole.[11] Others might have perceived a degree of effective pentapolarity in the 1930s (the 1920s, like the emerging 1990s, had little in the way of rival major bloc or major power enmities save the face-off between the West and the Bolsheviks or maybe a confrontation between Britain-France and Germany-USSR in the brief period between Rapallo and Locarno). Those poles were the United States, Britain-France, Germany, the USSR, and Japan, with rising Italy somewhat of a wild card.

There are some other major characteristics of the interwar period that appear to have affected the arms trade. Unlike the bulk of the Cold War period, there was an absence of long-term stable alliances. Moreover, prior to the late 1930s, alignments were not basically driven by ideology; even in the late 1930s, the Franco-Soviet alliance, with Britain as a silent partner, went across the grain of ideological lines.

Some other characteristics of the period were somewhat idiosyncratic, and in most respects, they reflected carryovers from the nineteenth cen-

9. Bruce Russett, *Trends in World Politics* (New York: Macmillan, 1965), p. 4.

10. Rosecrance, *Action and Reaction in World Politics*, p. 260, fig. 13.

11. Schweller, "Tripolarity and the Second World War."

tury. The arms trade was largely privatized in the sense that up to the mid-1930s most governments did not regulate arms sales. That is, arms sales were not normally used as a purposeful instrument of diplomacy as was later to be the case, after 1945, in connection with basing access, extension of political influence, and the like. Only a few scattered examples of the use of arms supplies to achieve basing access can be discerned: for instance, Japan's relationship with Siam in the late 1930s and Germany's ties to Spain at the same time. Otherwise, the fact that most of what we later came to call the Third World was under colonial control rendered the global strategic context of the interwar period a different situation from the one that would emerge after 1945.

Curiously, the interwar arms production and trade were more multinationalized than would be the case after 1945. This was an extension of pre-World War I patterns and was a correlate of the unregulated nature of the trade and of the more casual nature of diplomacy in a period relatively bereft of total war and total diplomacy. Many of the U.S. and European arms firms had foreign subsidiaries and other transnational connections. The major German firms were easily able to circumvent the restrictions imposed at Versailles by operating offshore subsidiaries in, among other places, Switzerland, Sweden, Turkey, and the Netherlands.[12]

Generally speaking, a laissez-faire economic ethos reigned during this period. In short, and in relation to the SIPRI arms sales policy typology, virtually all, if not all, of the major interwar powers had primarily economic rationales for arms sales.[13]

The interwar period was one that saw a major technological revolution in weaponry. There were tremendous advances in the capabilities of aircraft and tanks, and there were all manner of technological innovations ranging from bombsights to antitank guns to early radars and communications intercepts. What was most noteworthy, however, was the rapidity of the turnover of weapons generations. In all of the major arms-producing countries, qualitatively new prototypes of major equipment types were being developed every year or two. The then cheaper unit economics of arms production (a first-line fighter aircraft in the late 1930s cost about $20,000) allowed for production of numerous new aircraft, tanks, and other matériel by all of the major suppliers, which ramified into a very rapid turnover of weapons generations. Obsolescence came very quickly!

On the supplier side, the market for major weapons systems—across the board for various major weapons systems—was much less concentrated in the interwar period, as would accord with, relative to the postwar period, a greater distribution of power at the big-power level, arguably shading into a degree of multipolarity. In the combat aircraft category, the two largest interwar

12. Harkavy, *Arms Trade and International Systems*, chap. 2.

13. Stockholm International Peace Research Institute, *The Arms Trade with the Third World* (New York: Humanities Press, 1971), pp. 17-41.

suppliers, the United States and the United Kingdom, accounted for only 40 percent of the market in the 1930s, a far smaller share than would later obtain for the United States and the USSR after World War II. Adding the third- and fourth-biggest suppliers, France and Italy, the cumulative market share goes to 68 percent, also a low figure relative to the top four in the postwar period. This tendency, still pronounced but less stark, existed in the tank category, where France, the United Kingdom, the United States, and Italy were the largest four suppliers, and in several other categories of major weapons as well as with respect to overall volumes of arms supplies.[14]

As noted, the interwar arms trade, up to at least the mid-1930s, saw a large degree of discretion by private firms over arms sales. In effect, that meant that economic motives for sales transcended geopolitical ones, particularly in the absence of durable multilateral alliances and of drives for overseas basing access. Correspondingly, there was little in the way of security assistance or economic aid translatable into weapons purchases, which later phenomenon was hinged on ideologically based alliances and clientships and on government direction of arms sales diplomacy. Finally, regarding the interwar supplier markets, the low unit costs of weapons—medium-size nations such as Argentina or Romania

14. These and subsequent data for the interwar period are drawn from Harkavy, *Arms Trade and International Systems*, esp. chaps. 3 and 4. In turn, those data were drawn from the interwar military intelligence files located in the National Archives, Washington, DC.

fielded as many as 1000 combat aircraft—and the rapid pace of technological innovation translated into very quick changeovers of weapons generations. Almost every year, there were new aircraft and tank models by a large number of competing corporate producers. This rapid succession had a major impact on the market.

Regarding the patterns of sales between suppliers and recipients, several points stand out, which in turn may provide a preview of emerging trends in the 1990s. There were numerous cross-bloc, multiple-source acquisition patterns reflecting the primarily economic basis of the trade but also the absence of clearly demarcated bloc-related clientships. By the late 1930s, numerous nations in Latin America, Eastern Europe, Scandinavia, Asia, and the Middle East were acquiring weapons simultaneously from Western and Axis sources. Many of these relationships seemed almost in contradiction to prevailing political relations. Germany, for instance, was selling weapons to various European countries— the Netherlands, Denmark, Romania, Yugoslavia, Greece—that it was imminently to invade; indeed, it reacquired the weapons as a prize for its conquests. Japan, even in the late 1930s, was acquiring modern military technology of all sorts from American and European suppliers.

The existence of numerous multiple-source, cross-bloc acquisition patterns by the late 1930s served to mask somewhat one other important development during that period of gathering storm and escalating arms races. That was the gradually increasing role of the revisionist supplier powers—Germany, Italy, Japan—at the expense of the status quo nations emerging from World War I, particularly Britain and France.[15] The mid- to late 1930s saw numerous cases wherein particularly Germany and Italy, and particularly in Latin America and Eastern Europe, made major inroads into arms markets previously wholly dominated by Western arms firms. That trend correlated with the increasingly purposeful use of arms transfers by the Axis powers as a political instrument, a policy that previewed its more widespread use in the postwar period. Particularly noteworthy were the efforts by the Axis powers to utilize arms transfers in order to undermine the Western political position in Latin American nations such as Brazil, Argentina, Colombia, Chile, Peru, and several Central American states, some in proximity to the prized Panama Canal. The Soviet Union, meanwhile, acting as another revisionist state but one then more an importer than an exporter of weapons, had only some limited arms sales in nearby states, particularly Czechoslovakia and Afghanistan.

The combination of the absence of stable alliance relationships (or the expectation of such stability) and the ease of entry into arms production because of low unit costs had still other ramifications. Numerous medium-range powers, particularly in Europe, were able to develop and produce their own first-line aircraft and armored systems. In other words, the

insecurity of future supply wrought by rapidly shifting alignments impelled many nations to fend for themselves via autarkic production. Not only France and Italy, Germany and Britain, but also Belgium, the Netherlands, Poland, Lithuania, and Yugoslavia were producing indigenously designed combat aircraft. A related phenomenon was that some nations possessed of only modest technological and economic wherewithal were still able to license-produce some of the most advanced systems. China, Chile, and Turkey, for instance, license-produced top-of-the-line U.S. fighter aircraft in the late 1930s. Germany was able to conduct offshore submarine production in Turkey. There was a somewhat lesser overall dependence on weapons on the part of many middle-range and smaller states than later would be the case.

THE POSTWAR ARMS TRADE

Relative to the interwar, of course, the lengthy postwar period now concomitant with the history of the Cold War is a much longer period and one with political changes and phases that render difficult any overall generalizations.

Throughout much of the Cold War, the international system, particularly as pertains to military security affairs, could easily be characterized in terms of bloc bipolarity. But by the 1970s and 1980s, what had been a "tight bipolarity" in Kaplan's terms had become, relatively speaking, a "loose bipolarity" in that many newly decolonialized states had assumed a nonaligned posture, one conducive to

---

15. Schweller, "Tripolarity and the Second World War," is to be credited with emphasizing the importance of revisionist versus status quo orientations in relation to systems structure.

bargaining between the superpowers regarding influence, leverage, and, yes, arms markets. Still, the overall structure of alignments was largely defined in ideological terms, and those alignments were mostly stable over a lengthy period, even given such major aberrations as the Chinese defection from what had been the Sino-Soviet bloc, France's military withdrawal from the North Atlantic Treaty Organization (NATO), and the political vicissitudes and upheavals of some major Third World nations, such as Indonesia, Egypt, and Iran. Most arms trade client relations remained throughout, largely explicable by reference to relative political orientations toward Washington or Moscow or, in some cases, Beijing.

Otherwise, this lengthy period also saw the superpowers competing for arms markets in what the SIPRI typology referred to as a "geopolitical style" of arms selling. They engaged, indeed, in a totally global competition for political influence and for basing access, in the context of which arms sales became the primary coin of exchange. That was, however, mostly a two-power game, leaving secondary suppliers such as Britain, France, Italy, Germany, Sweden, and others to sell arms primarily for commercial purposes. But even there, many of the arms transactions involved were explicable within the general borders of Cold War politics, so that America's NATO allies were mostly constrained to carving out smaller markets in what largely were American bailiwicks.

Still, by the 1970s—and, perhaps to a degree, constituting a measure of a trend toward multipolarity and

away from the two-bloc ideologically driven model—there were a considerable number of Third World states that had acquired weapons simultaneously from both blocs, though in many cases involving some asymmetry favoring one side or the other. Perhaps close to half of the sub-Saharan African states came to fit that pattern. So, too, did such major arms recipients as India, Pakistan, Iran, Iraq, Jordan, Egypt, Libya, Algeria, and Peru, among others. But even in some of these cases, acquisitions from both sides represented not just a reflection of ideological evenhandedness but an effort to play off one superpower against the other in a game of influence and leverage. That general pattern held until the end of the Cold War, as demonstrated in Table 1, for the period 1987-91.

Unlike the interwar period, there was no progression from a period of relative peace and worldwide low levels of arming to one of escalating tensions and arms races. The arms races were there from the start. But the overall size of the arms market was heavily affected in the 1970s by another factor, namely, the OPEC-driven rise of oil prices, which created a huge market for arms in the Middle East, one that came to dominate the data for arms transfers.

On the supplier side, the highly oligopolistic nature of the market carried through the bulk of the mid-to late Cold War period. But some secular trends were visible from the early 1960s to the late 1980s, before the upheavals accompanying the end of the Cold War. In the 1960-70 period, the United States and USSR together accounted for some 80 per-

TABLE 1

SUPPLIER—RECIPIENT ARMS ACQUISITION PATTERNS, 1987-91

1 Sole Source: West Bloc	2 Predominant Source: Within the West Bloc	3 Predominant Source: Mostly West Bloc, Some East Bloc	4 Multiple Source: Within the West Bloc	5 Multiple Source: West and East Blocs	6 Multiple Source: Within the East Bloc	7 Predominant Source: Mostly East Bloc, Some West Bloc	8 Predominant Source: Within the East Bloc	9 Sole Source: East Bloc
Ivory Coast (FR)	Botswana (US)	Thailand (US)	Cameroon	Gambia		Algeria (USSR)	Burkina Faso (USSR)	Benin (USSR)
Malawi (UK)	Gabon (FR)	Egypt (US)	Chad	Liberia		Angola (USSR)	Ethiopia (USSR)	Burundi (USSR)
Tunisia (US)	Kenya (UK)		Senegal	Morocco		Zambia (USSR)	Mozambique (USSR)	Cape Verde (USSR)
Luxembourg (US)	Niger (US)		Indonesia	Nigeria		Burma (PRC)	Cambodia (USSR)	Congo (USSR)
UK (US)	Taiwan (US)		Malaysia	Somalia		Finland (USSR)	N. Korea (USSR)	Equatorial Guinea (USSR)
Malta (US)	Japan (US)		Greece	Sudan		Yugoslavia (USSR)	Bulgaria (USSR)	Guinea (USSR)
Barbados (US)	S. Korea (US)		Norway	Uganda		N. Yemen (USSR)	Czechoslovakia (USSR)	Guinea-Bissau (USSR)
Costa Rica (US)	Philippines (US)		Austria	Zaire		Bangladesh (PRC)	E. Germany (USSR)	Madagascar (USSR)
El Salvador (US)	Singapore (US)		Ireland	PRC		India (USSR)	Hungary (USSR)	Mauritius (USSR)
Guyana (US)	Belgium (US)		Sweden	Peru		Nepal (PRC)	Poland (USSR)	Rwanda (PRC)
Honduras (US)	Denmark (US)		Switzerland	Iran			Romania (USSR)	São Tomé (USSR)
Jamaica (US)	France (US)		Argentina	Iraq			Nicaragua (USSR)	Sierra Leone (PRC)
	W. Germany (US)		Bolivia	Jordan			Syria (USSR)	Tanzania (USSR)
	Italy (US)		Brazil	Kuwait				Zimbabwe (PRC)
	Netherlands (US)		Chile	Pakistan				Laos (USSR)
	Portugal (US)		Colombia	Sri Lanka				Vietnam (USSR)
	Spain (US)		Ecuador					Cuba (USSR)
	Turkey (US)		Panama					S. Yemen (USSR)
	Dominican Republic (US)		Paraguay					Afghanistan (USSR)
	Guatemala (US)		Uruguay					
	Mexico (US)		Venezuela					
	Bahrain (US)		Oman					
	Cyprus (FR)		Qatar					
	Israel (US)		Saudi Arabia					
	Lebanon (US)		UAE					
	Canada (US)		USA					
	Australia (US)							
	New Zealand (US)							

SOURCE: U.S., Arms Control and Disarmament Agency, *World Military Expenditure and Arms Transfers, 1991-1992* (Washington, DC: Government Printing Office, 1994).

NOTES: The countries in parentheses are suppliers; the other countries named are recipients. Not known or difficult to classify: Ghana, Mauritania, South Africa, Haiti, Togo, and Papua New Guinea.

cent of global arms sales, with the next two suppliers adding only about 5 percent of market share. Then, up to the 1983-86 period—this also was the peak of the Iran-Iraq war as well as after the main thrust of the OPEC oil boom—the combined superpower shares gradually dropped to near 60 percent, masking a precipitous drop in the U.S. share and some rise in the Soviet share. The third- and fourth-largest sellers then accounted for over 12 percent of the market. By the late 1980s, the combined U.S. and Soviet figures were again up—with a 42.5 percent share achieved by Moscow on the very eve of its collapse. Simultaneously, the combined shares of the third- and fourth-largest producers dropped back to the 7-8 percent range. Then came the end of the Cold War and also the pivotal Gulf war.

In much of the arms trade literature of the 1980s, there was reference to the "diffusion" of production and trading capabilities. That was inspired not only by the (temporary) increase in the roles of France, Britain, China, and Italy but also by the enhanced roles of European neutrals such as Sweden, Austria, and Switzerland and by the "indigenous" programs in the Third World represented by, among others, Israel, Brazil, South Africa, India, and the two Koreas. However, as the overall market declined at the end of the Cold War, the arms sales of these third-tier suppliers declined precipitously. As they were greatly dependent on export sales to sustain production because of limited home markets, these programs were placed in great jeopardy.

THE EMERGING INTERNATIONAL SYSTEM OF THE EARLY 1990s

As was previously stated, there is considerable variance in the manner in which academic analysts characterize, even in the most general terms, an emerging international system. This is all the more difficult a task because of the lack of congruence between military and economic power at the major-power level, itself somewhat of a historical anomaly.

But perhaps the 1989-91 watershed has ushered in even more profound changes than would constitute the norm. Rosecrance, in discussing the emergence of the trading state, perceives a historical alternation between periods seeing, respectively, predominantly security and economic competitions.[16] That indeed may point to the growing submergence of security competition; such a submergence would lend an entirely new meaning to structural concepts such as bipolarity or multipolarity. In such a milieu, Russett's former insistence on defining systems structure according to comparative gross national product data might acquire greater validity.

One seeming hallmark of the emerging period is the absence of rival alliance blocs.[17] NATO continues to exist, but who are its enemies? Indeed, who are now America's enemies? Are there indeed recent histori-

16. Richard Rosecrance, *The Rise of the Trading State* (New York: Basic Books, 1986).
17. These conceptual issues, in historical context, are discussed in Charles W. Kegley and Gregory Raymond, *A Multipolar Peace?* (New York: St. Martin's, 1994).

cal precedents for an utter lack of enmity on the part of the contending major powers? In the 1920s, a peaceful period, Germany and the USSR, maybe also Japan, were at least widely regarded as revisionist powers. Can the same be said today of Japan, China, Russia, or Germany, all at least potential rivals to the U.S. unipolar hegemony?

But outside the realm of the admittedly stilted academic language of systems analysis, some writers have attempted to outline the main characteristics of an emerging postwar era. William Maynes, editor of *Foreign Policy*, has produced a checklist for a "shape of the future," from which the following points would appear relevant to any analysis of the arms trade:

— there will be a decline in defense spending by the great powers and an increase by the small powers—"the latter will be striving to increase the tendency of the larger states to pause before threatening the smaller powers";

— the extant nuclear powers will engage in a coordinated effort to stop further proliferation—"a third attempt at collective security in this century with the focus on weapons of mass destruction";

— the role of the United Nations will grow, and with it the use of international law;

— geoeconomics will vie with geopolitics for importance—an impending three-bloc competition where Europe might become the world's powerhouse;

— China is more likely than any other nation to pose a challenge to international stability;

— the importance of Asia in the world will increase steadily, and if security concerns continue to decline in importance, U.S. bargaining power in Asia will steadily decrease, even as it needs Asia as a source of capital (but Asia must develop its own security order);

— there will be a struggle between finance and trade—the former is increasingly globalized, and the latter is becoming regionalized;

— the ability of the state to control economic activity at the national level seems to be declining; and

— in every region of the world, the United States will be present but decreasingly dominant—its "unipolar moment" will be very brief, and power will continue to be more evenly distributed as America's military dominance recedes and as others' economic performance improves.[18]

Perhaps of some importance is the question of what the impact of MTR will be on the arms trade. In a recent volume, Keith Krause concluded that over the past several centuries there have been three discernible "long cycles" or phases in arms production and trade. Each was inaugurated by a burst of military technological innovation; each then saw a hierarchical stratification of arms production and trade into some three tiers; each saw an ineluctable diffusion of weapons-

18. Charles William Maynes, "The World in the Year 2000: Prospects for Order or Disorder," in *The Nature of the Post-Cold War World* (Carlisle, PA: U.S. Army War College, Strategic Studies Institute, Mar. 1993).

producing capability—hence also diffusion of power—as a long cycle progressed.[19]

The advent of MTR leads many analysts to the presumption that we are at the beginning of a fourth cycle of weapons innovation and production. At the moment, the United States stands virtually alone as a first-tier producer of MTR weaponry and in its capability for integrating its major components: target acquisition systems, precision-guided munitions, and so forth. But there are now also emerging analyses of MTR—note some recent studies by the Washington-based Center for Strategic and International Studies and by Los Alamos National Laboratory—centered on its predicted impact on the future arms trade.[20]

Two points stand out in these studies. First is the assertion that, for the next 10-15 years, U.S. dominance of MTR technologies will remain virtually unchallenged, albeit with some diffusion of capabilities, pertaining not only to weapons themselves but also to related doctrinal and organizational matters. Second, regarding the four basic elements of MTR—information acquisition systems, command and control, precision weapons, and weapons platforms—the latter, which has long been at the heart of the arms trade, is considered

perhaps the least important. That reinforces comments rendered elsewhere in the present volume regarding the increasing importance both of upgrades and retrofits and of dual-use technologies important to the first two categories.

THE EMERGING ARMS
TRADE OF THE EARLY 1990s

Analyzing the transition between the late Cold War arms trade and the arms trade of the emerging post-Cold War period is no easy matter. The data are simply not yet available in the form we need to gauge the impact of these events on the arms trade. SIPRI's data are more up to date, ending with 1992, and are also disaggregated on a year-to-year basis, allowing one to deal with a dividing line around 1991. But those data are for major weapons systems only, and they do not easily lend themselves to further analysis of donor-recipient patterns on a country-by-country basis, save by reviewing the arms trade registers. The data published in the U.S. Arms Control and Disarmament Agency's *World Military Expenditures and Arms Transfers* are more comprehensive, including everything falling within a definition of arms transfers, and are felicitously disaggregated on a dyadic supplier-recipient basis. But they are not on an annualized basis; rather, the most recent data provide a picture of the cumulative 1987-91 deliveries, similar to the earlier year-by-year provision of five-year segments. That is a particular problem in that the 1987-91 data, which go up only to the end of the Cold War period, do not allow for comparative analysis of data on

19. Krause, *Arms and the State.*

20. Michael J. Mazarr et al., "Military Technical Revolution: A Structural Framework" (Final Report of the CSIS Study Group on the MTR, Center for Strategic and International Studies, Mar. 1993); Patrick J. Garrity, "Why the Gulf War Still Matters" (Report no. 16, Center for National Security Studies, Los Alamos National Laboratory, July 1993).

either side of the Cold War divide. Nevertheless, some patterns do emerge from a combined look at the data from these two sources.

On the supplier side, using the SIPRI data, one can clearly see the transition from a somewhat bipolar pattern to a unipolar pattern, with a watershed between 1990 and 1991.[21] Soviet sales of major conventional weapons still exceeded American sales up to 1989, were slightly below in 1990, and then dropped way below in 1991 and 1992. By the latter year, Soviet sales were less than one-quarter those of the United States and only slightly higher than those of Germany; also, they were not much higher than those of China. Looked at another way, U.S. sales were about equal to the sum of those of the next six suppliers: the USSR, Germany, China, France, the United Kingdom, and Czechoslovakia. Curiously, the 1987-91 data from the Arms Control and Disarmament Agency show the USSR to be clearly the leading supplier in what was still a duopolistic market, with the United Kingdom in third place, followed by France, China, and Germany. Relatively speaking, Germany and China appear on the rise, reinforcing our thesis noted earlier concerning rising, revisionist powers. The SIPRI data also clearly demonstrate the near collapse of the supplier roles of hitherto rising challengers such as Brazil, Israel, Sweden, Italy, and Spain, acting to reverse a long-heralded trend toward diffusion in the arms markets.

21. Stockholm International Peace Research Institute, *SIPRI Yearbook 1993* (New York: Oxford University Press, 1993), pp. 415-518.

Less clear are the emerging trends away from the Cold War donor-acquisition patterns. Those trends had remained fairly stable all the way from the 1960s to the end of the Cold War. Both superpowers had large numbers of client states that received all or most of their weapons from them or from other NATO or Warsaw Pact suppliers. These patterns were quite predictable. There were few surprises, and much of the arms trade could easily have been correlated with U.N. General Assembly votes.

Beginning in the 1960s and continuing to 1990, there were also a substantial number of dependent states that acquired arms in a cross-bloc pattern, varying widely from evenhandedness to some mitigation of predominant reliance on one or the other side. These trends were evidence of some shift from "tight" to "loose" bipolarity. Hence the multiple-source, cross-bloc pattern was evidenced in Gambia, Libya, Morocco, Nigeria, Somalia, Sudan, Uganda, Zaire, China, Peru, Iran, Iraq, Jordan, Kuwait, Pakistan, and Sri Lanka.

But after 1991, the end of the Cold War competition would allow for the prediction that these patterns would be greatly altered, presumably in the direction of a more random pattern dictated by the dominance of commercial over the previous mixed ideological and geopolitical considerations. That would, indeed, represent a return to patterns evidenced earlier, in the 1920s and prior to World War I. That trend might be slowed by the facts of some nations' desire to extend the previously existing supplier relationships so as not to have to undergo a wholesale transition from one supplier to another. The overall drop in the volume of arms traded, correlated to lower levels of regional warfare and arms-racing, would, of course, also have an impact.

Early indications are that exactly that is occurring. Arms flows are, as they were in the interwar period, being split off from prevailing patterns of political alignment, producing what only a couple of years ago would have been considered surprises. Russia has become a major supplier of weapons to China, involving high-performance aircraft among other things.[22] Moscow is also becoming a more significant supplier to Iran. The United States is now considering arms sales to former Warsaw Treaty Organization (WTO) states in Eastern Europe. Israel has resumed significant transfers to China,[23] even despite apparent earlier retransfer of Israeli-origin technology by Beijing to regional Arab rivals, and has also inaugurated some weapons deals with newly independent Estonia.[24] Soviet-origin weapons from the stocks of former East European WTO states are moving to and through Croatia to destinations in the Middle East,[25] and, indeed, Moscow may yet achieve some direct sales in Kuwait, which earlier had bought some Soviet weapons.

The recently published SIPRI arms trade registers for 1992 provide additional evidence of these changes.[26] Sri Lanka is acquiring arms simultaneously from Argentina, Czechoslovakia, and the United Kingdom. Thailand—formerly a U.S. stronghold in the Southeast Asia Treaty Organization—now acquires significant amounts of weapons from China and Czechoslovakia, along with France, the Netherlands, Spain, Switzerland, the United Kingdom, and the United States. The United Arab Emirates has ordered 500 BMP-3 armored fighting vehicles from Russia; Malaysia, 50 MiG-29s from Moscow.[27] Pakistan is armed by China, France, and the United States; Peru, by Czechoslovakia, the United States, and Russia; Myanmar, by China and Poland; Islamic Iran, by China, Russia, and North Korea; Algeria, by China and the United Kingdom. China's acquisitions—even as it has become a major supplier—are divided among Russia, Israel, the United States, and France.

22. Steven Erlanger, "Moscow Insists It Must Sell the Instruments of War to Pay the Costs of Peace," *New York Times*, 3 Feb. 1993.

23. William Branigin, "Asian Nations Express Concern about China's New Weapons and Bases," *Washington Post*, 31 Mar. 1993. China has requested assistance from Israel for aerial refueling technology, electronic warfare gear, and radar systems for fighter aircraft. Ibid.

24. Margaret Shapiro, "Against All Odds, Estonia Hums Along," *Washington Post National Weekly Edition*, 28 June-4 July 1993, p. 17, which refers to Estonia's signing a deal to buy NATO-type weapons from Israel.

25. Steve Coll, "In the Balkans, a Balance of Terror," *Washington Post National Weekly Edition*, 22-28 Feb., 1993, p. 16; U.S., Congress, House, Republican Research Committee, Task Force on Terrorism and Unconventional Warfare, "Nuclear Trafficking in Europe," 30 Nov. 1992.

26. E. Laurance, S. Wegeman, and H. Wulf, *Arms Watch: SIPRI Report on the First Year of the UN Register of Conventional Arms*, SIPRI Research Report no. 6, (New York: Oxford University Press, 1993), pp. 70-104.

27. Erlanger, "Moscow Insists It Must Sell the Instruments of War."

But these examples may also serve to obscure a larger trend. As the overall market has declined, and as the role of the former Communist powers—China somewhat excepted—has markedly declined, a larger number of dependent states are drawing their arms from a mix of former Western and/or neutral sources. In this sense, there is a marked difference from the interwar period, which saw many dependent states—in Latin America, the Near East, and Eastern Europe—drawing weapons simultaneously from Western and Axis-bloc sources, with the latter revisionist (and rapidly arming) states increasing their market shares.

Only in some respects, however, may the emerging patterns of the arms trade fully imitate the pre-World War II patterns. The growing mobility of capital, labor, and technology and the predominantly commercial nature of most transfers, is reminiscent even of nineteenth-century Europe. The unipolar dominance of the United States as a supplier, however, provides a difference. So, too, does the curious absence, for the time being, of serious security rivalries and enmities or the prospect of same.

The political content of the arms trade is now provided more by enmities, rivalries, and arms races in the Third World than by rivalries between suppliers. This was also true before 1914 in the Balkans and during the interwar period with respect to the rivalries between Brazil and Argentina and between Bolivia and Paraguay. But before World War II, much of what is now the Third World was under colonial control, which tended to suppress such regional rivalries. The politics of the arms trade is now largely defined by the attempts at achieving leverage with suppliers by either side of the divides between India and Pakistan, Iraq and Iran, the Arabs and Israel, and the contending ex-Yugoslav states. Meanwhile, only China, now considered the prime prospect of an upstart revisionist state, seems to be pursuing an extension of external access in connection with its arms sales, for the moment limited to moves in Burma obviously connected to a still-simmering regional rivalry with India.[28]

Contrary to the predictions of Rosecrance and others about the rise of a "trading state system," it remains to be seen whether future security rivalries will again propel an arms trade based significantly on geopolitical considerations. A possible later security rivalry between the United States and either Japan or China (or both of these countries) or a rivalry between the two Asian states might produce such an outcome. So might a resumption of rivalry between Russia and the West, or even a more comprehensive confrontation between the Islamic and Western worlds.

For the moment, however, the most basic realities are those of a depoliticization and denationalization of the arms trade. With reference to the former, one can point to a diminution of the former geopolitical impetuses to selling arms, at least as

28. Branigin, "Asian Nations Express Concern," p. 7, which refers to a naval base China is building with Burma on Hanggyi Island in the Bassein River and a monitoring station on Grand Coco Island in Myanmar waters just north of India's Andaman Islands.

applied to the superpowers, resulting in a largely commercially based arms transfer system. Regarding the latter, as outlined elsewhere in the present volume, the growing multinationalization of arms production and trade has made it more difficult to analyze the arms trade primarily in terms of national rivalries. For the long term, who can tell? That will likely hinge on whether or not traditional revisionist drives surface in Japan, China, Russia, or maybe Germany to challenge U.S.-based unipolarity, particularly regarding production of, and trade in, MTR weaponry. If that happens, more than the arms trade will be at stake, but that trade would again become a leading indicator or characteristic of a more traditional international system.

ANNALS, *AAPSS*, **535**, September 1994

Current Trends and Developments in the Arms Trade

By IAN ANTHONY

ABSTRACT: More attention has focused on the issue of arms transfers since Iraq, with an inventory based exclusively on foreign military technology, invaded Kuwait. Political and academic analysts of the issue are handicapped by the absence of an agreed set of data with which to work. Given that different analytical tasks require different data sets, this article reviews the types of data that could be of value. Using the aggregate data that are available, the article tries to identify trends in the trade in major conventional weapons and assess which of these trends are transient—an interim adjustment to the end of the Cold War—and which might be more long-lived. Finally, the article offers a projection of macrotrends over the medium term.

Dr. Ian Anthony is the project leader of the SIPRI Arms Production and Arms Transfer project. His most recent publications include The Future of the Defense Industries in Central and Eastern Europe *(1994) and* Arms Export Regulations *(1991).*

T HIS article will identify trends that have emerged over the past few years and try to assess which of them are robust and which represent an interim adjustment to the end of the Cold War.

Conclusions about the long term are inevitably tentative even though both arms procurement and the economy are characterized by long cycles that can be identified and therefore predicted. The movement from one generation of equipment to another has imposed a rhythm on global procurement patterns. Moreover, after these generational changes in the armed forces of major powers, the disposal of older items through heavily discounted foreign sales also appears to be in a cycle.

The political conditions in which this process took place in the 1950s and 1960s are different from those of the 1990s, and this complicates projections about developments in the arms trade. Global sources of supply greatly outstrip global demand for conventional weapons. Moreover, as the level of resource allocation for defense is politically determined, the downturn in military spending may not be reversed even when the major economies come out of recession. Government debt reduction and social welfare expenditures are both likely to have a stronger claim on any increased revenues than will defense ministries. This may apply not only among the countries of the Organization for Economic Cooperation and Development but also elsewhere.[1]

On the other hand, there is no evidence that the underlying demand for military equipment has been eliminated. On the contrary, many countries would like to rebuild and modernize their armed forces for a variety of reasons. In Central and Eastern Europe, countries face the challenge of a complete reorientation in defense policy, often reflecting their new boundaries as well as the new political environment in which they find themselves. Other countries find that a policy based on alignment with one or the other superpower during the Cold War is no longer tenable as a basis for planning national security.

It may be useful to address the reasons for trying to measure trends and developments in the arms trade at all, as the utility of this approach is often questioned. The contribution that the existing data collections can make to resolving analytical problems can be—and frequently is—overstated. Their value is in helping to identify issues and questions that deserve further and more detailed examination. They are a supplement

---

1. This case is argued for Western Europe in W. Walker and P. Gummett, eds., *Nationalism, Internationalism and the European Defence Market*, Chaillot Paper no. 9 (Paris: WEU

Institute for Security Studies, 1993). Central and Eastern Europe is discussed in Ian Anthony, ed., *The Future of the Defence Industries in Central and Eastern Europe*, SIPRI Research Report no. 7 (New York: Oxford University Press, 1994). Recent publications suggest that it also applies in the Middle East; see Yahya Sadowski, *Scuds or Butter? The Political Economy of Arms Control in the Middle East* (Washington, DC: Brookings Institution, 1993). A 1993 study of Saudi Arabia by the International Monetary Fund apparently concluded that high spending on imports is unsustainable given the growing cost of debt servicing and low oil prices, though this does not necessarily mean that military imports need be reduced.

to and not a substitute for other forms of analysis.

The primary purpose for collecting and publishing data on the arms trade is to feed into the debate on international security. While the decisions that determine the course of this debate are political, it is reasonable to demand that some systematic process of evaluation take place. The probability that decisions will be based on foolishness or ignorance is diminished by scrutiny and accountability. In most areas of public policy, this is uncontested, and, to permit scrutiny, national statistical bureaus collect vast amounts of information and store it in a systematic format. In the area of arms transfers, the sensitivity that governments still feel about releasing any information that may indicate military capability disallows systematic analysis using an agreed body of official data.

Countries that disclose information about arms exports remain the exception and not the rule. From a national perspective, in the majority of democracies even the legislature does not have access to information about national arms exports, undermining its ability to exercise effective oversight over this aspect of foreign and security policy. From an analytical perspective, cross-country comparisons using official data are impossible because the definition of arms exports is not standard. There are only two cases—Sweden and the United States—where governments are sufficiently forthcoming to permit detailed analysis of patterns in national exports using official data. Even Sweden, which produces detailed value statistics, is reluctant to disclose the numbers or types of items transferred.

MEASURING TRENDS IN THE INTERNATIONAL ARMS TRADE

The absence of acceptable official data is seen as a major handicap by some decision makers. In a recent statement, Senator John McCain observed, "If we are to deal with conventional arms transfers, we must have a realistic data base. We must have facts that are both relevant and accurate."[2] Under the most optimistic scenario, McCain is condemned to a long period of frustration. Nevertheless, the process of constructing a realistic database—something that can only be done by governments—has begun with the establishment of the United Nations Register of Conventional Arms in 1991.[3] In the future development of the U.N. register, the decisive factor will be whether sufficient political will exists among governments, first, to sustain the momentum developed during the first year of reporting and, second, to force their representatives to resolve some fundamental technical issues.

At present, there is no agreed definition of what types of equipment constitute conventional arms. The

2. John McCain, "The Need for Improved Analysis of Conventional Arms Transfers," in U.S., Congress, Senate, *Congressional Record*, 28 Apr. 1993, p. S5052.

3. E. Laurance, S. T. Wezeman, and H. Wulf, *Arms Watch: SIPRI Report on the First Year of the UN Register of Conventional Arms*, SIPRI Research Report no. 6 (New York: Oxford University Press, 1993).

narrow definition of arms would be linked purely to lethal equipment, but this usage is rare, as any effective military force depends on combat support equipment of various kinds and items that have civilian as well as military uses. There are also competing definitions of "international arms transfer" arising out of the fact that while the items may be classified as arms, the end user may be a police or paramilitary force, coast guard, or some other government agency.

While the United States, Russia, and China are largely self-sufficient in their arms production, in the other 184 countries of the world, international arms transfers have a decisive influence on the structure, capability, and readiness of the armed forces. As most governments regard the preparedness of their armed forces as the most important single component of national security, it is not unreasonable to say that the arms trade is a core issue in international security. However, there are many different reasons for being interested in the arms trade, and the measurement of trends should, ideally, be sensitive to the needs of the analysis. Clearly, those interested in burden sharing in the North Atlantic Treaty Organization need a different data set from the one needed by those interested in non-European conventional arms control.

At least six kinds of data are important to current debates on aspects of the arms trade. These are (1) data concerning excessive accumulations of offensive weapons systems; (2) data concerning advanced technology that can increase the capability of existing weapons platforms; (3) data on dual-use technologies—that is, technologies with either a civil or a military application; (4) data related to man-portable weapons; (5) data on the value of the arms trade; and (6) data on the changing organization of global industrial production. Each data type leads into complex and difficult problem areas.

Measuring excessive accumulations of offensive weapons systems

The U.N. register rests on the premise that international transfers of major conventional weapons are legitimate provided that they do not lead to excessive accumulations. There is also a consensus that, while the defensive use of force still has a legitimate role in international affairs, offensive doctrines and the aggressive use of force should be outlawed. This is a restatement of the principles adopted by all members of the United Nations through their acceptance of the U.N. Charter. This leads to obvious problems of definition.

Defining what is and what is not excessive cannot be done in the abstract or on a universal basis by a global body; wisely, the United Nations has not tried to provide any definition. As the case of Iraq illustrates, the definition of excessive armament certainly cannot be trusted to arms suppliers but can only emerge out of a dialogue between governments at the regional and subregional level. Similarly, the assessment of what types of weapons in what combinations and quantities are offensive has to be determined in a specific context.

*Measuring trends
in transfers of
advanced technology*

Establishing trends in transfers of advanced technology is a formidable challenge. The resolution that founded the U.N. register committed the United Nations to examine the issue of transparency in high technology with military applications. Consideration of this issue has been delegated to the Conference on Disarmament, and in 1992, informal meetings were held in an ad hoc committee. The initial discussions apparently underlined how hard it will be to find a concrete approach to this problem.

It is relatively easy to establish the broad categories into which advanced technology falls. A rudimentary list would include smart conventional weapons; stealthy weapons platforms; electronic warfare systems; and command, control, communications, and intelligence systems, both terrestrial and space based. The political constituency arguing for transparency in this area is weak in contrast to the commercial and military arguments against it.

The idea that after the Cold War the outcome of competition between nations or between corporations depends on economic, scientific, and technological strength is a powerful current perception. In the more narrow military arena, an equally strong notion is that technological advantage translates directly into battlefield success. Advanced technology is proprietary information owned by the corporations or—more often—the governments that paid for its development, and even if a method of defining advanced technology could be devised, governments have an interest in preventing the release of information about rates of acquisition and absorption.

In the absence of pressure for information release, the practical obstacles to measuring the movement of items are great. Many of the characteristics of a technology are invisible, such as increased speed in data processing, more effective software, or the tying together of several systems through data links.

These examples underline the extent to which advanced military technologies and the issue of dual-use technologies have come to overlap. Efforts to monitor the movement of mobile telecommunications systems and current-generation computers—especially microprocessors or software—have, thus far, defeated the efforts of the European Union to harmonize regulations on dual-use exports. After more than two years of intensive discussion between government experts, there is still no agreement, although many of the countries of the European Union have almost fifty years of experience with the Coordinating Committee on Multilateral Export Controls industrial list. Counterpressure from industrial lobbies who support a further deregulation of exports to enhance their competitiveness seems likely to block efforts at close monitoring of transfers of this kind.

*Measuring trends in
small-arms transfers*

Establishing trends in the transfers of small arms presents few definitional problems but formidable

TABLE 1
CONTAINERS HANDLED PER YEAR AT SELECTED PORTS

Country	Port	1984	1989	Percentage increase
Singapore	Singapore	1,552,184	4,364,000	181
Netherlands	Rotterdam	1,791,357	2,371,508	32
South Korea	Pusan	1,054,330	2,313,000	119
Belgium	Antwerp	965,003	1,473,746	53
Germany	Hamburg	854,318	1,306,989	53
United Kingdom	Felixstowe	495,410	957,634	93
Thailand	Bangkok	341,021	904,781	165
France	LeHavre	613,633	889,336	45
Spain	Barcelona	325,592	439,969	35

SOURCE: *Shipping Statistics* (Institute of Shipping Economics and Logistics, Bremen), p. 49 (Dec. 1990).

practical ones associated with government reluctance to release information, on the one hand, and the current nature of international trade, on the other.

The rapid and unbroken increase in the movement of standard-size closed containers through ports in countries with a domestic small-arms industry (see Table 1) underlines that monitoring of the legal trade can only occur with the consent and cooperation of governments and industry. Even if effective monitoring of the transfer of small arms could be achieved in these countries, the current situation in Central Europe and the former Soviet Union and the residual presence of large weapons stockpiles in Europe as well as places like Afghanistan, El Salvador, and Lebanon would still complicate the identification of trends in small-arms transfers.

*Measuring
financial flows*

Establishing an accurate picture of the financial flows associated with the arms trade is almost certainly impossible. It is also very doubtful that such a picture would have enough confidence to be useful in analysis.

Details about pricing are commercially sensitive secrets, and any published information is likely to have been deliberately highly aggregated in a way that makes it difficult to determine the price of any specific item. Moreover, as a variety of complex arrangements are likely to surround any one deal—such as government financing, private sector credit, partial payment in commodities, other types of offset arrangements or countertrade—even if the details are known, it would be many years before any final tally could be made. In the countries of the former Soviet Union, political pricing, in which money flows were arranged through bureaucrat-to-bureaucrat negotiations, has not been ended. The recent proliferation of contradictory official statements of revenue from arms exports that have come out of Russia should not be taken to mean that accurate information is now being generated. Moreover, the growing use of the government-to-government memoranda of understanding by European countries suggests that a process of government-industry collaboration and the close political management of trade is not becoming any less pervasive.

*Measuring trends in
    the transfers of
    production licenses*

The fact that customers can now establish many of the conditions for access to their market has brought changes in the industrial organization of the arms industry. One condition is that a proportion of production is devolved to recipients, but establishing exactly what this proportion consists of is a very difficult undertaking.

Devolved tasks could range from simple assembly to effective autonomy that would permit continued production without any assistance from the original supplier. Moreover, this is a dynamic process in which the competence of the customer may grow across time—though this competence is different in different cases depending on the level of aspiration of the recipient and the capacity for technology absorption of the recipient. In some cases, the nominal recipient is even able to sell product improvements back to the country of origin.

From this overview, it is clear that an enormous amount is not measured and will not be under the most optimistic scenario for increased transparency. Nonetheless, while our current indexes are calibrated crudely, they do permit general con-

clusions about broad trends and a framework in which to argue.

The following section examines trends contained in recent published studies by the main agencies attempting to measure the arms trade.

RECENT TRENDS IN THE
CONVENTIONAL ARMS TRADE

Among the groups that attempt to monitor the arms trade, it is agreed that the volume and value of transfers turned downward in the mid-1980s. Figure 1 compares global deliveries of arms as recorded by the Stockholm International Peace Research Institute (SIPRI) and the U.S. Arms Control and Disarmament Agency (ACDA). Figure 2 compares deliveries to developing countries as recorded by the Congressional Research Service (CRS) with deliveries to the same countries as recorded by SIPRI.

The match between the trends reported is remarkable, especially given the fact that the agencies concerned apply significantly different definitions of the arms trade. However, when comparisons are made between the specific country data available from the different agencies, many discrepancies appear for both exporters and importers. The perfect match between the aggregated data sets must therefore be a coincidence, reflecting the fact that the discrepancies cancel each other out. Nevertheless, in spite of these specific discrepancies, there are some broad findings that are common to each of the data sets.[4] The reduction in the overall

4. From this point, the comparison is between SIPRI and CRS data only. The most recent data available from ACDA end in 1989,

FIGURE 1
A COMPARISON OF SIPRI AND ACDA DATA

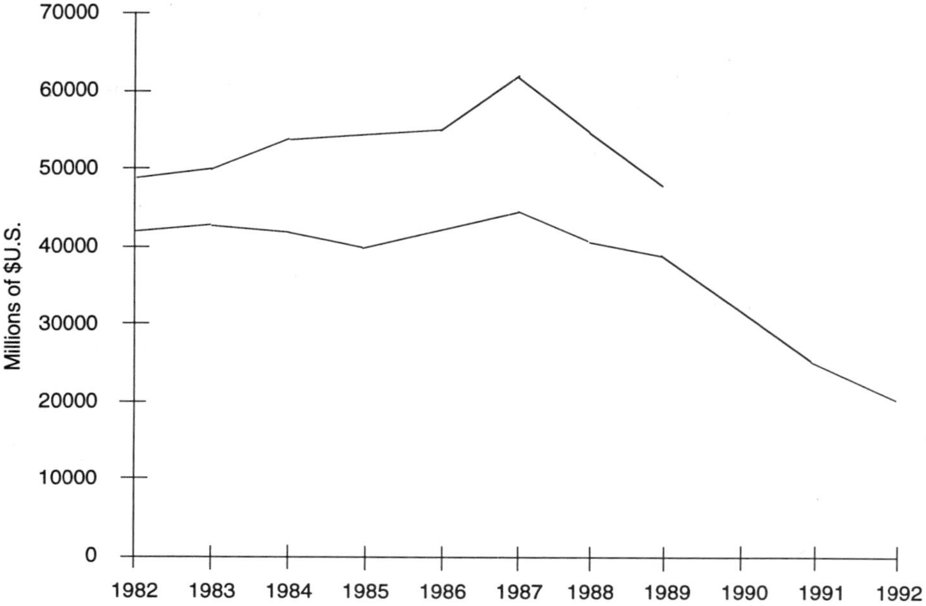

SOURCES: The SIPRI data are from the SIPRI arms trade database. The ACDA data are from U.S., Arms Control and Disarmament Agency, *World Military Expenditures and Arms Transfers 1990* (Washington, DC: Government Printing Office, 1991).

NOTE: SIPRI data are expressed in 1990 U.S. dollars; ACDA data in 1989 U.S. dollars.

value is primarily explained by the reduction in the scale of former Soviet arms transfers, though there is also agreement that the value of transfers from France has fallen significantly as well. However, the reduction in overall value began before the collapse of the Warsaw Treaty Organization and the dissolution of the Soviet Union. While the change in the central relationship is one of the most important factors in the downturn in the volume of the arms trade, it is not the only factor.

since when there have been fundamental changes in the global arms market.

From the late 1940s to 1990, the global arms trade was dominated by two superpowers, which used arms transfers to support wider foreign and security policies in the framework of the Cold War. In addition to being the two largest arms producers and arms exporters, the United States and the Soviet Union—as the leaders of alliances whose members also possessed significant defense industrial capacity—were able to influence the arms transfer policies of other important arms suppliers. Inevitably, the collapse of the Soviet Union and the change in U.S.-Soviet/Russian relations that resulted from

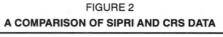

FIGURE 2
A COMPARISON OF SIPRI AND CRS DATA

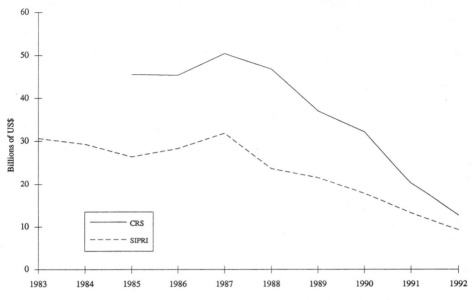

SOURCE: The SIPRI data are from the SIPRI arms trade database. The CRS data are from Richard F. Grimmett, *Conventional Arms Transfers to the Third World, 1985-92*, Report 93-656F (Washington, DC: Congressional Research Service, 1993).
    NOTE: SIPRI data are expressed in 1990 U.S. dollars; CRS data, in 1992 U.S. dollars.

it had a major impact on the arms trade. However, the international economic environment, coupled with the escalating cost of major systems, has been another factor constraining transfers. In addition, in some cases—notably, Latin America and parts of southern Africa—political changes that are not associated with the end of the Cold War have also depressed demand.

The arms trade is a highly concentrated activity involving a small number of exporters and a small number of importers. Among the exporters, it is a common finding that the United States is now the predominant supplier of arms and that a stable group of five countries—China, France, Germany, Russia, and the United Kingdom—represents an important second tier of exporters.

There is disagreement about the relative importance of several exporters, notably China and the United Kingdom. The discrepancy related to the United Kingdom is easier to explain, as the spike in CRS data for the period 1987-90 presumably reflects the implementation of the 1-Yamamah memoranda of understanding reached between the United Kingdom and Saudi Arabia in 1985 and 1988. Much of these related to military construction and training rather than hardware transfers, which were, from a U.K. perspective, disappointing. Several contracts anticipated in 1985—such as for the British version of the U.S. Blackhawk helicopter—have never been placed, while others were agreed in a modified form only in 1993.

The United Kingdom represents a challenge to the SIPRI method of measurement because its exports consist mainly of communication systems—notably tactical radios—and component sales to overseas subsidiaries of British companies, mostly defense electronics and aerospace engineering companies like GEC, Smiths Industries, and Lucas Aerospace. Neither product type is included in SIPRI figures, and the importance of the United Kingdom as a technology supplier is understated. The SIPRI method reflects the reduction in heavy engineering in the United Kingdom.

While the volume of Chinese exports to the Middle East fell after the 1980-88 Iraq-Iran war, China still has important Asian clients including Pakistan, Thailand, Myanmar, and Bangladesh. The figures recorded for China by the CRS presumably represent an estimate of real financial flows as bilateral transfers to these countries have been undertaken at friendship prices and represent a political rather than economic linkage.

Among importers there is broad agreement about which are the most important countries and similar levels of concentration. In the eight-year period 1985-92, the ten largest recipients in the developing world accounted for 63 percent of all deliveries according to SIPRI and 69 percent according to the CRS data. Compar-

ing the two for 1992, the ten largest recipients accounted for 78 percent of deliveries according to SIPRI, against 80 percent for CRS.

For the period 1985-92, eight countries are common to both SIPRI and CRS listings of the ten largest importers among developing countries: Afghanistan, Angola, Egypt, India, Iran, Iraq, Saudi Arabia, and Syria. SIPRI includes Israel and North Korea among the ten largest importers for this period, while the CRS lists Cuba and Vietnam. For 1992, seven countries are common to both lists: China, Egypt, India, Iran, Israel, Saudi Arabia, and Syria. SIPRI also lists Thailand, Pakistan, and South Korea among its top ten, while the CRS data include Taiwan, Kuwait, and the United Arab Emirates. In a comparable list from SIPRI for 1992, these countries would rank 11, 14, and 16, respectively.

Concentration in the global arms trade has increased to the point where, by 1992, only around 25 countries were active recipients of major weapons. (See Figure 3.) The members of this group have also changed. Of the 25 largest importers in 1983, only 9 remained in the 1992 listing. In 1983, there were no countries of the Conference on Security and Cooperation in Europe (CSCE) among the 10 largest arms recipients. In 1992, there were 4: Greece, Turkey, the United Kingdom, and the United States.

Looked at on a regional basis, Asian countries became progressively more important as arms importers during the decade of the 1980s. The Middle East, by contrast, has declined in importance relative

FIGURE 3

PERCENTAGE OF DELIVERIES TO THE 25 LARGEST RECIPIENTS, 1983-92.

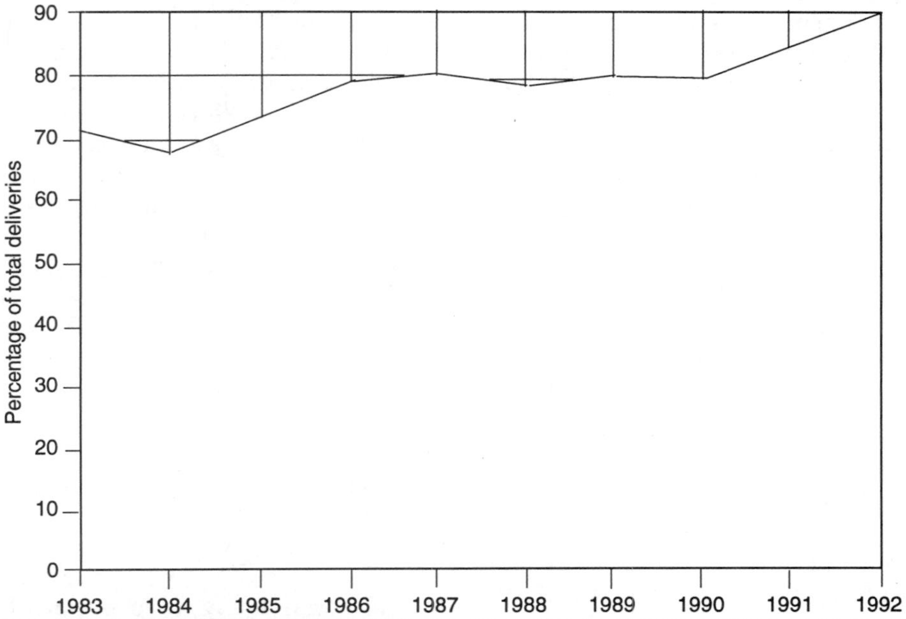

SOURCE: SIPRI arms trade database.

to both Asia and Europe.[5] The growing importance of European countries as importers reflects several recent developments.

Countries such as France and the United Kingdom have emerged as major arms importers largely because of the delivery of highly advanced systems such as the E-3 Sentry Airborne Early Warning aircraft from the United States. In spite of their historical role as leading designers, the cost and complexity of

5. While CRS data indicate that the importance of the Near East has remained constant, European countries are excluded from the country coverage, as are other important importers, notably Japan. The increasing importance of Asian countries in the CRS data indicates a decline in Latin American and sub-Saharan African sales.

major platforms of this type are beyond the national means of single European producers. No European country can now sustain more than one or two major programs to develop advanced systems at any one time.

The current importance of European countries as arms recipients also reflects the disposal of large quantities of material that is surplus either because of perceived changes in national requirements or because of arms control commitments under the 1990 Conventional Forces in Europe Treaty. Much of this equipment has become available with the draw-down of forces in Germany. The United States, Germany, and the Netherlands have been the principal suppliers, while the main destination for this equipment has been the southern and southeastern parts of Europe, with Greece and Turkey being particularly important.[6] While the demilitarization of Germany is well under way, the process still has some way to go. The European Disposal Office of the U.S. Department of Defense currently anticipates receiving 137,500 tons of major end items and 7500 tons of spare parts by 1995. Such equipment as cannot be reutilized by the U.S. armed forces will be sold or given away to disaster relief agencies and foreign countries.

MEDIUM- TO
LONG-TERM TRENDS

If the current pattern of the arms trade is dictated by the combination of continued demand but no purchasing power, then the trade will begin to rise as soon as the economic means are available. However, this is unlikely to occur quickly enough to prevent the major arms-producing countries from having to reduce their industrial capacities. This concentration will in turn have an impact on the international arms trade. Moreover, more and more customers are learning how to conduct their arms procurement in an efficient and effective manner. This development may be strengthened by a growing tendency toward closer scrutiny and accountability in national decision

6. The implementation of these transfers of secondhand equipment has been described in successive SIPRI Yearbooks in 1991, 1992, and 1993. For a full accounting of the destination of U.S. equipment over the past three years, see *Security Assistance: Excess Defense Articles for Foreign Countries*, GAO/NSIAS-93-164FS (Washington, DC: General Accounting Office, 1993).

making associated with the focus on good government.

Only manufacturers with deep pockets seem likely to be around if and when global military expenditure begins to grow again. If this is true, then the most financially secure producers are likely to have a diversified civil-military product base (permitting cross-subsidy between defense and civil divisions), low indebtedness, and tolerant taxpayers. Almost all of the arms producers in Central Europe seem certain to be eliminated by their combination of defense dependence and massive debt. The situation in Russia has been complicated by the size and political influence of the defense industry. While it may be right that only shock therapy will force the industrial sector in Russia to change its behavior, the industrial lobby is so powerful that the politics of survival still force President Yeltsin to subsidize the arms industry and maintain production without orders to sustain employment. However, current production capacity could not be sustained by foreign sales alone even in a buoyant global market. The production of systems for which there is no demand wastes resources, consumes capital, and postpones the difficult adjustments that must at some point be made. As a consequence, what Julian Cooper has called "a rapid and brutal downsizing of the defense industry" is inevitable in Russia.[7]

Sales of major new systems are increasingly likely to be conducted in

7. Julian Cooper, speaking at the workshop "Conventional Arms Proliferation in the 1990s," Carnegie Endowment for International Peace, Washington, DC, 9-10 July 1992.

partnership between government and industry. Arms purchases are also increasingly likely to be linked with other aspects of bilateral trade. In part, this reflects the difficulties of financing arms transfers, but it also underlines the political symbolism that both exporters and importers continue to attach to major defense contracts. Even though the arms trade makes up a trivial proportion of international economic activity—at the most generous estimate, it cannot represent more than 1.5 percent of global trade—major defense contracts continue to guarantee widespread public attention.

The importance of sales of major platforms vis-à-vis defense industrial activities that prolong the effective life of equipment currently in service is likely to decline. Further growth in the market for retrofits and upgrades tailored to specific major platforms seems inevitable.[8] While most major conventional weapons platforms are modified several times during their life, these modifications tend to be small in size. In the future, weapons platforms are likely to undergo major modification or almost total rebuilding. This reflects the fact that the aircraft, ship, or armored vehicle has a frame that lasts much longer than the engines, electronics, or weapons on it. Some upgrades offer almost the same combat power for an estimated 20-35 percent of the cost of a new system.

From an industry point of view, this market has favored small- and medium-sized companies that lack

the technical and financial resources to develop major new systems but that may be able to develop specific electronic subsystems. The complexity of this market is likely to grow as more companies—including those in countries such as Israel—learn how to modernize the tens of thousands of armored vehicles, artillery pieces, and land-based air defense systems produced in the former Soviet Union and still in service around the world. Under current conditions, major companies are likely to turn to this as a means of generating revenue, but the market is probably too dispersed to permit reconcentration.[9]

The sale of services rather than products also seems to be becoming more widespread. While this has been done nationally in several countries, in the future, governments may contract out to foreign suppliers repair and maintenance tasks previously performed by the armed services. Recipients may also make greater use of leasing arrangements, including the lease of major capabilities, in an effort to familiarize themselves with a technology before making a decision to buy it.

Another long-term development is a shift in the secondary centers of arms production away from Europe to Asia. While in most countries, the financial and technological obstacles

8. That is, modifying an already existent platform through the addition of new engines, electronics, and/or weapons.

9. The recent decision by Northrop to try and eliminate the Canadian company Bristol Aerospace as a rival for worldwide F-5 upgrades through litigation is a good example. If Northrop succeeds with Bristol Aerospace, other companies, including Bedek (Israel), Israel Aircraft Industries (Israel), Singapore Aerospace (Singapore), and Smiths Industries (United Kingdom), are all capable of performing similar upgrades.

to developing an arms industry are unlikely to be overcome, equipment modernization is affordable in several Asian countries, including China, India, Japan, South Korea, and Taiwan. Moreover, while imperfect, the information available suggests that all five countries increased their military research and development expenditure rapidly in the 1980s, albeit from a low baseline.

Even looking ahead 10-15 years, it is unlikely that Asian countries will occupy a place in the arms market comparable to their current dominance in some civil sectors. They are, however, likely to play a greater role than they do today. Moreover, while China, India, and Japan have sizable national requirements, Indonesia, Singapore, South Korea, and Taiwan have limited domestic demand for military equipment. The existence of production capacities in excess of domestic demand will create pressures to export.

Finally, the arms trade is likely to continue to expand to include more and different types of equipment and technology. Notable recent additions have included the development of a market for images taken from space by civilian satellites. The possibility that a U.S. military reconnaissance satellite might be sold to the United Arab Emirates and rumors that similar discussions are under way with South Korea and Spain also hint at a potential future development.

ANNALS, *AAPSS*, **535**, September 1994

The Internationalization
of the Arms Industry

By ELISABETH SKÖNS and HERBERT WULF

ABSTRACT: In the current environment of excess capacity in the arms industry in combination with a continuing trend of rising research and development costs in this sector, companies have become increasingly active in attempting to apply strategies of internationalization to arms-producing activities. At the same time, the end of the Cold War has led to a relaxation in government attitudes toward military technology transfers within a broad group of industrialized countries. This article discusses three basic forms of internationalization: exports, foreign direct investment, and international cooperation arrangements. Cross-border merger and acquisition activities are mainly concentrated in Western Europe, in particular in the aerospace and electronics sectors, but there are also examples of international restructuring outside these areas. International cooperation projects with the Russian arms industry have been limited in number and scope, due to their uncertain future prospects.

Elisabeth Sköns is a researcher on the Stockholm International Peace Research Institute (SIPRI) arms transfer and arms production project. Previously, she was a researcher at the Research Service of the Swedish Parliament. She is the author or coauthor of chapters in several editions of the SIPRI Yearbook.

Herbert Wulf is director of the Bonn International Center for Conversion. Previously, he was leader of the SIPRI project on arms transfers and arms production. He is editor of the SIPRI book Arms Industry Limited *(1993).*

A new development in the global arms industry is the occurrence since the late 1980s of international takeovers and joint ventures. Cross-border merger and acquisition activities are mainly concentrated in Western Europe, but there are examples of international restructuring in other sectors as well. While there have been many instances of cross-border cooperation between companies at the levels of subcontracting, licensing, and collaboration in advanced weapons research and production, the trend toward increasing joint ventures is a new phenomenon.

This development has attracted broad attention, since it breaks with the current notion of the defense industrial base as a national asset. It raises a number of essential questions regarding the structure of the arms industry. Is this a stable trend that will continue in Western Europe? Will the geographical scope of this development expand to include the rest of the countries in the North Atlantic Treaty Organization, the Organization for Economic Cooperation and Development (OECD), the Commonwealth of Independent States, and the developing world? Are the observed cases of international takeovers and joint ventures isolated cases, or are they part of a broader pattern of industrial internationalization?

The focus of this article is on the companies. Their international interaction is the point of departure for the analysis of implications for government policy. In the current arms industrial environment of excess capacity in combination with a continuing trend of rising research and development costs in this sector, companies have become increasingly active in attempting to apply strategies of internationalization to arms-producing activities. At the same time, the end of the Cold War has led to a relaxation in government attitudes toward military technology transfers within a broad group of industrialized countries. At least within this group of countries, new developments seem to be initiated on the company level, while governments take a more reactive role.

The scope of this article is not sufficiently broad to cover developments in other than the major arms-producing countries. This leaves out China and the newly industrialized countries in East Asia, a region in which some argue that important changes are under way in arms production.

CONCEPTS AND ISSUES
OF INTERNATIONALIZATION

The internationalization of industrial activities is a broad concept covering a range of different company activities involving actors in more than one country. These activities can take different forms, including foreign trade, foreign investment, cross-border mergers and acquisitions, international subcontracting, international licensing, international joint ventures, and international interfirm agreements. Some of these forms overlap with others, but they still serve well in the conceptualization of internationalization.

The internationalization of industry by OECD countries during the postwar era has developed in three main phases with regard to the most expansive form of industrial internationalization. These are the phases of foreign trade, foreign direct investment (FDI), and international interfirm alliances.

The great expansion in foreign trade through the late 1960s was followed by a strong growth in foreign investment—mainly in production facilities—in the 1960s and the early 1970s, followed by another peak in the mid-1980s. These were the decades of company expansion into multinational, or transnational, corporations. During the current, third, phase of internationalization, these two forms have been complemented by new patterns of international industrial linkages. Joint ventures, subcontracting, licensing, and interfirm agreements are the more common examples of these international networks. International interfirm agreements seem to be the form of internationalization that has expanded most in the 1990s.[1]

The internationalization of the arms industry has not proceeded at the same pace as the rest of industry. It is true that trends in the internationalization of industrial activities vary by industrial sector, but even within the same industrial sector, trends differ between the arms-producing activities and nonmilitary, or so-called commercial, production. The trend in international interfirm agreements is more difficult to interpret, mainly because it encompasses such a variety of types of agreement.

1. See, for example, Organization for Economic Cooperation and Development, *Globalisation of Industrial Activities* (Paris: Organization for Economic Cooperation and Development, 1992).

The reasons for this difference are related not only to differences in demand but also to the specific characteristics of the market for arms industrial goods and services. Both these factors are basically the result of government intervention: economic and political/legislative. The economic factors include the degree of state ownership, government-sponsored company research and development (R&D), and the specific procurement practices and contracts applied for military equipment. The legislation concerns the production and transfer of military technologies. These factors all act as impediments to internationalization. A difference between foreign trade in military and nonmilitary products, which is likely to have the opposite effect, is the existence of offsets. While in commercial trade, offset practices are regarded as negative trade distortions to be avoided, they are increasingly common in international arms transfer contracts. To the extent that offsets include arms-producing activities, they would foster their internationalization.

In general, it can be assumed that, without government intervention, the internationalization of arms-producing activities would more closely parallel that of the industrial sector of which it is a part. This assumption is reinforced by the fact that most arms-producing activities take place in companies with civilian production in the same industrial sector.

MEASURING THE
INTERNATIONALIZATION OF
ARMS-PRODUCING COMPANIES

Measures of industrial internationalization relate to the type of internationalization. The degree of internationalization of a company or a country in terms of foreign trade is measured primarily by export shares of total sales or output. Import penetration is another valid measure, depending on the perspective. The degree of internationalization by FDI is measured by the foreign subsidiaries controlled by the parent company as a share of the total economic activity of the transnational corporation or the national economy. The variables commonly used include output, value added, employment, and assets.[2] There are no good measures for the trends in interfirm agreements. Lists of international interfirm agreements provide an indication of the volume and direction of activities, but means of aggregation and a frame of reference are missing.[3]

*Concepts of exports
    and foreign sales used in
    company annual reports*

Although the concept of exports is itself straightforward, defined as cross-border sales, it is not a straightforward concept at all in the context of transnational corporations. First, there are exports from the home country of the parent company. These can be to external customers and/or to its foreign subsidiaries (intracompany exports). Second, there are

2. See, for example, U.N. Centre on Transnational Corporations (UNCTC), *The Process of Transnationalization and Transnational Mergers*, UNCTC Current Studies, series A, no. 8 (New York: UNCTC, 1989), p. 3 ff.
3. A meaningful aggregation cannot be made unless the type, importance (in terms of, for example, technology), or size (for example, production value) of the agreement can be identified and measured.

sales by foreign subsidiaries. These can be domestic sales in the country of the subsidiary, intracompany export sales, exports to external customers in the country of the parent company, or exports to other countries. Third, there is foreign output, or turnover, which is the value of production in foreign subsidiaries. Sales by foreign subsidiaries are the combined value of their own output and the net purchases from their parent company. For production subsidiaries, the difference between output and sales is usually small.

Companies usually provide data on exports, on sales by foreign subsidiaries, or on total foreign sales as the sum of the two former minus intracompany sales, but seldom on all three of these. Therefore, the only set of data that can be constructed for a relatively large number of companies is for a least value of foreign sales, indicating a minimum degree of dependence on foreign markets.

OUT OF ECONOMIC NECESSITY:
INTERNATIONALIZATION IN
WESTERN EUROPE AND RUSSIA

Declining arms procurement budgets and shrinking arms exports have made it impossible in Western Europe to sustain the arms industrial base of the 1970s and 1980s and to maintain several industrial competitors for each weapons requirement of the armed forces. In Russia, procurement cuts have been dramatic and the scope for conversion to nonmilitary production has proved limited. Internationalization of the arms industry is one of the strategies applied in these countries.

Strategies of the major companies in Western Europe

A variety of strategies were adopted by West European companies since the downsizing of industry began at around 1988-89, ranging from an emphasis on exports and promotion of the core defense business to diversification, conversion, and plant closures.[4]

The kind of strategies varied widely in the different European countries, but even more so in a comparison of small and large companies. A study of the situation of the European arms industry concluded in 1992: "The development of national champions (monopoly suppliers in individual European countries) and proliferating transnational ties were the two dominant trends in the European defence industry in the 1980s."[5] These two strategies—national concentration and internationalization—were and still are the typical reaction of big companies. Major companies tried to improve their business position by increasing their share in a shrinking market at the expense of small- and medium-size companies. Smaller arms-producing companies were purchased at the national level, and cross-border mergers and acquisitions occurred to an unprecedented degree within the arms industry.[6]

If these developments are realistically described, the results are major consequences for the future structure of the industry and for exports and export control. It seems that, for the first time, the 1990s might see the emergence of an integrated West European arms industry. A coordinated West European approach to weapons development, production, procurement, and industry has been attempted for decades. It has never materialized, despite promises and political action plans. Since the need for adjustment has become apparent, it seems that industry is now prepared to take the necessary action. In several of the interviews conducted for this article, company representatives emphasized that while governments in Europe are still at the level of discussing a restructured and streamlined European arms industry, a European arms procurement agency within the Western European Union, and harmonized export regulation in the European Union (EU), industry is not prepared to wait for such an agreement, but is acting now, out of economic necessity, by engaging in intensified international linkages, particularly through FDI.

For many companies, the route to survival is sought in new cooperation structures that go beyond the previously well-known single program collaborations or the concentration on families of products. These traditional types of cross-boundary activ-

4. This process is succinctly described by Jorg Huffschmid and Werner Voß, "Militarische Beschaffungen, Waffenhandel, Rustungskonversion in der EG," *Progress* (Institute fur Wirtschaftsforschung-Studien), no. 7, pp. 41-55 (1991).

5. James B. Steinberg, *The Transformation of the European Defense Industry: Emerging Trends and Prospects for Future U.S.-European Competition and Collaboration* R-4141-ACQ (Santa Monica, CA: RAND, 1992), p. x.

6. Elisabeth Sköns, "Internationalisation of the West European Arms Industry," in *Arms Industry Limited*, ed. Herbert Wulf (New York: Oxford University Press, 1993), pp. 160-90.

ity could be seen as "main alliances" to concentrate on major projects.[7] In the 1990s, the large West European companies are becoming more and more interconnected, not only at the level of joint development or production but also at the capital investment level.[8] Looking at the trend in mergers and acquisitions and the formation of joint stock companies, it seems that West European companies have now decided to concentrate—in certain sectors, even monopolize—to remain internationally competitive.

In parts of the arms industry, but by no means in all sectors, genuine European companies are emerging. The most prominent examples are listed, as follows.

In missile development and production, the focus is on Euromissile, set up by Aérospatiale and Deutsche Aerospace (DASA) in 1972, and the planned merger of the tactical missile business of Matra and BAe. Industry spokespersons hint that this so-called two-plus-two solution may not be far-reaching enough. To compete with their much larger U.S. ri-

vals, such as Martin Marietta or Raytheon, Europe's four largest missile producers may have to merge into one company.[9]

Restructuring is also taking place in the helicopter sector. Of the four major West European helicopter producers—Aérospatiale, DASA, Westland, and Agusta—two have merged with the establishment of Eurocopter, combining the helicopter branches of Aérospatiale and DASA in a company with 11,950 employees and 11.6 billion French francs turnover in 1992.[10] According to the chairman of Eurocopter, this merger makes Eurocopter " 'Europe's largest helicopter manufacturer and the world's largest exporter.' "[11] As Eurocopter's share of the world military helicopter market has plunged from 20 to 15 percent during 1991-92, it could well be that a West European-wide merger is on the agenda.[12]

The aerospace engine sector is characterized by networks of project-oriented cooperation rather than by changes in industry structure. In this sector, the partner companies are not limited to Western Europe. Traditional international ties, dating back to the 1960s, link SNECMA (France)

7. The term "main alliance" is used and described in great detail, particularly for the aerospace sector of the West European arms industry, in David Fouquet, Manuel Kohnstamm, and Michael Noelke, eds., *Dual-Use Industries in Europe* (Brussels: European Community, 1991), pp. A-81-A-93. For a recent description of the different types of collaborative arrangements, see William Walker and Philip Gummett, *Nationalism, Internationalism and the European Defence Market*, Challiot Papers, no. 9 (Paris: Western European Union, Institute for Security Studies, 1993).

8. A notable predecessor of the present trend of joint ventures is Euromissile, a company owned by DASA (previously MBB) and Aérospatiale, dating back to 1972 and set up to develop and produce missiles.

9. An unnamed French industry spokesperson is quoted in *Defense News*, 10-16 May 1993, p. 3. Dr. Thomas Enders of DASA argued similarly in a telephone conversation with one of the authors on 6 Aug. 1993 and characterized the formula of the two-plus-two arrangement as not being sufficient to operate competitively on the global market.

10. *Eurocopter Group 1992 Annual Report* (Paris: Eurocopter S.A., 1993), pp. 3, 17.

11. Jean-Francois Bigay, quoted in *Jane's Defence Weekly*, 24 Oct. 1992, p. 40.

12. Different shares are being published. This percentage is taken from *Interavia Air Letter*, 22 Apr. 1993, p. 1.

with General Electric (United States); MTU (Federal Republic of Germany) with Pratt & Whitney (United States), and Turbomeca (France) with Rolls Royce (United Kingdom). At least three international companies have been formed more recently, mostly for the management of specific projects: Eurojet Turbo was formed in 1986 by MTU, Rolls Royce, FiatAvio of Italy, and ITP of Spain to produce the engine for the Eurofighter; MTU Turbomeca Rolls Royce was established in 1989 to produce the engine for the Tiger/Gerfaut helicopter; and BMW/Rolls Royce was founded in 1990. International cooperation in engine programs goes beyond these companies and involves companies in Belgium, the Netherlands, and Japan. In contrast to the previously mentioned sectors, the formation of one or two major companies in the aerospace engine sector that would dominate the West European market does not seem to be a short-term option.

Concentration in the small arms and ammunition sector has taken place over the past few years. France's GIAT Industries and British Royal Ordnance (a subsidiary of BAe) are emerging as the major producers. GIAT bought the Belgian small arms producer Herstal, and British Aerospace bought the German small arms producer Heckler & Koch. With the small number of producers in Western Europe, these acquisitions have led to a concentration of industry.

In the military electronics sector, internationalization started earlier than in any other arms-producing sector and also seems to have proceeded further, perhaps because the military production part is more integrated with its civil counterpart in electronics. The major companies in this sector—Thomson, GEC, Matra, and Siemens—are not primarily arms producers but high-technology companies that operate globally.

In other sectors of the arms industry, both national and international concentration have taken place to a much lesser degree. Despite the limitations of the Conventional Forces in Europe Treaty concerning the holdings of tanks, several major tank producers remain basically national champions, hoping to survive at competitors' expense. All these companies have, during 1993, met in a number of competitions for new-generation tanks, primarily in the Middle East and in Europe. The offered offsets have been very generous, perhaps indicating the reality that in the absence of cooperation one or two of these companies will have to shut down their production lines for tanks in the near future.

In the production of combat ships, companies are still structured along national lines and hope to survive mainly with the support of government subsidies—for their production of mercantile ships—and exports of warships.

Internationalization of the large companies has already taken place to a great extent. There are strong interconnections between most major companies in Western Europe. This does not, however, mean that a structured and streamlined European industry with Eurocompanies is already in existence. On the contrary, the companies are tough competitors, particularly in exports.

*Russian international
cooperation projects*

Faced with drastic military procurement cuts in Russia and limited scope for conversion to nonmilitary production, Russia's arms plants are desperately trying to prevent closures and to secure their existence by implementing two strategies beside nonmilitary production: export of finished products and cooperation with Western firms in selected technological fields.

Both of these strategies have their limitations, however. Despite frantic activities by industry in arms trade fairs in several countries of the world and active promotion of exports by politicians, the actual number of deals has been limited, and exports of arms from Russia are but a small fraction of the previous exports by the Soviet Union.[13] The second initiative has also been, so far, an unpredictable source of income. Many Western arms-producing firms, particularly in the aerospace sector, have surveyed the potential of their counterparts in Russia, but the agreed projects in arms production have so far been limited in number and scope. This is not due to unattractive technology offers by the Russian firms; on the contrary, there are many interesting technology fields, and, according to a professional journal, Russia's aerospace capabilities are "extensive and world-class."[14]

Instead, international cooperation has been limited by two factors. First,

13. Ian Anthony et al., "Arms Production and Arms Trade," in *SIPRI Yearbook, 1993* (New York: Oxford University Press, 1993), pp. 444-45.

14. *Air Force Magazine*, p. 60 (Aug. 1993).

the political and legal situation in Russia has constrained investment by Western companies. The instability of the political system and the slow process of the privatization of industry have led Western companies to hesitate to move forward in a decisive way. Second, and possibly more important, the business prospects of Western companies have been —and remain—poor. Western companies suffering from overcapacities are interested in joint ventures in Russia only if such cooperation promises to solve some of their difficulties.

The few important military projects reportedly agreed by late 1993 are agreements listed in Table 1.

The status of a number of projects is not always clear. Often memoranda of understanding have been signed or intentions have been expressed. Whether or not they will be realized, and if so, to what extent, is currently an open question.

PATTERNS OF INTERNATIONALIZATION

Foreign sales as a form of internationalization in the arms industry have since the late 1980s been complemented by an increasing extent of international company acquisitions and cross-border interfirm cooperation. The trend in international interfirm agreements is more difficult to identify, mainly because it encompasses such a variety of types of agreement.

*Dependence on foreign
markets of arms-
producing companies*

The foreign sales dependence of the top 42 arms-producing compa-

TABLE 1

INTERNATIONAL COOPERATION PROJECTS OF THE RUSSIAN MILITARY AEROSPACE INDUSTRY

Russian Partner	Western Partner	Partner Country	Date	Status	Purpose
Kamov	Eurocopter	France	1992	Agreed	Develop a new light multipurpose helicopter
Kamov	Group Vector	Switzerland United States	1992	Agreed	Build Ka-50 Hokum helicopters abroad and market in selected countries
Mikoyan GosNIIAS	Hughes Rediffusion Simulation	United Kingdom	1992	Agreed	Hughes Rediffusion Simulation to develop training and simulation systems for Russian aircraft, including MiG-29, MiG-31 fighters
Mikoyan	Promavia	Belgium	1992	Agreed	Market and possibly assemble the Promavia-designed ATTA-3000 advanced trainer
Mikoyan	SNECMA	France	1993	Agreed	Develop and build MiG-AT trainer with Larzac engines
Mikoyan	Auxilec (Thomson-CSF)	France	1993	Plans announced	Auxilec to supply avionics for MiG-AT trainer
Mikoyan	Messier-Bugatti (SNECMA)	France	1993	Plans announced	Messier-Bugatti to supply landing gear for MiG-AT
Mikoyan	Thomson-CSF	France	1993	Plans announced	Thomson to offer upgrades for MiG-21 fighters
Mil	Brooke Group	United States	1992	Joint venture formed	Provide technical support and spares to operators of Mil helicopters
Mil Kazan Klimov	Eurocopter	France	1992	Agreed	Eurocopter to integrate cockpit, avionics, and passenger system of Mil-developed Mi-38 helicopter and adapt it for the international civilian market; production by Kazan; military version considered
Perm (PNPP) Aviadvigatel	Pratt & Whitney (UTC)	Canada United States	1993	Agreed	Pratt & Whitney to help develop improved version of Perm PS-90P engine; first East-West engine venture
Yakovlev	Aermacchi	Italy	1992	Plans announced	Develop Yak-130 military trainer; first East-West military airframe venture

SOURCE: Stockholm International Peace Research Institute archives.

51

TABLE 2

FOREIGN SALES OF SELECTED ARMS-PRODUCING COMPANIES, 1991 OR 1992

		Foreign Sales Share of Total Sales	
		High (≥ 40%)	Low (< 40%)
		(A)	(C)
		Israel Aircraft Industries (88/ ≥ 81)	DCN (100/ < 10)
		Thomson-CSF (77/55)	Newport News (100/low)
		Dassault Aviation (74/ ≥ 53)	Ordnance Factories (96/ < 1)
		Litton (60/40)	Alliant Tech Systems (93/4)
	High (≥ 40%)	Alenia (55/ ≥ 49)	Loral (90/21)
		MBB (51/41)	Northrop (90/low)
		DASA (49/63)	General Dynamics (80/ ≥ 18)
		Oerlikon-Buhrle (46/74)	E-Systems (78/ > 9)
		Aérospatiale (40/ ≥ 68)	Grumman (72/7)
		British Aerospace (40/ > 66)	Lockheed (70/10)
Arms sales			GIAT (61/ ≥ 35)
share of			GM Hughes Electronics (57/ ≥ 18)
total sales			McDonnell Douglas (55/ ≥ 29)
			Raytheon (55/19)
		(B)	(D)
		SNECMA Groupe (31/57)	TRW (35/32)
		Rolls Royce (27/70)	Rockwell (34/19)
		Matra Groupe (26/ ≥ 52)	Texas Instruments (29/30)
		GEC (24/62)	CEA Industrie (25/28)
	Low (< 40%)	Unisys (20/51)	Westinghouse (18/22)
		United Technologies (19/40)	Tenneco (16/ ≥ 5)
		Boeing (17/58)	Mitsubishi Heavy Industries (14/22)
		Daimler Benz (7/57)	General Electric (10/19)
		Alcatel-Alsthom (4/ ≥ 58)	INI (7/ ≥ 31)

SOURCES: Company annual reports and, for Litton, *Defense News*, 19 July 1993. The data for this table were compiled by Bjorn Kuhne.

NOTE: The first figure in parentheses after the company name stands for the share of arms sales; the second stands for the share of exports; both figures are percentages.

nies on the Stockholm International Peace Research Institute's Top 100 List, for which data were available, is shown in Table 2. The relationships in this table indicate the following:

1. Companies with a high arms sales share (boxes A and C) do not have a lower foreign sales share than companies that are more diversified into commercial products.

2. Many of the companies with a low dependence on arms sales (B and D) either are in sectors in which the gap between military and nonmilitary technologies is small, such as aero-engines—for example, General Electric, Rolls Royce, and SNECMA—and electronics—Alcatel, GEC, Matra, TRW, Texas Instruments, Unisys, and Westinghouse—or are typical technology conglomerates,

such as United Technologies, Daimler Benz, Mitsubishi, and INI.

3. European companies have a high dependence on foreign sales. Among the 18 European companies in Table 3, only 4 are in the categories for low foreign sales shares (C-D): CEA Industrie, DCN, GIAT and INI. One of these, GIAT, which has an export share of 35 percent, is now rapidly increasing this share.[15]

4. U.S. companies, especially the aerospace giants, tend to be in the high arms sales, low foreign sales category (C). These companies specialize in arms production, and most of their products are sold in the domestic market. There are only four U.S. companies in the category with high foreign sales share, and only one of these, Litton, depends on arms sales for more than 20 percent of its total sales.

5. For non-OECD companies, there is no pattern, since only two non-OECD companies are represented in the table, Israel Aircraft Industries and Ordnance Factories of India.

Foreign direct
investment

Besides a surge of international takeovers in the West European arms industry, there have also been examples of transatlantic acquisitions and a few cases involving arms-producing companies in the developing countries cooperating with companies from the West. How can we interpret these cases? Do they indicate the emergence of a new and broad trend in the international defense industrial base? Or is this a phenomenon

15. *La Tribune Desfosses*, 15 Feb. 1993, p. 1.

of limited extent, geographically restricted to Western Europe or even to the EU or NATO countries, and timewise confined to an interim post-Cold War period of excess arms production capacity and relaxed government attitudes?

Recent developments in FDI in the arms industry appear to fall into two major types in terms of driving forces. First, there are the international takeovers of companies in the same field of production, vertically or horizontally. This is the type of development taking place mainly within Western Europe. Second, there is establishment of foreign subsidiaries or joint ventures for local assembly, production, marketing, or after-sales services. This type of development has a broader geographic spread. The first type represents an extension of industrial concentration from the national to the international level and is driven by rising R&D costs, excess production capacity, and the need for economies of scale. The second type represents a traditional objective of FDI as a substitute for exports.

Both these types of driving forces are strongly prevalent in the arms industry at present. Soaring unit costs and excess production capacity are probably even more significant in the military part of the aerospace industry than in the commercial part, although both are plagued with problems. The necessity to achieve economies of scale is strong also in most other arms-producing sectors. Three major sources of motivation for individual firms to invest in production in other countries as a substitute for exports are very pronounced in most arms-producing sectors. These sources are trade barriers, technical and legal; transportation costs; and after-sales services. The arms trade system is characterized by legal and political restrictions, high transportation costs of complete systems, and, in particular, high dependence on after-sales services, such as for maintenance and repairs.

Global industry at large is marked by two main developments. The first is the redirection of corporate strategy away from product diversification and geographical consolidation to product consolidation and geographical diversification, mainly through mergers and acquisitions.[16] Second, and with some overlap, the previous one-way flow of investment from the United States to the rest of the world has been replaced by significant FDI flows to the United States from both Europe and Japan, resulting in a triad of FDI flows between the three main trading blocs in the world: Europe, Japan/Southeast Asia, and North America. Substantial investment flows have also emerged within each part of this triad, often via mergers and acquisitions.[17]

Again, rigid comparisons with the arms industry are difficult to make due to lack of data specific to the arms industry. However, most analysts of the arms industry would probably agree on the following observations. In both North America and Western

Europe, we find intraregional flows of foreign investment in the arms industry. In North America, this is not a new development. Several of the major U.S. defense contractors have production facilities in Canada. In Western Europe, there is the new and marked expansion in international takeovers, at least in the military electronics and aerospace industries.[18] Within the Southeast Asian region, there appear as yet to be no significant investment flows in the arms industry. While there are numerous examples of intraregional mergers and acquisitions in the North American and West European arms industry, this is rare in the Southeast Asian region.[19] One factor behind this is probably the fact that Japan, which would be the natural center for such flows, has restrictive policies for the export of arms and military technologies.

As regards flows between regions of the triad, these appear to be much weaker in the arms industry. For the same reasons as previously mentioned, Japan is not a major actor in this field, in contrast to civil production. Instead, there are external flows from the United States and Western Europe into several countries in Southeast Asia, mainly for marketing activities but also for com-

16. UNCTC, *Process of Transnationalization and Transnational Mergers*, pp. 63-64.

17. UNCTC, *World Investment Report. The Triad in Foreign Direct Investment* (New York: United Nations, 1991), summarized in Margaret Sharp, "Industrial Policy in a Global Environment," *International Spectator*, 28(2): 26-27 (Apr.-June 1993).

18. For a description of the restructuring of the West European arms industry, see Susan Willett and William Walker, "Restructuring of the European Defence Industrial Base," *Defence Economics*, 4(2): 141-60 (1993).

19. See tables on international mergers and acquisitions in *SIPRI Yearbook 1990* (New York: Oxford University Press, 1990), pp. 336-37; *SIPRI Yearbook 1991* (New York: Oxford University Press, 1991), pp. 289-90; *SIPRI Yearbook 1993*, pp. 440-41.

ponent manufacture and assembly.[20] U.S. arms-producing subsidiaries in Europe are neither an unusual nor a new phenomenon, but U.S. takeovers of European companies are rare.[21] U.S. FDI flows to Japan seem to be more or less nonexistent in the arms industry. While globalization is one of the strategies considered for and by U.S. arms producers, these producers appear to be more interested in direct arms exports and more informal international cooperation arrangements than in takeovers of foreign companies.[22]

In the opposite direction, from Western Europe to the United States, the investment flows appear to have increased. Several European arms-producing companies have established a number of subsidiaries in the United States, and there have been examples of minor takeovers and several joint ventures. The limits to this development were defined, at least temporarily, by the well-known case of the attempt by the French electronics firm Thomson-CSF to acquire the missile division of the U.S. LTV Corporation. U.S. policymakers are now wrestling with the design of a long-term policy on foreign takeovers of critical U.S. industries.[23] On balance, however, the scope for future transatlantic ownership links involving any degree of control over development or manufacturing capacity for military equipment is limited.

International interfirm cooperation

While the concept of international interfirm cooperation, or alliances, is used in different ways by different authors, most of these include international joint ventures, subcontracting, licensing, and international interfirm agreements.

A significant number of international joint ventures in arms-producing activities have been set up during recent years. This appears to be a new development in the arms industry. Does this mean that the arms industry is entering the same phase as the rest of industry, where international interfirm agreements are becoming the most important form of internationalization in the 1990s?

International joint ventures and interfirm agreements, just like the FDI flows, can be categorized in two types. First, there is cooperation between rival firms for joint development of expensive new weapons systems and to share the related costs and risks. In many cases, such cooperation is an alternative to international concentration by mergers and acquisitions, which have been subject to political difficulties. Examples in-

20. Susan Willett, "Dragons' Fire and Tigers' Claws: Arms Trade and Production in Far East Asia," in *Post-Cold War Security Issues in the Asia-Pacific*, ed. Colin McInnes and Mark G. Rolls, special issue of *Journal of Arms Control and Contemporary Security Policy*, 15(2) (Aug. 1994).

21. This observation is based on the SIPRI company archives, which include files on about 500 arms-producing companies.

22. Judith Reppy, "Unmanaged Change in the Defence Industry," in *Arms Industry Limited*, ed. Wulf, pp. 56-57.

23. The issues involved are described and a framework for decision making is proposed in Theodore H. Moran, "Foreign Acquisitions of Critical U.S. Industries: Where Should the United States Draw the Line?" *Washington Quarterly*, 16(2): 61-71 (Spring 1993).

clude Euromissile, Eurocopter, and the EH Industries. Second, there are the joint venture structures formed as a result of large arms deals in which the buyer country has requested and achieved some localization of production—of parts, components, subsystems, assembly, or complete systems—such as the joint ventures of Tai and Tusas in Turkey to produce F-16 aircraft and engines under license. This is not a new development. These cases represent the establishment of new production lines and are not part of an international concentration process or the result of rising R&D costs. This type of venture could be expected to increase as a result of recipient leverage but not due to industrial factors on the supplier side.

If it is true that international alliances are a second-best alternative to international concentration of ownership,[24] then a change in government policy on foreign ownership in the arms industry will probably result in increased transnationalization through international mergers and acquisitions. That is, more liberal government policies would probably result in a wave of international takeovers in the arms industry.

IMPLICATIONS FOR THE
ARMS TRADE OF RECENT TRENDS
IN INTERNATIONALIZATION

Arrangements to control the flow of arms and technology are based on

24. Which also appears to be the implication of the data shown by P. Dussauge and B. Garette, "Industrial Alliances in Aerospace and Defence: An Empirical Study of Strategic and Organizational Patterns," Defence Economics, 4(2): 45-62.

national legislation. International arrangements, especially if based on interfirm agreements, make export control more difficult. The flow of difficult-to-control blueprints, technology, components, and subsystems is increased by such cross-national cooperation, and the final product, the finished weapons system, can be exported from the country with the most relaxed export control. Export control of the end product from another country by a country supplying component or technology inputs would require a complete redefinition of the lists of items in national arms export legislation or an elaborate system of end-user certificates for such components.

The impact on the implementation of existing rules would be strongest for international R&D projects, since there are a number of difficulties involved in defining the local and foreign content of the output of such projects and in regulating transfers accordingly.

Common export rules can also be seen as a precondition for further internationalization. Thomas Enders of DASA believes that, unless there are common rules and guidelines for exports, there will never be a truly European arms industry. Even the most advanced Eurocompanies, such as Eurocopter, are likely to be renationalized or at least French-dominated, not only because Aérospatiale's capital share is 60 percent but also because the German partner has to cope with more restrictive export regulations, while the French partner can rely on strong government support for exports. In the long run, Enders suggests, the German arms industry could even be reduced to a component supplier and lose its capability as a systems integrator.[25]

The European Defence Industries Group (EDIG), a Brussels-based association of West European arms producers, calls for an open European defense market in which "the European defence industry should have a preferred position within the [European] Community" and "a common set of rules governing the export of defence equipment."[26] EDIG Secretary General Graham Woodcock, of British Aerospace, has underlined the need for common rules for exports outside the EU. According to him, exports are at present regulated only for certain joint projects where government-to-government agreements have been signed. What industry would like to see are similar agreements that would be applied in general for company-to-company agreements.[27] Such an umbrella approval for dual-use and arms exports out-side the EU is, however, unlikely to be given, since it contradicts existing legislation in several countries.

What happens in East-West weapons development, production, and marketing cooperation can have sharp international repercussions. The Russian arms export policy has changed in several important ways. Soviet arms deliveries were seen as a foreign policy instrument in the struggle between the two military blocs. The situation is, of course, totally different today, and hard currency income is the overriding goal. There is a policy dilemma of economic pressures for expanded exports and technology cooperation versus political motives for restraint. International cooperative agreements as described previously are intended to enable survival of development and production facilities. Their aim is to intensify business activities, and they are thus a potential threat to arms export restrictions. It is, however, not at all certain that this trend will gather momentum or that it will have the intended effect of revitalizing the Russian defense industrial base.

As regards other geographical areas in the international arms trade market, generalizations from trends in Western Europe or even OECD countries must be avoided and the pattern in these regions analyzed on the basis of their specific conditions.

25. Thomas Enders, DASA, telephone conversation with one of the authors, 6 Aug. 1993.

26. Quoted from an unpublished paper of the European Defence Industries Group, presented by the president of EDIG, Jan Bosma, at the seminar "Future Options for the European Defence Market," West European Union Institute for Security Studies, Paris, 20-30 Apr. 1993, pp. 1, 2.

27. Graham Woodcock, EDIG, telephone conversation with one of the authors, 6 Aug. 1993.

ANNALS, *AAPSS*, **535**, September 1994

Developments in the Global Supply of Arms: Opportunity and Motivation

By MICHAEL BRZOSKA and FREDERIC S. PEARSON

ABSTRACT: Likely trends in the supply side of the arms trade are examined, considering the opportunities and motives available to key actors and the changing international system that constrains their options. Among suppliers, the United States remains predominant, if somewhat more commercially than hegemonically oriented than in the past. Despite reassertive efforts and lower prices in the arms field, Russian export prospects are questionable, given uncertainties over budgetary investments, lagging technology, and potentially unreliable parts production or supply. West European sales are likely to remain confined to niches, since there still are no single unified European Union production and marketing mechanisms. China, the least predictable supplier, remains on an economic arms sales push. The depressed market for third-tier suppliers seems likely to persist. The global move to restructure defense industries is likely to lead to a shift from overproduction of finished arms, with many dual-use products emerging instead.

Michael Brzoska is a senior research scholar at the Center for the Study of Wars, Armaments and Development of the Institute of Political Science, University of Hamburg, Germany. Frederic S. Pearson is director of the Center for Peace and Conflict Studies and professor of political science at Wayne State University in Detroit. The two have col- laborated on a number of studies of arms transfers, including Arms and Warfare: Escalation, De-escalation, Negotiation *(1994).*

IN a sense, it seems a waste of time to take a hard look at the selling side of the trade in arms. Arms exports, after all, are an outgrowth of the arms production sector, and today there are large overcapacities.[1] Isn't everybody trying to sell as hard as they can?

While it is true that in the early 1990s the size of the decreasing international arms market is predominantly determined from the demand side, with buyers having more choice and less money than for several decades, there are still important questions on the supply side. Arms production and the resultant trade entail at once motives of state security (domestic or foreign), economic welfare (either governmental concern for the general domestic economy or firms' concern about their own survival and profits), and technological advancement (a form of prestige and a ticket to the top ranks of today's trading economies).[2] How is the pursuit of these goals affected? Who is losing which markets and policy options? How does the restructuring of supply affect prospects of arms transfer control? Will the economic pressure to export grow or decrease?

Even more interesting is the longer run. In the tumultuous international situation of the early 1990s, the foundations are laid for the arms transfer system of the next century. Nobody knows yet what it will look like. If past experiences are anything to go by, we have three contenders. Number one is a largely commercialized arms transfer system, where arms are traded almost like all other goods. Number two is a highly restrictive system, where the trade in arms and related technology are considered exceptional. Number three is a power-oriented system where arms are given to friends but not to adversaries. Of course, a hybrid system combining certain of these features is distinctly possible.

Predicting developments in global arms supplies naturally entails a bit of crystal ball gazing, informed as much as possible by detectable emerging trends and policies. Prudent analysis should take actors and systems into account. Policy is made by actors, but often their moves are precipitated by the restrictions of a system. We will proceed here by looking first at actors and then at international arms transfers in a systems perspective, taking the links between these actors into consideration in both the shorter and the longer term. In the process, an important and useful distinction will be made between states' opportunities and motives to export arms.

1. See Herbert Wulf, ed., *Arms Industry Limited* (London: Oxford University Press, 1993).

2. For discussion of arms export motives, see, for example, Edward Kolodziej, "Arms Transfers and International Politics: The Interdependence of Independence," in *Arms Transfers in the Modern World*, ed. Stephanie G. Neuman and Robert E. Harkavy (New York: Praeger, 1980); Frederic Pearson and Edward Kolodziej, *The Political Economy of Making and Marketing Arms: A Test for the Systemic Parameters of Order and Welfare*, Occasional Paper 4/89 (St. Louis: University of Missouri, Center for International Studies, Apr. 1989); Keith Krause, *Arms and the State: Patterns of Military Production and Trade* (New York: Cambridge University Press, 1992).

SUPPLIERS

Future arms trade patterns are likely to depend upon who has the capabilities and occasion, along with the economic or strategic impetus to export. One key factor under opportunity would be the type and quantity of weapons produced and procured by supplier states, and therefore likely to be available for export.

United States

As far as capabilities are concerned, the United States is paramount, in terms of both generic military technologies and modern weapons systems. The key American advantages are the world's largest military research and development budget and a large, protected domestic market. The extent of government subsidies and the length of production runs provide U.S. arms industries with competitive advantages.

Extensive restructuring of companies has taken place due to the end of the Cold War and shrinking markets, however, and it is likely to continue.[3] Current indicators, such as reports on profitability, indicate that the fewer large corporate entities remaining in the arms business are more competitive on the world market than U.S. companies were during the "fat years" of the early and mid-1980s.[4] Already, American firms have dramatically increased their shares of the international trade in conventional weapons.[5] Some of this has been by default, with the demise of the USSR, but some of it also results from concerted and persistent sales campaigns, under the Clinton administration even involving high officials such as the secretary of commerce, who promoted weapons sales on an early trip to Europe.[6] The current and future U.S. position in international arms markets benefits from Washington's determination to maintain armed forces capable of at least 1-2 simultaneous regional involvements. In addition, President Clinton appeared to slow the pace of defense budget cutbacks in his budget proposal for fiscal year 1995.

Recent U.S. Air Force sales policy proposals also indicate a heightened desire for commercial payoff in the transfer of excess used fighter air-

3. It has been estimated within the industry that 75-80 percent of existing American weapons contractors, including subcontractors, could disappear from the arms market completely or become part of larger, more aggressive companies. Calvin Sims, "For Weapons Makers, a Time to Deal," *New York Times,* 17 Jan. 1993.

4. See Philip Finnegan, "U.S. Firms Profit in Worldwide Consolidation," *Defense News,* 19-25 January 1993, pp. 1, 18. Quote reprinted courtesy of *Defense News.* Copyright by Army Times Publishing Company, Springfield, Virginia.

5. Richard Grimmett, *Conventional Arms Transfers to the Third World* (Washington, DC: Congressional Research Service, 1993); Stockholm International Peace Research Institute, *SIPRI Yearbook 1993: Armament and Disarmament* (New York: Oxford University Press, 1993), pp. 443-48.

6. In the industry, it is acknowledged that Ronald Brown was the first commerce secretary to associate himself with arms exports. See John D. Morocco, "U.S. Strives for Balance in Defense Export Policy," *Aviation Week and Space Technology,* 7 June 1993, p. 91. On disagreements within the administration about the commercial viability of arms sales, see "Clinton Administration Gives Mixed Signals on Arms Trade," *Arms Trade News* (Council for a Livable World Education Fund) (June 1993).

craft. The plan is to upgrade aircraft that would previously have been shipped to allies and friends at cut-rate prices. The upgraded fighters would then be sold at depreciated market value, with the proceeds used to help pay for new Air Force equipment.[7]

Not only will U.S. industry have a competitive edge in many parts of the arms market, but Washington also is likely to retain some of its strategic goals through the supply of arms, this being a partially "hegemonic approach" to arms transfers. President Clinton evidently was talked out of supplying arms to Bosnian Muslims in 1993, but, clearly, such attempts to manipulate regional political outcomes through arms supply are still open to consideration. The Clinton team has been reluctant to commit to major changes in arms transfer policy. It seems set to follow the course of cautious expansion established during George Bush's presidency, with some shifts in the public presentation away from foreign policy considerations to domestic economic issues and with due regard for what it considers excessive supply by others, such as North Korean and Chinese missiles and Russian missile technology.

Arms still are used to pursue various forms of influence; this strategy includes hesitant efforts to build a "world order" through, or in conjunction with, the United Nations. Bargaining power is used to protect foreign assets, including remaining bases, and to reward clients' favorable behavior—for instance, in underwriting a further Arab-Israeli peace ac-cord. Longer-term attempts at structural influence continue to be discussed in relation to client states' observation of human rights and democracy, furthering of market-friendly policies, and stable international commodity markets.[8]

Two factors could limit U.S. dominance in the international arms market in the longer run. One is the power dilemma resulting from the interest in keeping a dominant world military position. That interest could be undermined by looser, more commercially driven, weapons sales, including sales of the most modern systems and the know-how to make them.[9] Therefore, administrations historically have maintained a restrictive technology export policy except with respect to close allies. One consequence has been a low U.S. profile among exporters of licenses. Prospective buyers turned to more forthcoming sellers in the past and may try to do so in the future. Consequently, the United States is the natural champion of restrictions on the transfer of those types of military technology that might threaten its military superiority. While obviously preferring multilateral limits, Washington also has been willing to enact unilateral technology controls as they relate both to certain types of technology and to specific countries.

8. An indicator is the justification for U.S. military assistance as reported in *Congressional Presentation for Security Assistance, Fiscal Year 1994* (Washington, DC: Department of State and Defense Security Assistance Agency, 1993).

9. This concern is strongly argued in Ashton B. Carter, William J. Perry, and John D. Steinbrunner, *A New Concept of Cooperative Security*, Brookings Occasional Papers (Washington, DC: Brookings Institution, 1992).

7. Barbara Opall, "USAF May Curtail Bargain Fighter Exports," *Defense News*, 31 Jan.-6 Feb. 1994, pp. 1, 20.

The other limiting factor comprises the technology dilemma and the associated costs resulting from the weight of arms production in U.S. industry. It is often argued that—compared to major competitors such as Japan and Germany—disproportionate shares of American military research and development in government R&D and the high demand for the best and the brightest among scientists and engineers have been reasons for the relative decline of U.S. civilian industry.[10] With the trend of incorporating more dual-use technologies in weapons and support systems, military technology has become more dependent on civilian industry. Therefore, the market for military goods is likely to shift further away from products originating with traditional weapons makers and toward more competition between makers of sensors, electronics, or computer hard- and software.[11] U.S. defense suppliers may lose market shares in these expanding fields to West European and Japanese suppliers. Yet the overall strength of American high-technology industry might allow the continued dominance of American defense sales, with newer firms entering the field from the civilian side.

Declining U.S. weapons procurement budgets also could mean that fewer copies of advanced designs will be built unless needed in crisis. Instead, reliance is likely to be put on "concept and technological demonstrations" and prototypes.[12] Therefore, the time before systems would be released on the export market could be extended, since fewer copies will be built and become excess or obsolete. Allies and clients might be included in discussions on whether actually to produce a weapons system, with joint up-front funding sought if it is to be available for export.

The former Soviet Union

In the 1970s and 1980s, the Soviet Union was the world's largest weapons exporter. Russia, as the successor state with by far the largest share in arms production, has seen arms exports from factories on its territory shrink from a high of more than $20 billion per year in the mid-1980s to the range of $3-4 billion in the early 1990s. Part of the remaining income from arms sales derives from the supply of surplus equipment, so the impact on the order books of Russian arms manufacturers is even more

10. See, for example, U.S., Congress, Office of Technology Assessment, *Building Future Security* (Washington, DC: Government Printing Office, 1992).

11. See, for example, Philip Gummett and Judith Reppy, eds., *The Relations between Defence and Civil Technologies* (Dordrecht: Kluwer, 1988).

12. The Defense Department has moved toward categories of technology initiatives and prototyping based on anticipated needs. Recently announced categories include rapid force projection; precision space targeting; advanced joint planning, command, and control; Korean challenges; simulated theaters of war; unmanned vehicles; countermine capabilities; and cruise missile defenses. See Robert Holzer and Stephen C. LeSueur, "DoD Spotlights New Prototyping Approach," *Defense News*, 31 Jan.-6 Feb. 1994, pp. 6, 18. Quote reprinted courtesy of *Defense News*. Copyright by Army Times Publishing Company, Springfield, Virginia.

dramatic than is apparent in these figures.[13]

Russian leaders, including, after some oscillation, President Yeltsin, have declared their intention to push for more arms exports as more or less the only quick way to earn foreign exchange through industry. Prospects that exports will rebound are small, though. First, Soviet arms exports never really amounted to what available statistics seemed to show. A large part of these exports were grants to poor allies, often involved in wars. Although weapons were almost always delivered on credit terms, it was often understood that debts would never be paid. Many other customers received weaponry at bargain prices.[14] To some extent, arms exports were a way to subsidize the oversized Soviet arms industry. Now that such exports have been put on a commercial basis, the bulk of former recipients are unlikely cash customers. Others continue to expect low prices.

Second, prospective customers lack confidence in the long-run viability of Russian suppliers. Original procurement often is only a small part of weapons life-cycle costs. Un-certainty concerning flows of spare parts and the inability of the supplier to offer cyclical updates reduces the chances of Russian sales. These doubts are linked to the question of future Russian military R&D funding and the ability to keep the best engineers and technologists in the arms sector; this question, of course, hinges in turn partly on the results of political struggle in Moscow between "reformers" and "arch-nationalists."[15]

Third, few Russian weapons are fully competitive with Western counterparts. For instance, while modern fighter aircraft such as the MiG-29 have performance characteristics comparable with U.S. aircraft, their maintenance costs are much higher. Also, their avionics are 10-15 years behind Western standards.[16] Not all possible recipients are concerned about this deficiency, however. For instance, Moscow's best customer in the 1990s, China, is content with copying the level of technology now attained by the Russian arms industry. Those buyers requiring less sophisticated weapons, such as armored personnel carriers, can live with what Moscow offers. In addi-

13. These are official governmental figures; see Konstantin Sorokin, "Russische Rüstungsindustrie sucht Überleben im Export," *Europäische Sicherheit*, 42:238 (Apr. 1993). Of course, the low international valuation of the ruble provides arms producers with comparatively large ruble incomes from small dollar receipts.

14. Issues of grants and credits in arms exports are discussed in Michael Brzoska, "Military Aid, Trade and Developing Country Debt," in *Research Symposium on Military Expenditures*, World Bank Discussion Paper no. 185, ed. Geoffrey Lamb with Valeriana Kallab (Washington, DC: World Bank, 1992).

15. Reformers generally see the arms sector as a liability, which, despite relatively advanced technology, drains needed research and development funding from the consumer economy, while nationalists see it both as a mass employer and as a strategic asset that should be used as a source of technology and foreign exchange. See, for example, Alexei Izyumov, "The Soviet Union: Arms Control and Conversion—Plan and Reality," in *Arms Industry Limited*, ed. Wulf, pp. 109-20.

16. The German Air Force inherited a squadron of MiG-29 fighters in October 1990 and thoroughly tested them. See, for example, Manfred Opel, "Die MiG-29 Fulcrum der NVA," *Wehrtechnik*, 22(10):48-54 (1993).

tion, there is the possibility of fitting Western electronics and other subsystems to Soviet weapons; explorations of Western-Russian joint arms ventures already are under way.[17] While ex-Soviet weapons upgrades have become frequent among Moscow's customers, the uncertain future of the Russian arms industry has so far discouraged longer-term collaboration between Western component suppliers and Russian manufacturers. Of course, certain Russian components also might be profitably incorporated into Western arms systems.

These problems for Russian arms sellers even accompanied their most spectacular export success in the early 1990s, the sale of 18 MiG-29 fighter aircraft to Malaysia in mid-1993 amid stiff worldwide competition. For the first time, Moscow achieved a major competitive commercial sale of sophisticated weaponry outside the traditional Soviet sphere of clients such as India, Syria, or Finland. While the MiGs constituted an acceptably advanced technology, the real Russian advantage in this deal was low prices, partly payable in Malaysian commodities. Still the Malaysians hedged their bets both on reputed quality and supplier follow-up capabilities by adding eight U.S. F/A-18 attack jets to the purchase mix. Also, the Russian aircraft were to be fitted with Western avionics.[18]

Despite these grave marketing problems, Russian arms exports

could have been larger if Moscow had not followed the Western and U.N. lead on declared and undeclared arms embargoes. Iran, the former Yugoslav republics, Libya, or Iraq might pay well if Russia delivered what these traditional Soviet customers wanted. But the current leadership is convinced that the political price would be too large. Western economic aid and investments are weightier than what could be gained from selling to these and similar customers. Therefore, Moscow has gone from a hegemonic approach toward arms transfers to a dependent commercial approach, but with some regard for international sensibilities and arms proliferation problems.

Western Europe

In Western Europe, the dominant response to declining domestic demand has been extensive restructuring on a regional level.[19] Effects on competitiveness and exports have been mixed; there is yet no West European arms market. Companies continue to operate in protected national markets. Governments are not willing to yield control over an industrial sector deemed economically, technologically, and politically important at a time of persistent unemployment, despite numerous statements to the contrary.[20]

17. See both civilian and military projects in "East/West Aerospace Ventures on the Rise," *Aviation Week and Space Technology*, 23 Aug. 1993, pp. 51-59.

18. Daniel Sneider, "Russians Extol Fighter Sale," *Defense News*, 5-11 July 1992, pp. 1, 20.

19. See Elisabeth Sköns and Herbert Wulf, "The Internationalization of the Arms Industry," this issue of *The Annals* of the American Academy of Political and Social Science.

20. See, for instance, Michael Brzoska and Peter Lock, *Restructuring of Arms Production in Western Europe* (New York: Oxford University Press, 1992).

Indeed, it is not clear whether a common Western European defense market would enhance competitiveness.[21] True, a larger market could result in longer production runs over which larger research and development costs could be distributed. But the few international companies could act as a tight oligopoly in a secure market with a high protective fence around it. Given the size of military R&D budgets, in the long run Western Europe will be hard-pressed to keep up with the United States in the full range of latest military technologies.[22] Difficulties getting the Euro-fighter and Euro-AWACs technologies off the ground over the past decade are illustrative.

It is likely that West European producers will continue to be more successful in various market niches, such as helicopters, ships, submarines and missiles, and dual-use technologies, than in the most prominent of modern weapons systems, such as fighter aircraft or radar systems. West European sellers retain competitive advantages over others in a number of dual-use technologies—for instance, engines, automotive equipment, and some types of industrial electronics—as well as arms production equipment, such as numerically controlled machine tools.

While the West European arms industry is slowly becoming more integrated, the harmonization of arms export policies lags behind. European Community (EC) member states could not agree on much about arms export matters before the Maastricht summit in November 1991. Harmonization of regulations and policies was classified as a prerequisite for a true Common Foreign and Security Policy and designated as a priority for future work in the European Union (EU). An intergovernmental working group on arms exports was established but has not been able to reconcile differences. At the time of writing, the Community was not able to agree on an EU regulation on the export of dual-use goods, a policy area that definitely falls under Community jurisdiction since the introduction of the Single Market on 1 January 1993.[23] A Commission proposal for such regulation in August 1992 was not accepted by the Council of Ministers, although it left full authority to license exports with member states. The differences in arms export policies between EU member countries are smaller in the early 1990s than they were in the 1980s, but neither France nor the United Kingdom is prepared to yield national sovereignty in a sector still considered strategically important.

It seems unlikely that the differences can be ironed out in the near future. Despite vociferous criticism of the French conservative govern-

21. See Andrew Moravcsik, "The European Armaments Industry at the Crossroads," *Survival*, 32(1):65-85 (1990).

22. There has lately been a surge of critical books on arms production in France, a nonissue until the late 1980s. See, for example, Francois Chesnais, ed., *Compétitivité internationale et dépenses militaires* (Paris: Economica, 1990); Jean-Paul Hebért, *Stratégie francaise de l'armement* (Paris: Fondation pour les Etudes de Defense National, 1990).

23. The best publicly available account is Paul Eavis, ed., *Arms and Dual-Use Export from the EC: A Common Policy for Regulation and Control* (Bristol, U.K.: Saferworld, Dec. 1992).

ment's "neglect" in 1993, for example, the French arms industry remains too large and technologically important for Paris to jeopardize through a restrictive arms export policy. Germany, on the other hand, remains committed to a restrictive arms export policy, though still heavily reliant on international coproduction and licensing arrangements. Disagreements are largely confined to the current EU membership; countries intending to join the Union, such as Sweden and Austria, which were thought to complicate defense cooperation because of their declared neutrality, are now quite willing to accept whatever conditions the EU sets. However, larger issues, such as post-Maastricht difficulties in EU economic integration and hesitation over a Common Foreign and Security Policy, budgetary stringency, and difficulties in absorbing former East Bloc neighbors, give pause to easy assumptions of trans-European defense production and marketing.

In EU arms export policy harmonization, politicians are much behind corporate managers, and it is unlikely that the gap will close soon. The likely outcome is arms export corporate partnership, selling via the state that has the least restrictive regulations. Governments with more stringent rules or case determinations are already allowing transnational industrial cooperation for exports. Under the pressure of companies threatening to transfer jobs out of the area, governments are likely to sanction more such license shopping while, on paper, keeping national regulations strict.

China

China is the least predictable of the major arms exporters. In terms of employment and output numbers, China has one of the largest arms industries in the world, yet the Chinese also must import significant arms technologies. For export, Chinese producers have specialized in relatively low-technology items. Examples are new and upgraded missile systems for use against sea and land targets. While not as sophisticated as the latest cruise and stealth devices, this equipment, nevertheless, at least nominally moves recipients up into the higher ranks of offensive capability. Also, Chinese producers have aimed at increasing technology levels by combining Chinese platforms and weapons with Western subsystems. A number of companies have been set up for this purpose in Southeast Asian states.

Since the late 1970s, economic interests have dominated Chinese arms exports. Sectors of the Chinese military were authorized to export arms to support their own arms acquisition costs, and export decisions evidently were decentralized. Most of the lucrative deals were with the Middle Eastern states, for example, Iran, in which, mainly for political reasons, other suppliers were reluctant to compete. Since the end of the Cold War, Chinese export policy has oscillated between accepting and challenging new international norms, for instance, in the context of U.N. arms embargoes and negotiations over restraints on conventional arms exports among the five permanent Security Council members. Exports have declined, but more because of slack demand for Chinese weapons than because of Chinese unwillingness to deliver.[24]

Other suppliers

The decline in global arms markets from the mid-1980s, due to rising debts, both ongoing and settled wars and disputes, completed procurement cycles, and domestic budget problems, caused great hardship for the armament sectors of third-tier suppliers such as Israel and Brazil and also for former Warsaw Pact states in Europe. A diverse array of states, both politically and with respect to security policy and industrial capabilities, they are all marked by their comparatively limited funds to develop more than a few arms technologies.

Correspondingly, exports of modern arms are limited to a few types, while at least some suppliers, such as the former Warsaw Pact states, can deliver large quantities of outdated weapons and ammunition. Currently, demand for such systems is low, but an increase in the level of fighting in the many low-level wars in Africa, Asia, and Central Europe, or a major war fought in World War I style, might increase demand, as did the 1980-88 Iraq-Iran war.

Niche suppliers can complicate Western defense planning, as North Korea has done with missiles to the Middle East, or Ukraine could do with an aircraft carrier sale to China.

But with the end of the Cold War, the United States and its allies are less willing to tolerate arms transfers from small-scale suppliers. One example was the sale of 300 tanks from then-Czechoslovakia to Syria, which met with strong American and West European objections. Similar opposition has hindered Polish sales, even as Western aid to convert from war to civilian production was slow to arrive. The reaction among smaller suppliers was well captured in the widely quoted words of the then Czech minister of trade and industry: "They preached to us to drink water while they themselves were drinking wine."[25]

ARMS EXPORTERS IN THE INTERNATIONAL SYSTEM

We now change the level of analysis to include, specifically, relations between suppliers. Such relations are only part of a systemic analysis of the arms trade,[26] but they are important in shaping the basis of actors' behavior. For instance, substantial restrictions on global arms exports can come about only if the major exporters agree on it. The likely out-

24. Nods to limiting supply and assertions of military cutbacks evidently were designed to reassure a suspicious American government. See, for example, R. Bates Gill, "Curbing Beijing's Arms Sales," Orbis, 36:879-96 (Summer 1992).

25. While Washington urged restraint on East European states, many of which wished to comply in order to boost chances for membership in the North Atlantic Treaty Organization, it was noted that the United States itself was selling arms at record levels. See Raymond Bonner, "U.S. Tries to Stem East Europe Arms," New York Times, 13 Feb. 1994. See also Ariane Genillard, "Question of Arms Points up Czechoslovak Divisions," Financial Times, 11 Mar. 1992, p. 2.

26. The latter is the subject of Robert E. Harkavy, "The Changing International System and the Arms Trade," this issue of The Annals of the American Academy of Political and Social Science.

come of restriction by one supplier is a mere redistribution of market shares. This has happened numerous times in the past; an example is the case of Iran in the 1980s, when U.S. arms exports were substituted with arms from a number of European and third-tier suppliers.

In addition, international politics are to some extent guided by mutual example. Along with explicit rules and norms, of which there are few in the arms trade, some implicit codes of preferred behavior exist.[27] For example, high barriers against supplies to states or factions at war that are not direct allies work to diminish arms transfers.

Finally, the network of international arms production and transfers is a subsystem of the larger international system, with its many links and hierarchies. After the Cold War, the United States was the sole superpower with global security interests and military reach. At the same time, of the two dominant factors shaping the arms trade system and state behavior in it, the pursuit of wealth has gained in prominence, at least temporarily, over the pursuit of power.[28] During the Cold War, the United States and USSR were technologically dominant in the military

sphere, but they allowed some diffusion of technology, through licenses and coproduction among allies or close political associates. These smaller power allies, able to design equipment on their own, developed a distinctly more commercial approach to distributing arms than that of the superpowers, out of the necessity of supporting military research and development with far smaller domestic markets and resources. Thus, arms technologies gradually proliferated, proving progressively more difficult to control.

The relations between suppliers only influence actors' behavior; they do not necessarily determine it. Other factors, such as the general prevailing structure of international security, economic systems, and domestic politics, can be decisive at particular times. The most striking example illustrating this point is Japan, which has become a regional power of some importance and has assumed a growing role in international politics. Given their civilian-based design and manufacturing capabilities, Japanese companies could easily become formidable global arms competitors.[29] Yet there are no strong indications that Japan will change its policy of not exporting finished arms and restricting the exports of dual-use goods.[30]

27. There is much academic controversy about rules and norms in international politics. See, for example, Friedrich V. Kratochwil, *Rules, Norms and Decisions* (New York: Cambridge University Press, 1988).

28. The classic work on arms and systems change is Robert Harkavy, *The Arms Trade and International Systems* (Cambridge, MA: Ballinger, 1975). Important new additions are Krause, *Arms and the State*, and Edward J. Laurance, *The International Arms Trade* (New York: Lexington Books, 1992).

29. See Masako Ikegami-Anderson, "Japan: A Latent But Large Supplier of Dual Use Technology," in *Arms Industry Limited*, ed. Wulf.

30. See, for example, Hideo Sato, "Japan's Role in the Post Cold War Period," *Current History*, 90:145-48, 179 (Apr. 1991); and, more generally, Hans W. Maull, "Germany and Japan: The New Civilian Powers," *Foreign Affairs*, 69:91-106 (Winter 1990/91).

Differing behavioral patterns can coexist. In a major study on the arms trade published in the early 1970s, researchers distinguished three types of actors in arms transfers: hegemonic, economic, and restrictive.[31] Trends appear to indicate that economic and restrictive concerns have come to greater prominence in the post-Cold War period, but that hegemonic efforts continue—as with U.S. pressure to limit arms to certain recipients, such as Iran and Syria, or to offset North Korea in an Asian balance of power. Various approaches will continue to coexist, but it is crucial to examine the evolving relative importance of the three policy approaches to arms transfers.

Economic aspects

From at least the 1970s, the international arms trade has become more commercialized. The United States, Britain, and the Soviet Union widened the scope of their arms transfer policies to embrace sales from an economic standpoint. Some traditional suppliers, notably France, also began to market exports as policy neutral, with customers not forced to choose between East and West. New suppliers appeared on the market.[32] The Cold War's end, with the attendant loss of motives to support a side in the East-West conflict through arms exports, as well as the large overcapaci-

31. Stockholm International Peace Research Institute, *The Arms Trade with the Third World* (Stockholm: Almqvist & Wicksell, 1971).

32. See, for example, Michael Brzoska and Thomas Ohlson, *Arms Transfers to the Third World, 1971-85* (New York: Oxford University Press, 1987).

ties resulting from reduced defense procurement, strengthened this trend toward a commercially driven arms export system.

Therefore, some observers expected arms transfers to escalate again in the early 1990s. Extensive U.S. sales to the Middle East before and after the second Gulf war and U.S. fighter aircraft sales to Taiwan have been watched as early signs of an impending arms market boom. The available statistics indicate otherwise, however, as the market continues to shrink—largely because of lack of funds on the recipient side but also because of suppliers' policies.

Supplier restriction

The large overcapacity in arms production in the early 1990s has not yet resulted in a full breakdown of the level of restraint that developed during the Cold War and after the second Gulf war. Although available information is far from complete, it seems that in the early 1990s a comparatively high level of constraint in international arms trade coincided with large overcapacities. Another new development was the widespread support among suppliers for transparency in the arms transfer system, in the form of a U.N. registry.

Restrictions work on two levels. One is specific technologies (vertical proliferation), and the other concerns specific countries (horizontal proliferation). Only a few explicit restrictions on the transfer of conventional arms technologies have been agreed to by suppliers, covering technologies such as missiles above certain ranges or equipment deemed particularly harmful. The expansion of the membership of and the adherence to the rules—by Russia, for example—of the Missile Technology Control Regime is one indicator of constraint in the international arms system.[33]

The growing willingness to agree to and honor international arms embargoes is another indicator of growing restraint in the international arms trade. A seldom used instrument during the Cold War, such embargoes were declared, though with only mixed results, on a number of states in the 1990s because of aggression (Iraq), internal wars (Somalia, Liberia, the former Yugoslavia), human rights violations (Haiti, Sudan), and support of terrorism (Libya). It also seems that informal arms export bans, encouraged by the United States but without legal or internationally agreed political basis—for instance, on Iran and some Islamic Soviet successor states—had a restrictive influence on export policies of at least some other states, particularly in Western Europe.

HEGEMONISM AND
A NEW COLD WAR?

None of this amounts to a truly restrictive international arms trans-

fer regime. The Cold War's end is not the end of history. Arms supplies remain an important policy instrument, and they are used as such globally by the United States and regionally by a number of suppliers. Earlier we distinguished between arms exports for (1) bargaining power, as over access to foreign bases; (2) structural power, as in attempts to manipulate the strategic policies of the recipient state; and (3) hegemonic power, as in efforts to engineer favorable regional and global power balances and internal policies in recipient countries. Prior studies have shown only the first of these to be predictably feasible, with the other two quite problematic.[34] Still, the second and third forms of influence are pursued, in arms control as well as arms transfer efforts, as when U.S. arms transfer decisions are openly linked to the pursuit of such goals as human rights.[35]

33. The original rationale of the Missile Technology Control Regime (MTCR) was that it strengthened nonproliferation of nuclear weapons by controlling the preferred means of delivery. But the MTCR also has been cited in cases without a clear nuclear connection, such as reported Chinese deliveries to Syria. Russia complied with U.S. requests when it canceled the sale of controversial rocket motors to India in 1993, though perhaps after useful technology already had been exchanged. See Elaine Sciolino, "Russia Is Halting Arms-Linked Sale," *New York Times*, 17 July 1993.

34. Keith Krause, "Military Statecraft: Power and Influence in Soviet and American Arms Transfer Relationships," *International Studies Quarterly*, 35:313-36 (Sept. 1991); John Sislin, "The Elusive Link between Military Assistance and Political Compliance" (Ph.D. diss., Indiana University, 1993).

35. A parallel discussion is occurring on development aid. Both national and international aid agencies and international financial institutions are now committed to consider economic waste through military spending, including arms imports, as a criterion in deciding on the level of financial support to give to a poor state. For a comprehensive discussion, see Nicole Ball, *Pressing for Peace: Can Aid Induce Reform*? Policy Essay no. 6 (Washington, DC: Overseas Development Council, 1992); on recent U.S. policy, see Simon Payaslian, "Human Rights and U.S. Distribution of Foreign Economic and Military Assistance" (Ph.D. diss., Wayne State University, 1992).

A closer look reveals that influence attempts and restrictions have been highly selective. While a number of arms embargoes against, for example, states with internal wars and states violating human rights have been agreed upon, there is no evident intention by the major powers to make this a general rule. Technology transfer controls in the dual-use field have been tightened by Western industrialized countries toward most nonindustrialized countries, although the original rationale of preventing West-East technology transfers is no longer applicable. Major powers can be expected to continue to try to dampen the supply of certain technologies to volatile regions marked by political and military struggles, but only when they threaten to get out of these powers' control.

Some observers, especially from Third World countries such as India, are interpreting this pattern as a kind of "new cold war," now between the North and the South, with dual-use and higher technology as the major battleground. While not consistent with all of the facts—for instance, the extensive arms and dual-use technology transfers that continue to reach developing countries, including India—this view captures the element of growing fear and mutual distrust in North-South relations.[36]

At several points in the discussion so far, we have touched upon the crucial role of the United States. Two trends continue to make the U.S.

hegemonic in the postwar international arms transfer system. One is America's dominant role because of the unique marriage of technological capabilities and strategic interests. The other is the political and economic vulnerability of most other suppliers. To take the least obvious example of the EU member states, the precarious internal policy balance—with declarative commitment to a harmonized arms export policy and extensive industrial cooperation, on the one hand, and dependence on national arms production and continuing national sovereignty over arms exports, on the other hand—makes EU members' arms transfer decisions vulnerable even to comparatively little outside pressure. It is difficult for individual governments to ignore their EU partners' or North Atlantic Treaty Organization/ American calls for embargoes of certain states, for example, Argentina during the Falklands/Malvinas fighting; yet if the United States sells comparatively freely, the balance between EU member states also tends to tilt toward more liberal export policies. The current ambiguity in restriction versus expansion of arms markets is partially a reflection of U.S. indecisiveness about its own arms transfer policy.

THE LONGER RUN

Seen purely from the aspect of export capacities, analysis of the future of arms exports has to consider two stages. Currently, there is great overcapacity in almost all of the arms-producing states and especially in the former Soviet Union, and this

36. See Michael Moodie, "Constraining Conventional Arms Transfers," this issue of *The Annals* of the American Academy of Political and Social Science.

will remain so for a few years. But since arms exports at current levels do little to employ these capacities, and because domestic demand is likely to decrease further, capacity will be cut drastically. Already, as Sköns and Wulf detail in this volume, massive industrial restructuring, mergers, and, sometimes, downsizing are taking place in the arms field.[37]

From the late 1990s, conversion and closures could lead to a less imbalanced market for complete weapons systems. Contradictory trends caution against simple assumptions, though. On the one hand, many arms producers will diversify into related areas of production and thereby remain capable of supplying dual-use technologies and coming back into the arms market at short notice. But unless the worldwide economic situation deteriorates sharply, the shift from overcapacity in devoted arms industries to more competitors in the much larger dual-use goods market should lessen the economic impetus to supply foreign military forces.

On the other hand, pressure for economies of scale for remaining weapons production will grow under conditions of reduced domestic arms procurement, thus reinforcing the urge to export in order to enlarge sales as much as possible. Therefore, for most suppliers the overall volume

37. Robert Holzer, "U.S. Navy Targets Hybrid Weapons," *Defense News*, 29 Nov.-5 Dec. 1993, p. 4.

of foreign sales will probably drop, but the search for foreign buyers will continue to be intense, aggressive, and competitive.

A common denominator in these lines of argumentation is technology. The perception of military and civilian science and technology as keys to overall economic development and future political influence will shape opportunities and motivations to export arms in the long run. But directions are unclear.

The spectacle of American smart weapons during and after the Gulf war has, at least for the time being, reinforced the importance of specific military technology, accelerating a move among many armed forces toward acquisition both of advanced weapons systems or capabilities to defend against them and of corresponding electronic control capabilities. Dedicated advanced military technologies are identifiable and still comparatively easy to control. Yet with dual-use technologies dominant, and with the difficulty of predicting the ultimate use of components, control and restriction of technologies will become more difficult.

None of these trends necessarily implies significantly more weapons and arms technology proliferation. Political and strategic motives for restraint will remain important, and the arms transfer system also is shaped by recipients—whose motivations and capabilities to import were not discussed here.

ANNALS, *AAPSS*, **535**, September 1994

Middle Eastern Arms Recipients in the Post-Cold War World

By KEITH KRAUSE

ABSTRACT: Arms transfers to the Middle East have been high on the international agenda since the Gulf war and the end of the Cold War. But the precise nature of recent developments, and the underlying motivations and forces that have produced the current pattern of weapons proliferation in the region, are poorly understood. A close examination of the data suggests that arms transfers to the Middle East have actually declined in the 1990s, following similar patterns manifest around the world. In addition, by shifting the focus away from arms transfers, toward overall changes in weapons arsenals and the relationship between weapons and armed forces, one can gain some insight into the underlying motives that drive regional arms acquisitions. These motives can be regional, systemic, or internal, and they interact in such a way as to enormously complicate the process of security building in the Middle East.

Keith Krause is an associate professor of political science at York University, Toronto. His work has concentrated on historical and conceptual issues surrounding the global arms transfer system. In addition to several articles and chapters, he is the author of Arms and the State: Patterns of Military Production and Trade *(1992). His current research focuses on military development and conflict in the Middle East. He is the deputy director of the Centre for International and Strategic Studies, York University.*

THE end of the Cold War and the 1990-91 war in the Persian Gulf have catalyzed a near flood of scholarly and policy-oriented analysis on the arms race or the proliferation of weapons in the Middle East.[1] The revival of a Middle Eastern peace process, with its focus—at one multilateral table—on questions of regional security, confidence building, and arms control, has also highlighted the potentially destabilizing impact of large and sophisticated regional arsenals.[2] Attention among extraregional powers has likewise focused on how they can act in concert to reduce the destabilizing impact of past and present great-power rivalries in the region and perhaps even play a role in pushing the various regional conflicts toward some resolution.[3] Although the post-Gulf war

initiatives to control the arms trade were usually cast in global terms, specific concern with the Middle East was manifest.[4] Implicit in almost all of this work is an argument that events may have created a ripe moment for tackling both the visible manifestations and the underlying sources of some of the many conflicts in the region.

It is too early to evaluate the success or failure of the various policy initiatives, but already the optimism of 1991-92 has given way to caution and skepticism. On a scholarly level, the end of the Cold War and the Persian Gulf conflict have also sown great analytic confusion. Analysts cannot agree on whether or not the spurt of weapons acquisitions by some Middle Eastern states—notably Gulf states—in 1990-92 is a short-term blip in a longer secular decline in weapons transfers to the region or a reversal of the apparent decline of the mid- to late 1980s. Likewise, they cannot agree on whether the end of the Cold War and the collapse of the

1. See Anthony Cordesman, *Weapons of Mass Destruction in the Middle East* (London: Brassey's, 1991); Geoffrey Kemp, *The Control of the Middle East Arms Race* (Washington, DC: Carnegie Endowment for International Peace, 1991); Avner Cohen and Marvin Miller, "Nuclear Shadows in the Middle East: Prospects for Arms Control in the Wake of the Gulf Crisis," *Security Studies*, 1(1):54-77 (Autumn 1991).

2. For an analysis of the Middle East regional arms control process through the fall of 1992, see Keith Krause, "The Evolution of Arms Control in the Middle East," in *Confidence-Building in the Middle East*, ed. David Dewitt and Gabriel Ben-Dor (Boulder, CO: Westview Press, 1994), pp. 267-90.

3. See President Bush's address to the Air Force Academy, 29 May 1991, and the accompanying White House fact sheet unveiling his "comprehensive arms control policy for the Middle East." These efforts also include the meetings, now in limbo, of the five permanent members of the United Nations Security Council to develop a framework for consultation on arms transfers to the Middle East. For a summary of this, see Natalie Goldring, "Transfer of

Advanced Technology and Sophisticated Weapons" (Paper delivered at the U.N. Conference on Disarmament Issues, Kyoto, Apr. 1993).

4. See, inter alia, Geoffrey Kemp, "The Middle East Arms Race: Can It Be Controlled," *Middle East Journal*, 45(3):441-56 (Summer 1991); Congressional Research Service, *Middle East Arms Control and Related Issues*, Report 91-384F (Washington, DC: Congressional Research Service, 1991); Dore Gold, ed., *Arms Control in the Middle East* (Boulder, CO: Westview Press, 1991); Alan Platt, ed., *Arms Control and Confidence Building in the Middle East* (Washington, DC: U.S. Institute of Peace, 1992); Frank Barnaby, "Arms Control after the Gulf War," *Conflict Studies 240* (London: Research Institute for the Study of Conflict and Terrorism, 1991); *Middle East Report*, no. 177, special issue *Arms Race or Arms Control?* (July-Aug. 1992).

Soviet Union will intensify the global arms trade, as the states of Eastern and Central Europe seek desperately to earn hard currency through their only globally competitive export, or whether the ending of superpower rivalries in the developing world will eliminate a potent cause of regional insecurity and reduce the incentive to acquire modern weapons.[5]

In order to resolve some of these puzzles, one must have a better understanding of the dynamic forces that have produced the current pattern of weapons proliferation in the Middle East than is provided by the existing literature. Briefly, the literature suffers from four main weaknesses. First, its trend analysis concentrates on the trade in weapons rather than on shifts in the composition or size of regional arsenals. This reflects the policy-relevant thrust of the literature, which is often directed toward the major arms suppliers, but it hardly generates a sound analysis of the factors contributing to insecurity in the region. The second weakness is a tendency to focus unduly on the weapons themselves and on the most prominent or so-called destabilizing ones—ballistic missiles, nuclear and chemical weapons, nuclear-capable aircraft—without paying enough attention to the underlying political and social processes that generate arms acquisitions. As was clear from public analysis during the Gulf war, this confused appearance with reality; it mistook the number of Iraqi soldiers for the existence of an effective military force, or the number of its tanks and aircraft for the threat it posed to neighboring states.

Third, overmuch attention has been paid to possible means of controlling or slowing the diffusion of modern weapons, before an adequate understanding has been achieved of why states acquire weapons and what motivates their security policies. As Stephanie Neuman has pointed out, the study of defense planning (of which arms acquisitions are one aspect) in the developing world has not been subject to careful comparative social science analysis and has tended to focus on narrow current issues or on the particular interests of external powers. It has not attempted to determine what perceptions and structures shape the security policymaking processes of states in the developing world.[6] Finally, the literature has concentrated on interstate conflicts as the primary explanation of arms acquisitions and military buildups, excluding in the process other domestic and systemic determinants of security policies.[7]

Not all of these issues can be resolved here, but this article will attempt to overcome some of the most obvious pitfalls by analyzing the acquisition of modern military technologies by Middle Eastern states and the growth of the accompanying military establishments. It will begin

5. For different perspectives on these various questions, see Mark Kramer, "The Global Arms Trade after the Persian Gulf War," *Security Studies*, 2(2):260-309 (Winter 1992); Peter Almquist and Edwin Bacon, "Arms Exports in a Post-Soviet Market," *Arms Control Today*, pp. 12-17 (July-Aug. 1992); Goldring, "Transfer of Advanced Technology," passim.

6. Stephanie Neuman, ed., *Defense Planning in Less-Industrialized States* (Lexington, MA: Lexington Books, 1984), p. 3.

7. For a classic example of this, see Kemp, *Control of the Middle East Arms Race*, pp. 17-18.

by presenting an overview of the qualitative and quantitative expansion of military arsenals in the Middle East since 1970. Against this backdrop, I will then discuss patterns of arms transfers to the Middle East in the late 1980s and outline the competing judgments of their significance. The final section will sketch a way of understanding the causes and consequences of these patterns of military development in the Middle East in a broader analytic and conceptual context.[8]

MILITARY DEVELOPMENT IN
THE MIDDLE EAST SINCE 1970

From the mass of data that could be assembled on military establishments in the Middle East, three types of information are relevant for our purposes: the growth in weapons arsenals, changes in the sophistication of arsenals, and changes in the size of armed forces. These data provide the backdrop needed to examine

8. The concept of military development is analogous to economic development, which is not just a set of statistical indicators—gross national product per capita, and so forth—but a policy issue of alternative choices that states can make and a field of study with competing ideologies of development and a set of theoretical tools. Thus, at its most basic level, "military development" would mean the growth and modernization of armed forces. It is also, however, the broader process that is catalyzed by the diffusion of modern military technologies and techniques of organization to the developing world, and it encompasses such things as choices about military doctrines (mass versus elite armies, defensive versus offensive force postures); the development of ancillary social and political institutions (civil-military relations, a military educational system, a fiscal apparatus for the state); and choices between different concepts of security (who or what represents the threat and how best to counter it).

and hypothesize about the role of external powers in security relations in the Middle East.

The conventional approach to arms transfers and regional security begins with an assessment of the flow of arms into the region, with major suppliers and recipients lined up together.[9] Already this implies that the conflict dynamic is outward oriented and that external powers play a major role in shaping the regional security agenda. Although this might, in some cases, be true, a better starting point is to assess the stocks of arms in the region, in order to evaluate patterns of military buildup and regional security more directly from the perspective of regional actors. Without more detailed analysis than can be performed here, one cannot explain the factors behind the different rates of military buildup, but at least some hypotheses for further examination can be adduced. The numbers themselves cannot provide explanations, but they can direct analysis toward particular hypotheses or problem areas.

Table 1 presents an overview of the military buildup in the Middle East since 1970, broken down by weapons system. The Middle East has also

9. See, for example, John McFadden, "The Strategic Arena," in *The Powers in the Middle East*, ed. Bernard Reich (New York: Praeger, 1987), pp. 47-50; Paul Ferrari et al., *U.S. Arms Exports: Policies and Contractors* (Cambridge, MA: Ballinger, 1988), pp. 151-77. The data from the Stockholm International Peace Research Institute, the Arms Control and Disarmament Agency, and the Congressional Research Service are also presented in this fashion. For a good, albeit dated, survey that does not fall into this trap, see Joe Stork and Jim Paul, "Arms Sales and the Militarization of the Middle East," *MERIP Reports*, pp. 5-15 (Feb. 1983).

TABLE 1
THE EXPANSION OF ARSENALS IN THE MIDDLE EAST, 1970-91

	1970	1975	1980	1985	1990
North Africa					
Main battle tanks	476	1,020	3,330	3,933+	3,800
Other armored fighting vehicles	825+	1,964+	5,073+	6,007+	6,885+
Combat aircraft	247	405	683	973	958
Helicopters	87+	139	319	398+	579
Naval vessels	4	3	7	19	18
Core Middle East					
Main battle tanks	3,535	7,045	8,139+	10,949+	13,239+
Other armored fighting vehicles	4,000	8,084+	10,022+	16,049+	20,529+
Combat aircraft	1,141+	1,424+	1,621	1,476+	1,757
Helicopters	165+	324	509+	687+	820
Naval vessels	10	8	10	12	7
Persian Gulf					
Main battle tanks	700+	2,805+	6,408	5,797+	8,285+
Other armored fighting vehicles	380+	4,116+	5,979+	8,892+	17,556+
Combat aircraft	372+	765	1,227	1,213	1,467
Helicopters	113+	410	1,295	650+	1,341+
Naval vessels	11	11	12	18	21
Middle East totals					
Main battle tanks	4,711+	10,870+	17,877	20,679+	25,324+
Other armored fighting vehicles	5,205+	14,164+	21,074+	30,948+	44,970+
Combat aircraft	1,768+	2,594+	3,531	3,662+	4,182
Helicopters	365+	873	2,123+	1,735+	2,740+
Naval vessels	25	22	29	49	46

SOURCES: *The Military Balance* (London: International Institute for Strategic Studies, various years); *Jane's Armour and Artillery*, 1988-89 ed.; *The Middle East Military Balance* (Jerusalem: Jerusalem Post, various years); *Jane's All the World's Navies* (various years). The data were compiled by Ken Boutin.

NOTES: States are allocated as follows: North Africa comprises Algeria, Libya, Morocco, Sudan, and Tunisia; the core Middle East comprises Egypt, Israel, Jordan, Lebanon, and Syria; and the Persian Gulf comprises Iran, Iraq, Saudi Arabia, and the Gulf states. The data contained in the *Military Balance* are often ambiguous, and subject to annual correction. These figures are trend indicators only.

been divided into three subregions: North Africa, comprising Algeria, Libya, Morocco, Sudan, and Tunisia; the core Middle East, comprising Egypt, Israel, Jordan, Lebanon, and Syria; and the Persian Gulf, comprising Iran, Iraq, Saudi Arabia, and the Gulf states. This table highlights that the expansion of military arsenals in the region has been extremely uneven and not always connected to obvious potential security threats. In the early 1970s, the core Middle East doubled its stock of tanks, armored vehicles, and helicopters, a development that is not surprising in the aftermath of the 1973 Arab-Israeli war. But arsenals in North Africa and the Persian Gulf grew at an even faster rate, in the absence of any involvement in interstate war or even, in North Africa, of its imminent threat.[10] One could object that the base size of arsenals was much larger in the Arab-Israeli context and hence the rate of growth likely to be slower, but while this makes some sense for the first half of the 1970s, by 1975, the gap in relative numbers had narrowed sufficiently that other factors must be sought to explain the dramatically different growth rates. Between 1975 and 1980, most weapons system stockpiles doubled or tripled in size in both the Persian Gulf and North Africa, while in the Arab-Israeli context, they grew by 14 to 57 percent.

If military acquisitions are in any sense a response to perceived threats, then the subregional security environment would have had to have been extraordinarily tense in the late 1960s and early 1970s to justify such military buildups. This was not the case in either the Persian Gulf or North Africa.[11] The alternative explanation that is usually advanced to explain the high levels of weapons acquisitions is the new wealth of the oil-producing states, most of whom were the most prominent recipients of arms in the 1970s

10. The only exception is the rate of growth of helicopter stockpiles, which grew more quickly in the core Middle East than in North Africa.

11. On the pre-1970 strategic climate, see J. C. Hurewitz, *Middle East Politics: The Military Dimension* (New York: Praeger, 1969); Geoffrey Kemp, "Strategy and Arms Levels, 1945-1967," in *Soviet-American Rivalry in the Middle East*, ed. J. C. Hurewitz (New York: Praeger, 1969), pp. 21-54. On the Persian Gulf, see Anthony Cordesman, *The Gulf and the Search for Strategic Stability* (London: Mansell, 1984), pp. 85-147. The literature on these conflicts is, of course, vast, and I do not intend to discuss in detail their particular dynamics.

and 1980s. The problem with this, however, is that the ability to pay for weapons facilitates their acquisition but cannot be the sole motivation for acquiring them.

In the 1980s, matters became slightly more complicated. The 1981-82 Lebanon war spurred arms acquisitions by Israel and Syria, although these were concentrated in armored vehicles, tanks, and helicopters. The Iran-Iraq war resulted in a decline in the size of arsenals from battle losses in the early 1980s (although figures are imprecise here), but these were rebuilt to prewar levels by 1990; a redistribution among the regional actors also occurred, since Iran remained relatively weak. The Gulf, however, assumed great importance in the global arms market, with more than $100 billion in imports between 1980 and 1988 (or about 25 percent of total global arms transfers!). North African arms acquisitions subsided to relatively low growth rates or even small declines throughout the 1980s. The core Middle East continued its steady buildup, although at the end of the decade average annual increases in arsenals are in the order of 5-6 percent. Given the changing age profile of the arsenal (and the reluctance to scrap weapons), this might not have reflected any increase in military capability whatever for North Africa and the core Middle East.

Assessing changes in the sophistication of weapons stocks in the Middle East is fraught with problems, and the information is difficult to present in a clear fashion. General imprecision in the available information makes several weapons systems—at

TABLE 2
PERCENTAGE OF ARSENAL COMPRISED OF FIRST-CLASS EQUIPMENT

	1970-71	1975-76	1980-81	1985-86	1990-91
North Africa					
Main battle tanks	0	0	0	10	11
Other armored fighting vehicles	20	12	12	12	8
Combat aircraft	0	0	27	0	2
Helicopters	0	29	24	30	27
Naval vessels	0	33	57	68	6
Core Middle East					
Main battle tanks	0	0	1	15	9
Other armored fighting vehicles	15	3	0	1	2
Combat aircraft	4	5	8	11	13
Helicopters	12	66	4	13	15
Naval vessels	0	0	0	11	29
Persian Gulf					
Main battle tanks	0	11	17	13	12
Other armored fighting vehicles	61	0	9	22	1
Combat aircraft	11	5	14	9	17
Helicopters	9	44	55	17	12
Naval vessels	36	36	0	44	38

SOURCES: *Military Balance* (various years); *Jane's Armour and Artillery*, 1988-89 ed.; *Middle East Military Balance* (various years); *Jane's All the World's Navies* (various years). The data were compiled by Ken Boutin.

NOTES: First-class equipment is defined as material that is near the forefront of existing technologies, although not necessarily the state of the art. It should be underlined that this is a dynamic definition; evidently, the state of the art in 1970 is significantly different from that of 1990. The figures in this table are trend indicators only.

times the majority—impossible to classify. It is also difficult to assess the relative sophistication of weapons, especially when these may have been modified for export or by the recipient. Finally, the standards selected—such as "state of the art" or "obsolete"—are themselves moving targets and must be adjusted over time. In spite of this, it is worthwhile to attempt to chart changes in the sophistication of Middle Eastern arsenals, if only to determine if the growth in sophistication is as dramatic or as linear as some analyses suggest.

Table 2 assesses the percentage of weapons holdings that could be con-sidered first class at different periods between 1970 and 1990. The methodology used to determine a ranking of first class is primarily qualitative: it involves categorizing all the equipment available within a given weapons system category according to its age, overall capabilities, and relationship to the state of the art. Thus, for example, in 1990, the T-72, Merkava, and Khalid (Chieftain-derived) main battle tanks represented the first-class tanks deployed in the Middle East, although these were not quite state of the art at that time (behind the M-1, T-80, and Leclerc). In 1970, by contrast, the M-60, T-62, Chieftain, and AMX-30 were first class.[12] This method, although subjective, is an approximation of the kind of relative assessments that would be made by military planners in these states, as they assessed the sophistication of their weapons holdings relative to those possessed by regional rivals or by more advanced states.[13] It is not meant to assess relative combat capabilities, which obviously depend on a range of other factors.

Some interesting conclusions can be drawn from Table 2. First, the percentage of holdings of sophisticated weapons is actually small in almost all weapons categories. By the early 1990s, sophisticated weapons accounted for less than 20 percent of holdings in 12 to 15 categories, the aberrations being helicopters in North Africa and naval vessels in the Persian Gulf and core Middle East. One concrete example is the following: before the Gulf war, it was clear that 80 percent of Iraq's tanks were of pre-1970s vintage, while only about 30 percent of its combat aircraft were modern or more sophisticated types.[14] This does not mean

that the weapons are not usable, but it explains clearly why Middle Eastern arms clients ceaselessly seek more advanced weapons: from their perspective, their armies are not particularly well equipped, and ongoing modernization programs merely keep pace with the broader development of military technology.

More important, these figures increase substantially the uncertainty in threat assessment for defense planners: how many obsolescent tanks or aircraft will it take to eliminate or counter a small number of more sophisticated opponents? The Gulf war suggests that one ought to put a great premium on technological superiority and the concomitant training required, especially in command and control and weapons targeting systems, areas in which most Middle Eastern armed forces are weak. From the perspective of regional arms control, these figures suggest that it would still be possible for arms suppliers to "suffocate" regional arms races near existing levels of technological sophistication, as the number of suppliers of the most advanced weapons is relatively small and their global diffusion relatively limited.[15]

Although the relative sophistication of the region's arsenals—that is, relative to the most advanced weapons available—has not increased dramatically since the early 1970s, in absolute terms the increase in destructive potential is overwhelming and has been demonstrated by the general tendency toward more in-

---

12. These data were compiled by Ken Boutin. A complete breakdown of how weapons systems were classified is available from the author.

13. How this works can be illustrated by Singapore's 1993 decision to upgrade its fighter plane purchases from the F-16A/B to the F-16C/D variant. This decision appears to have been influenced primarily by Malaysia's acquisition of M-29s and F/A-18Ds. *Jane's Defence Weekly*, 27 Nov. 1993.

14. *The Military Balance, 1990-1991* (London: International Institute for Strategic Studies, 1991), pp. 105-6. I have considered only the T-72 tanks to be sophisticated, and the Mirage F-1, Su-24 and 25, and MiG-29 to be modern aircraft.

15. Keith Krause, *Arms and the State* (New York: Cambridge University Press, 1992), pp. 187-92.

tense, ferocious, and destructive battles and wars in the region since 1967 (the decade-long stalemate between Iran and Iraq is a partial exception). Coupled with this has been a selective quest, on the part of some states, for nuclear, chemical, or biological weapons or advanced ballistic missiles. The enforced disarmament activities carried out by the United Nations Special Commission in Iraq have brought to light the depth and intensity of Iraq's nuclear program and have highlighted those of other regional actors.[16] Israel possesses a nuclear arsenal; Iran is suspected of conducting a long-term nuclear weapons development program; and at various times, Algeria and Libya have also sought nuclear weapons.[17] Up to six Middle Eastern states are alleged to have an offensive chemical weapons capability.[18] Ballistic missile proliferation in the region is also proceeding, notwithstanding the dismantling of Iraq's capabilities: Israel possesses missiles with a range of up to 2000 kilometers; Saudi Arabia possesses missiles with a range up to 2800 kilo-

meters; and Syria, Libya, Iran, and Egypt possess weapons with ranges between 200 and 900 kilometers.[19]

Arms acquisitions must also be considered against the growth of the region's armed forces. The acquisition of weapons was part of a broader process of expansion of armed forces throughout the Middle East, as former colonial constabularies were converted into mobilized (and often mass) armies. The number of soldiers in the region grew from less than 1 million in 1963 to 3.7 million by 1989.[20] In the states involved in the Arab-Israeli conflict (the core Middle East), in the aftermath of the 1967 and 1973 wars, the armed forces almost doubled in size, reaching by 1980 almost 1 million soldiers and remaining more or less constant since. A quick glance at Table 1, however, shows that arsenals, especially for ground forces, continued to increase through the 1980s in spite of this relative stability in force size. In the Persian Gulf, on the other hand, armed forces doubled in size during the 1980s (primarily as a consequence of the Iran-Iraq war), and arsenals also increased, albeit not as rapidly. In North Africa, armed forces

16. David Albright and Mark Hibbs, "Iraq's Nuclear Hide-and-Seek," *Bulletin of the Atomic Scientists*, pp. 14-23 (Sept. 1991); idem, "Iraq's Bomb: Blueprints and Artifacts," ibid., pp. 30-40 (Jan.-Feb. 1992).

17. On the Middle East in general, see Avner Cohen and Marvin Miller, "Nuclear Shadows in the Middle East: Prospects for Arms Control in the Wake of the Gulf Crisis," *Security Studies*, 1(1):54-77 (Autumn 1991); Leonard Spector, "Nuclear Proliferation in the Middle East," *Orbis*, 36(2):181-98 (Spring 1992). See also Cordesman, *Weapons of Mass Destruction*.

18. These are Iraq, Israel, Iran, Libya, and Egypt. Elisa Harris, "Towards a Comprehensive Strategy for Halting Chemical and Biological Weapons Proliferation," *Arms Control*, 12(2):129 (Sept. 1991).

19. Martin Navias, *Ballistic Missile Proliferation in the Third World*, Adelphi paper 252 (London: International Institute for Strategic Studies, 1990); A. J. Miller, "Towards Armageddon: The Proliferation of Unconventional Weapons and Ballistic Missiles in the Middle East," *Journal of Strategic Studies*, 12(4):387-404 (1989); Steve Fetter, "Ballistic Missiles and Weapons of Mass Destruction," *International Security*, 16(1):5-42 (Summer 1991).

20. Figures in this paragraph from U.S., Arms Control and Disarmament Agency, *World Military Expenditures and Arms Transfers* (Washington, DC: Arms Control and Disarmament Agency, various years).

grew at a steady pace between the early 1960s and the mid-1980s, with some decline since then. Overall, however, the picture is of a region in which military forces have grown more rapidly than corresponding populations or even perhaps threats.

Evidently, without a much more detailed analysis of particular states and conflicts, it is impossible to determine why particular patterns of force planning and weapons acquisitions have been adopted. The main point, however, is to highlight that it makes little sense to discuss weapons flows to a region without at least reflecting on the broader context of defense and security planning. Prima facie, this analysis suggests that the process of weapons acquisition has not always been well connected to overall defense planning. For example, concerning the Persian Gulf, one could argue that the huge flood of arms acquisitions throughout the 1970s was fueled by the absence of financial constraints on the oil states, since—with the exception of Iran and Iraq—they were not accompanied by a parallel increase in the size of the armed forces. Even acknowledging the role of sophisticated weapons as a force multiplier, this suggests that weapons led force expansion. In the core Middle East, by contrast, arsenals continued to grow in the 1980s and to increase in sophistication as a result of ongoing conflicts, especially the Lebanon war and Syrian-Israeli clashes. This growth was facilitated, but not caused, by the willingness of the United States and Soviet Union to supply large quantities of sophisticated weapons on generous terms to Egypt, Syria, and Israel.[21]

If correct, these hypotheses, at a minimum, give credence to the argument that regional conflicts can be exacerbated by the activities of external powers, who justify their behavior in terms of creating and maintaining regional stability. At a maximum, it suggests that what might be at work is a more systemic phenomenon, in which security policies—specifically, defense plans and arms acquisition policies—might be distorted by what Michael Barnett and Alexander Wendt have called "capital-intensive militarization."[22]

ARMS TRANSFERS TO
THE MIDDLE EAST
SINCE THE GULF WAR

The Gulf war unleashed a flurry of arms transfer activity on the part of both suppliers and recipients in the Middle East. Early hopes of controlling the arms trade to the region dimmed, in particular as the United States signed multi-billion-dollar agreements with its clients for ad-

21. I am arguing that the external forces—the willingness of superpowers to reduce the opportunity costs of weapons acquisitions by their clients—were a necessary, but not sufficient, condition for the arms buildup of the 1980s.
22. See Michael Barnett and Alexander Wendt, "Dependent State Formation and Third World Militarization," *Review of International Studies*, 19:321-47 (1993). Interesting confirmation of this also comes from John Harvey, "Regional Ballistic Missiles and Advanced Strike Aircraft: Comparing Military Effectiveness," *International Security*, 17(2):41-83 (Fall 1992). Harvey argues that the attractiveness of ballistic missiles to Third World states cannot be explained by their combat effectiveness, which is lower than that of advanced strike aircraft. See also Fetter, "Ballistic Missiles and Weapons of Mass Destruction."

TABLE 3

MIDDLE EASTERN ARMS TRANSFER AGREEMENTS, 1989-92
(in millions of current U.S. dollars)

Region or Subregion	Recipient	U.S.	Russia	China	Western Europe	Other Europe	Others	Total
North Africa								
	Algeria	—	500	—	—	—	—	500
	Libya	—	—	100	—	—	200	300
	Morocco	100	—	—	100	500	—	700
	Tunisia	100	—	—	—	—	—	100
	Total	200	500	100	100	500	200	1,600
Core Middle East								
	Egypt	7,000	100	—	—	200	—	7,300
	Israel	1,000	—	—	1,200	100	—	2,300
	Jordan	—	—	—	—	—	—	—
	Lebanon	—	—	—	—	—	—	—
	Syria	—	500	—	—	400	200	1,100
	Total	8,000	600	—	1,200	700	200	10,700
Persian Gulf								
	Bahrain	300	—	—	—	—	—	300
	Iran	—	4,300	1,100	100	500	700	6,700
	Iraq	—	200	—	500	100	900	1,700
	Kuwait	1,700	—	—	700	500	—	2,900
	Oman	100	—	—	600	—	—	700
	Qatar	—	—	—	—	—	—	—
	Saudi Arabia	24,800	200	300	8,000	2,400	200	35,900
	United Arab Emirates	600	300	—	200	—	400	1,500
	Yemen	—	100	—	—	—	—	100
	Total	25,800	5,100	1,400	9,400	3,000	2,200	49,800
Middle East Total		34,000	6,200	1,500	10,700	4,200	2,600	62,100

SOURCE: Richard Grimmett, *Conventional Arms Transfers to the Third World*, Report 93-656F (Washington, DC: Congressional Research Service, July 1993), p. 57.

vanced weapons systems. Other Western suppliers, sensing a window of opportunity, moved in to clinch

23. For contemporary discussion, see "War Sets off Fresh Arms Race in the Gulf," *Observer* (London), 28 Apr. 1991; "Where It Stops, No One Knows," *Jerusalem Report*, 1 Aug. 1991; "Arms Race Shows No Let-Up," *Times* (London), 4 Nov. 1991; John Williams, *The Middle East Peace Process and the Arms Trade: A Fatal Contradiction?* (London: Saferworld Foundation, Aug. 1992).

substantial long-term deals.[23] Public commentary was almost universal in characterizing this as a "new arms race" in the Middle East.

But have developments in the Middle East since the late 1980s marked a dramatic departure from previous trends? Table 3 fills in this picture with data on agreements to transfer arms to the Middle East for the 1989-92 period. The figures in

Table 3 are significant: compared with the previous four-year period, which had already shown declines from the high levels of the early 1980s, the volume of arms to be transferred under agreements signed in the most recent period declined by one-third—from $94.3 billion to $62.1 billion! The figures for weapons deliveries have an identical pattern: deliveries declined from $86.9 billion for 1985-88 to $52.2 billion for 1989-92.[24] Given that many agreements signed recently are for weapons to be delivered over several years and that current agreements are almost always subject to downward revision, it seems more plausible to consider developments of the early 1990s in a different light. Although suppliers are eager to lock in long-term deals in a declining market in order to guarantee the survival of particular firms or production lines, the main determinant of arms transfers is financial: suppliers are not offering easy terms and most recipients (Iraq and Iran, in particular), however much they may want to acquire weapons, are financially strapped or have limited access to advanced weapons. Where in all of this is the new arms race in the Middle East?

The most important states in this scenario are Saudi Arabia, Iraq, and Iran.[25] Between 1985 and 1992, the Saudis signed $63.6 billion worth of

weapons agreements and took delivery of $52.4 billion worth of arms. This annual average of almost $8 billion in agreements and $6.5 billion in deliveries represented roughly 18-19 percent of total acquisitions by the developing world. The U.S. State Department is projecting Saudi agreements for 1994, however, at only $2.75 billion, and current Saudi financial woes suggest that it will have difficulty paying for all the weapons it has contracted for since 1990.[26] These developments suggest a continued decline in weapons transfers to the region. Iran and Iraq, however, could change this picture somewhat. With respect to Iraq, in the 1985-92 period, it contracted for $21.3 billion worth of weapons and took delivery of $27.2 billion in weapons. Since the Gulf war, however, it has been under a near-complete embargo. Iran, despite laboring under the restrictions imposed by the West during the Iran-Iraq war, managed to contract for $17.4 billion worth of weapons and acquire $13.5 billion worth during this period. Both of these states have significant pent-up demand that could boost arms transfers to the region, if current political conditions were to change drastically. On balance, however, they are unlikely to fill the gap left by declining Saudi acquisitions, and overall weapons transfers to the region will thus likely decline.

This impression is reinforced by aggregate global data. Arms transfer agreements with the developing

24. All data in this section are from Richard Grimmett, *Conventional Arms Transfers to the Third World*, Report 93-656F (Washington, DC: Congressional Research Service, 1993), pp. 57, 68.

25. Israel, which has a large domestic arms industry, imports relatively small quantities of arms.

26. See the extensive analysis in the *New York Times*, 23 Aug. 1993. The Saudis have already canceled or postponed several recent contracts and are purchasing their weapons on credit!

world declined steadily from more than $60 billion in 1985 to less than $20 billion in 1992, with the only blip in this decline occurring in 1990.[27] Deliveries show a similar decline, although the upsurge in agreements in 1990 may push totals somewhat higher for the next few years. At a minimum, this evidence challenges the popular view of developments since the Gulf war; at a maximum, it forces us to rethink the link between arms transfers, arms races, and regional security. Radically different conclusions, however, can be drawn from this evidence depending upon which causes or consequences one considers to be most important.

ARMS TRANSFERS TO THE MIDDLE EAST: CAUSES AND CONSEQUENCES

With this information one can begin to assess the motives that drive arms acquisitions and races in the Middle East. It is difficult to generalize about these patterns since they are governed by a complex constellation of political or security considerations unique to each state. As Robert Rothstein points out in a broader context, "there is no such thing as 'the' security problem in the Third World: differentiation within the Third World itself is growing . . . and there are unique factors in each case that make grand generalizations inherently suspect."[28] One can identify,

however, three possible sets of motives that states have for acquiring arms:

— regional: driven by the need to fight wars or guarantee security against specified external threats;
— systemic: driven by supplier-client relationships, technological factors, or the pursuit of status and hegemony;
— internal: driven by the need to secure the regime against internal threats or the desire to use military development as a vehicle for social and economic modernization.[29]

Detailed case studies of arms acquisitions by each Middle Eastern state would be required in order to classify all the states properly, and even then a great deal of uncertainty would remain. In addition, these motives can be mixed, with particular weapons—such as a small number of sophisticated fighters—being acquired for prestige, while the bulk of procurement could be directed to specific perceived security threats. But the analytic utility of these three categories can be outlined against

27. Grimmett, *Conventional Arms Transfers*, p. 18.

28. Robert Rothstein, "National Security, Domestic Resource Constraints and Elite Choices in the Third World," in *Defense, Security and Development*, ed. Saadet Deger and Robert West (New York: St. Martin's Press, 1987), p. 141.

29. This account draws on Krause, *Arms and the State*, pp. 193-98. These motivations have been dealt with differently by many authors concerned with explaining not only arms acquisitions but also military expenditures. For a general account, see Andrew Pierre, *The Global Politics of Arms Sales* (Princeton, NJ: Princeton University Press, 1982), pp. 131-35, 136-271; Stockholm International Peace Research Institute, *The Arms Trade with the Third World* (Stockholm: Almqvist & Wiksell, 1971), pp. 41-85. For a detailed statistical correlative analysis, see Robert McKinlay, *Third World Military Expenditure: Determinants and Implications* (London: Pinter, 1989).

this backdrop of recent trends in arms transfers to the Middle East, in order to highlight the many dimensions of the debates concerning the causes and consequences of arms transfers.

Although it is impossible to present definitive conclusions, it should be noted that most analyses of arms and the Middle East focus only on the first of the categories, regional conflict.[30] This exclusive focus on the interstate military dimensions of the regional security agenda in the Middle East is increasingly indefensible. As Mohammed Ayoob has observed, defense and security policies in the Third World are often not determined by threats emanating from other states but from threats to the survival of the regime in power.[31] Thus, when attempting to understand the role of arms transfers in broader political processes, one needs to expand the scope of the phenomena considered relevant.

30. See, inter alia, Kemp, *Control of the Middle East Arms Race*; Cordesman, *Weapons of Mass Destruction*; Gold, ed., *Arms Control in the Middle East*.

31. For cogent analysis of the security problematique in the developing world, see Mohammed Ayoob, "Security in the Third World: The Worm about to Turn," *International Affairs* (London), 60(1):41-51 (1983-84); Ed Azar and Chung-In Moon, "Third World National Security: Toward a New Conceptual Framework," *International Interactions*, 11:103-35 (1984). See also Edward Azar and Chung-In Moon, eds., *National Security in the Third World* (Aldershot: Edward Elgar, 1988); Mohammed Ayoob, ed., *Regional Security in the Third World* (Boulder, CO: Westview Press, 1986), pp. 3-23.

*Arms transfers
 and regional
 interstate conflict*

The realm of regional interstate conflicts is the conventional domain in which arms transfers and military establishments are assessed, their primary missions being to deter or defend against attacks from, or be used in battle against, other states. No doubt, military expenditures and the importation of modern weapons are concrete manifestations of the quest for security in the developing world, and the type of arsenals possessed by states in the same "security complex" can have a crucial impact on conflict and its management or resolution. Regional actors' perceptions of security threats are in part determined by the military capabilities of other actors in the same "security complex."[32] The security dilemma of these states also rests on subjective perceptions of intentions —conditioned by a shared history— but the acuteness of the security dilemma is intimately tied to the military potential of possible opponents.

Arms transfers to states that do not produce weapons can be treated as a measure of arms-racing behavior, which in turn either signals or exacerbates regional conflicts and tensions. Certainly, a large proportion of the arms acquisitions of Israel, Egypt, Jordan, Algeria, Morocco, Tunisia, Saudi Arabia, Kuwait, and the Gulf emirates can be explained by interstate rivalries and suspicions. Their arms acquisitions may or may not have been defensive in nature,

32. Barry Buzan, *People, States and Fear*, 2d ed. (London: Harvester Wheatsheaf, 1991), pp. 187-95.

but they cannot be explained by exclusive reference to systemic or internal security concerns. On this account, the lack of hard evidence for a renewed Middle Eastern arms race means that one could argue that the regional security environment is improving in the 1990s: that the economic concerns gripping the states of the region, and the possible progressive spread of the Middle East peace process, will indirectly and directly address the roots of the region's conflicts. Efforts by external parties to limit transfers to the regions may not have yet contributed to this process, but they can be encouraged as insurance against future changes in the regional security environment.

This picture does not appear so sanguine, however, when one looks either at specific subregions in the Middle East or at the overall regional arsenals. On the subregional level, both Morocco and Algeria are engaged in active force modernization efforts, perhaps related to their rivalry in the Western Sahara. Likewise, one could expect increased efforts by Iraq to acquire arms when and if it is freed from the U.N. embargo, and Iran's ongoing acquisitions speak to a renewed bid for regional hegemony.[33] With respect to regional arsenals, what is particularly noteworthy is the large number of recent agreements for the most sophisticated weapons in the suppliers' arsenals. Transfers of such weapons as T-72 and M1-A2 tanks or MiG-29 and F-18 fighters suggest a potential race to acquire advanced tanks, bombers, and fighter aircraft, many of which have never before been exported. At a time when overall force levels are stable or even declining, the effort channeled into technological upgrading implies that the region's pattern of high levels of military competition has not changed fundamentally, despite the lower level of resources that may be devoted to it.

*Arms transfers
and systemic
imperatives*

Certain states in the Middle East have advanced claims to global status and were privileged clients of the superpowers in this quest throughout the Cold War. The most prominent example was the Shah's Iran, which until 1979 was engaged in a massive weapons buildup that could not be supported by the country's economic and military infrastructure. Weapons acquisitions in this case could only be explained by this drive for status and regional dominance and by the encouragement it received from the United States.[34] Two other states that have also advanced such claims are Iraq, under Saddam Hussein, and Libya, albeit on a smaller scale. In the Lib-

33. For details on Iranian acquisitions, see Kramer, "Global Arms Trade," pp. 267-69. Egypt's large acquisitions of the early 1990s have been in many cases delayed or canceled, due to financial problems. Ibid., p. 264.

34. For details on the Iranian case, see Keith Krause, "Military Statecraft: Power and Influence in Soviet and American Arms Transfer Relationships," *International Studies Quarterly*, 35(3):326-28 (Sept. 1991); Stephanie Neuman, "Arms Transfers, Indigenous Defence Production and Dependency: The Case of Iran," in *The Security of the Persian Gulf*, ed. Hossein Amirsadeghi (London: Croom Helm, 1981), pp. 131-150.

yan case, evidence suggests that weapons acquisitions outstripped any rational process of defense planning and threat assessment, as equipment was either left in storage or operated by foreigners. In the Iraqi case, the weapons buildup was in part driven by rivalries with Iran and the decade-long Iran-Iraq war, but also by the Iraqi leader's bid to establish a position of leadership in the Arab world. The result in all cases was a bloated military establishment that consumed a large proportion of available resources—even if high oil prices reduced the guns-butter trade-off—and that was unable to use effectively the arsenal that had been constructed.

This characterization of systemic imperatives could be filled in with a more rigorous assessment of the relationship between specific arms acquisitions and security policy decisions. For example, one could argue that rational security policies would lead to arms acquisitions that are related to the threats a state faced, that are suited to potential battlefield conditions, and that could be used by its forces with a reasonable amount of training and support. Acquisitions that do not meet these criteria would prompt a search for other explanations, which could, of course, be either systemic or internal. Systemic motivations would be evidenced by the rhetoric of regional great powers, as has been offered by Iran or India, for example, or by attempts to acquire prestige weapons with no discernible military utility, such as advanced fighter aircraft without the pilots to fly them.

Arms transfers
   and internal
   sources of insecurity

The security policies of Middle Eastern states have not been determined solely by regional or systemic imperatives, especially in states such as Syria and Iraq. Perhaps the most disturbing developments in the Middle East do not concern arms transfers or weapons arsenals at all but rather stem from the broader process of military development in which these are embedded. Two sources of insecurity are most evident: those stemming from the weakness of regimes that have a narrow base of political support and those associated with weak states in which the institutions or very existence of the state are in question due to ethnic or religious fragmentation. The classic example would be Iraq: a state with large Kurdish and Shia minorities, repressed by the ruling elite, which itself is narrowly rooted in the Tikriti clan. Other similar weak states (qua states) would include Syria, Jordan, Lebanon, and the Sudan.[35] In all these cases, the military has emerged as a significant prop of the state, existing in a symbiotic relationship with the ruling elite. Sometimes the military rules by itself; sometimes it acts as the power behind the throne; and it always receives significant resources.

35. Libya is a slightly different case, with the legitimacy of the Ghadhafi regime being reinforced by a strong ideology and military, but it still may constitute a weak state.

In states such as these, military development and arms acquisitions are fueled not only by the need to respond to external threats but also by this internal or state-building dimension. What often results is a hypertrophied military establishment, with tentacles of influence reaching into all levels of society. Syria, Libya, Iraq, and Jordan, for example, all have more than 20 soldiers per 1000 population (1989 data) and are among the top 10 states in this category.[36] The world average is 5.4 soldiers per 1000. In most of these states and throughout the Middle East, defense expenditures remain above 10 percent of gross national product.[37]

The lines of causality are not easy to discern here, although three things are clear. First, arms transfers and the arsenals that are created are not just a product of rational assessment of external threats; instead, they result from a complex internal set of political choices over how resources are to be allocated. Analysts know little about which actors possess the greatest influence in these decisions, what sort of understanding of how to achieve security they possess, and what role external forces play in shaping choices. Second, the type and scale of arms transfers is in part a consequence of internal political struggles over who rules and who threatens; this conclusion turns on its head the argument that arms transfers are an indicator of arms-racing behavior between states.[38] Third, the high levels of political violence and repression and the intense political role of the military in many Middle Eastern states—such as Syria and Iraq—cannot be isolated from the high levels of weapons, soldiers, or military expenditures that are indicated by these figures.[39] This is obviously more complex than a simplistic linkage between arms imports and internal repression—and arms imports may be a symptom, not a cause!—but any analysis of security in the Middle East that does not at least draw attention to the links between the external and domestic dimensions of security would be incomplete.

36. The actual figures are: Jordan, 60.5; Iraq, 55.3; Syria, 33.3; Libya, 21.0. Yemen (Aden) was also in the top 10, with 34.9. The figures are from U.S., Arms Control and Disarmament Agency, *World Military Expenditures and Arms Transfers 1990* (Washington, DC: Arms Control and Disarmament Agency, 1991), p. 41.

37. Ibid. The global average for military expenditures as a percentage of gross national product was 4.9 percent; the average for the developing world was 4.3 percent.

38. The identical conclusion was reached by some analysts of the superpower competition in the Cold War and by the literature on organizational/bureaucratic politics. See Jacek Kugler and A.F.K. Organski, *The War Ledger* (Chicago: University of Chicago Press, 1984), chap. 4.

39. I have eschewed the imprecise term "militarization" because there is intense debate over its meaning. For an overview, see Andrew Ross, "Dimensions of Militarization in the Third World," *Armed Forces and Society*, 13(4):561-78 (Summer 1987). For details on specific Middle Eastern states, see Samir al-Khalil, *Republic of Fear* (Berkeley: University of California Press, 1989); Elisabeth Picard, "Arab Military in Politics: From Revolutionary Plot to Authoritarian State," in *Beyond Coercion: The Durability of the Arab State*, ed. Adeed Dawisha and I. William Zartman (New York: Croom Helm, 1988), pp. 116-46.

CONCLUSION

It is extremely difficult to disentangle these motives for arms acquisitions, and a full account would require detailed case studies of changing patterns of security policies and arms acquisitions. From a regional security perspective, however, what is most important is that one state may purchase weapons for reasons of prestige or to suppress internal dissent, yet the security dilemma may drive its neighbors inevitably to interpret this as a possible threat. Expensive and unnecessary arms races could be triggered, and the result might even be an armed conflict. Libyan arms acquisitions in the late 1970s and the early 1980s, for example, created unease in Egypt and Algeria and possibly contributed to increased arms acquisitions in these states. Only after the poor Libyan performance in the Chad war—and perhaps external intervention in the form of American bombing—did this perceived threat subside.[40] Likewise,

40. *Strategic Survey, 1987-88* (London: International Institute for Strategic Studies, 1988), pp. 187-88.

there is little doubt that the Shah's drive for regional hegemony was strongly opposed by Iraq and that Iraqi weapons buildups played some part in Israeli demands for arms and probably in Syrian and Saudi arms demands as well. A similar process might be at work in Syria, where the internal imperatives of regime security have created a military establishment that is viewed suspiciously by all Syria's neighbors.

What this review of the contemporary evidence on arms transfers and weapons proliferation in the Middle East does tell us, however, is that we need more sophisticated means of analyzing and understanding the complex processes behind the global diffusion of weapons. To date, most work has concentrated on the supplier or producer side of this process. The Middle Eastern experience suggests that the main task, though, is to understand the dynamic forces at work in the process of military development from the perspective of recipient states. Only from this analysis can one assess the impact of arms transfers on the security of regions, states, and peoples.

ANNALS, *AAPSS*, **535**, September 1994

Arms Transfers, Military Assistance, and Defense Industries: Socioeconomic Burden or Opportunity?

By STEPHANIE G. NEUMAN

ABSTRACT: More than thirty years of research on the positive or negative consequences of various military activities for the civilian sector has failed to yield strong and unambiguous evidence one way or the other. This article briefly describes the history of this guns-versus-butter controversy, noting the close relationship between U.S. policy needs and the response of the research community. The article then focuses on the debate over the role that arms transfers, military assistance, and defense industries play in Third World economic growth and development. Finally, it assesses the relevance of the debate for today's post-Cold War world.

Stephanie G. Neuman is a senior research scholar and director of the Comparative Defense Studies Program at Columbia University, as well as an adjunct professor of international and security affairs. She publishes widely in the field of arms transfers and military production. Some of her most recent publications include "Controlling the Arms Trade: Idealistic Dream or Real Politik?" Washington Quarterly (Summer 1993); and "Globalization and the Proliferation of Military Technology," in U.S. Domestic and National Security Agendas: Into the 21st Century, ed. Sam Sarkesian (1994).

A N intense, often angry, debate over the impact on society of military activities and spending has absorbed the energies of large numbers of social scientists, researchers, and policy analysts for many years. This article first briefly describes the history of this guns-versus-butter controversy and its current status. Then the focus turns to the major questions asked and the kinds of answers given regarding the specific role that arms transfers, military assistance, and defense industries play in Third World economic growth and development. Finally, the debate in today's changing post-Cold War world is assessed.

THE HISTORICAL SETTING

It is often held that scholarly research is a product of the arcane, self-generated ideas of an intellectual community divorced from the everyday policy dilemmas of government. An intellectual history of the defense-development field, however, suggests that the substance and degree of scholarly interest have been closely correlated with the needs and concerns of the U.S. policymaking community. Perhaps the reason was the available research money, fraternization between policy analysts and academics at conferences, or just the intellectual climate of the times, but what engaged U.S. policymakers during the Cold War also absorbed the attention of important segments of the scholarly research community.

Prior to World War II

Scant policy or scholarly notice was given to the relationship between the military sector and economic development before the late 1940s. After World War II, however, a number of factors moved American policymakers and, with a short lag, the scholarly community to examine the subject more closely.

The 1950s

In the 1950s, the growing size of the public sector obliged U.S. policymakers to explain and justify why federal spending was increasing at a rate that appeared to be spinning out of control. Two-thirds of the federal budget was now being spent on welfare and defense alone (see Table 1).

Moreover, statistical estimates of military spending, at least in the developed world,[1] had become more widely available. This provided policymakers and social scientists the ability to analyze a major source of government spending in all its dimensions, especially its impact on other sectors of the economy.

The increasing number of newly independent Third World states appearing on the international scene at this time also presented challenging analytical and political dilemmas for Western policy elites: How could economic development be stimulated and some form of political stability be achieved in these regions? What advice should be given to encourage both? How should financial and technical assistance be targeted? These

1. In the Third World there was an absence of official statistics prior to the 1950s, in part because many states were only newly independent. V. Bulmer-Thomas, "Economic Development over the Long Run: Central America since 1920," *Journal of Latin American Studies*, 15:269 (Nov. 1983)

TABLE 1
**SOCIAL WELFARE AND DEFENSE OUTLAYS AS PERCENTAGE
OF TOTAL U.S. FEDERAL GOVERNMENT OUTLAYS**

	1950	1960	1970	1980	1989
Social welfare	37.4*	38.4*	46.5[†]	57.1[†]	53.0[†]
Defense	29.1*	52.2[†]	41.8[†]	22.7[†]	26.2[†]
Total	66.5	90.6	88.3	79.8	79.2

NOTE: Social welfare outlays include the following categories: social insurance, public aid, health and medical programs, veterans programs, education, housing, and other social welfare.
*Statistical Abstract of the United States, 1980, pp. 329, 366.
[†]Statistical Abstract of the United States, 1992, pp. 356, 336.

were questions with significant policy implications for which decision makers could find few answers.

The 1960s

It was not until the 1960s, however, that Western scholars began to pay serious attention to these questions. Again, external factors and policy considerations seemed to serve as the intellectual catalysts. First, the Cold War had intensified, and Third World countries had now acquired strategic significance for the United States and the Soviet Union. Superpower competition had become a zero-sum game in which a political gain for one was considered a political loss for the other. What happened in the Third World now mattered, as the Vietnam war, then only in the beginning stages, was to painfully demonstrate to the American public later on.

Second, and not unrelated to the Cold War, were the escalating military expenditures worldwide. How to allocate public resources had become a major question for policymakers everywhere. How much should be spent on defense as opposed to other budgeted items? In the United States, social welfare spending was on the rise, but military expenditures were growing more rapidly, from 29 percent of government spending in 1950 to 52 percent in 1960. Together these items now composed 91 percent of total U.S. federal spending. (See Table 1.)

In the less solvent Third World, military expenditures had risen sharply, but economic development had improved only in a few cases and in some countries had declined. Between 1963 and 1967, the growth rate of Third World military expenditures was 9.1 percent, in contrast to 2.9 percent for gross national product per capita.[2]

Furthermore, military coups, occurring with some regularity throughout the Third World, were complicating the analytical problem. Policymakers and social scientists were unsure what impact the military takeovers would have on political development and economic growth or how the United States

2. U.S., Arms Control and Disarmament Agency, *World Military Expenditures and Arms Trade, 1963-1973* (Washington, DC: Government Printing Office, 1975).

should react to them. Given the newly discovered strategic importance of the Third World, resource allocation in less developed countries (LDCs) had also become a concern to U.S. policymakers.

In response to these events, the exigencies of the Cold War and the uneasy sense in Washington that the initiative for bettering conditions in the Third World lay with the United States, the U.S. government sponsored area studies programs to train experts and encourage research on the Third World.[3] The United Nations, too, supported related research during this period. The hope was that policy-relevant findings would emerge with solutions for these questions.

A number of studies on the Third World were produced during the 1960s, many of which focused on the role of the military in developing countries. Joseph Johnson's book, *The Role of the Military in Underdeveloped Countries*, emerged as the classic work of its time. It articulated the optimistic view that the military would have a modernizing effect on society and therefore an indirect, positive impact on the economy.[4]

It was also during this period that Emile Benoit began U.N.-sponsored research for his controversial book, *Defense and Economic Growth in Developing Countries*. This volume was to ignite the debate on defense spending versus development when it was finally published in 1973.[5]

The mid-1970s

By the mid-1970s, U.S. policymakers and academics were still uncertain about how to encourage economic growth in the Third World and what part the military played in the development process. The findings in the largely English-language literature were inconclusive, while events in the real world were demanding a policy response. Thanks to the 1973 oil boom, Third World countries' share of world military expenditures had risen to about one-quarter, in contrast to only 9 percent in 1963, while growth rates lagged behind.[6]

The persistence of this trend generated genuine puzzlement within government and academic circles. Given the continuous rise of defense expenditures worldwide and slow development, it seemed only logical to conclude that the former adversely affected the latter. Military expenditures and development were now assumed to be directly related and inversely correlated. Resources spent on defense must come at the expense of something else. Therefore, butter was being traded off for guns with negative consequences for society.

Only a small minority challenged this view. One scholar, in a puckish

---

3. The Fulbright-Hayes Act of 1961, for example, was designed to promote teaching and professional research in other countries by U.S. scholars and improve their knowledge of foreign languages and cultures.

4. J. J. Johnson, ed., *The Role of the Military in Underdeveloped Countries* (Princeton, NJ: Princeton University Press, 1962).

5. Emile Benoit, *Defense and Economic Growth in Developing Countries* (Lexington, MA: Lexington Books, 1973).

6. Arms Control and Disarmament Agency, *World Military Expenditures and Arms Trade, 1963-73*; idem, *World Military Expenditures and Arms Transfers, 1972-82* (Washington, DC: Government Printing Office, 1984).

mood over coffee one day, estimated the ratio of believers in the new orthodoxy to challengers as 95 to 5.[7] The scholarly literature, although skewed in one direction during this period, was distributed on a continuum between two distinct and opposing worldviews. At one extreme were the political realists and at the other, the dependency theorists, with an array of nuanced positions falling in between.[8] In the late 1960s and early 1970s, the balance was tipped toward the dependency end of the spectrum.

7. Gavin Kennedy, personal conversation, Washington, DC, 1987.
8. The political realists viewed sovereign nation-states as rational, unitary actors pursuing national interests, regardless of their form of government or type of economic organization. In a self-help, anarchic international system, they maintained, weapons are necessary tools in the struggle to survive and to achieve order and stability. Order is a precondition for economic development, but development is ultimately decided by domestic capabilities and resources. Inequalities between states are an inevitable byproduct of the uneven distribution of these resources and capabilities.
Dependency theorists, like the realists, regard states as the primary actors in the world, but they see them as representing class rather than national interests. From this perspective, states are not unitary but stratified actors. Classes form across state borders and compete for control within countries and among them. Governments pursue not an abstract national interest but the economic and political interests of a dominant class or classes. Arms represent an instrument of repression whereby the weak are subordinated to the strong. The world system is dominated by capitalism. Underdevelopment is seen as a by-product of that system, although scholars differ over the relative importance of domestic versus external forces. To achieve development and greater equality, they contend, the domestic or international status quo needs to change.

The 1980s

By the late 1970s, the debate had expanded to include the entire military sector. Much of the literature now reflected the view that not only defense spending but also military regimes, arms transfers, military assistance, and defense industries were responsible for negative development in the Third World. Inductive, quantitative, cross-national studies using various correlational and structural models were launched to decide the issue one way or the other. More political realists and some neutral empiricists joined the fray, and although a spirited methodological debate resulted, the findings of these studies, too, remained contradictory and inconclusive.[9] Significant theoretical insight into the relationship between the civil and military sectors continued to elude the field.

9. See, for example, B. Biwas and R. Ram, "Military Expenditures and Economic Growth in Less Developed Countries: An Augmented Model and Further Evidence," *Economic Development and Cultural Change*, 34:361-72 (Jan. 1986); Saadet Deger, "Economic Development and Defense Expenditure," *Economic Development and Cultural Change*, 36:179-96 (Oct. 1986); W. J. Dixon and B. E. Moon, "The Military Burden and Basic Human Needs," *Journal of Conflict Resolution*, 30(4):650-84 (Dec. 1986); Peter C. Frederiksen and Robert E. Looney, "Defense Expenditures and Economic Growth in Developing Countries," *Armed Forces and Society*, 9:633-46 (Summer 1983); D. Lim, "Another Look at Growth and Defense in Less Developed Countries," *Economic Development and Cultural Change*, 31:377-84 (Jan. 1983); Erich Weede, "Military Participation Ratios, Human Capital Formation, and Economic Growth: A Cross-National Analysis," *Journal of Political and Military Sociology*, 11:11-19 (Spring 1983).

The 1990s

With the ebbing of the Cold War, the controversy has become less heated. Emerging today is a tentative consensus, even between former antagonists, that the relationship between the military sector and development —if there is one—is more complex than originally believed and that different research approaches are needed.

THE DEBATE, PART 1: THE ARMS TRADE, PROCUREMENT, AND MILITARY ASSISTANCE

Whereas the role of the military and the level of defense expenditures occupied the attention of analysts in the 1960s and early 1970s, the military procurements of the Middle East oil states after 1973, particularly those of the Shah of Iran, added another dimension to the controversy. What part did arms transfers and military assistance play in the development and growth process of Third World states? Were the effects positive or negative? For the most part, the debate remained partisan. The lines had already been drawn. Those who viewed the military and defense spending as either detrimental or beneficial to development and social welfare held similar views about the impact of military assistance and arms procurement.

The negative impact

Those who hold that arms transfers, procurement, and military assistance have a negative effect on society accept, for the most part, the zero-sum pie assumption of the economists. Government spending on defense (guns) and social programs (butter) compete for the same limited government budget and thus must constrain each other.

Opportunity costs, the drain on foreign exchange, and domestic resources. The main argument claims that the opportunity costs[10] associated with arms procurement in general, and arms imports in particular, are too high. Resources used for military purposes compete for resources that otherwise could have been available for socioeconomic development.[11] The escalating demand for ever more sophisticated weapons and the rising price of these imported weapons put pressure on central budgetary expenditures, leaving fewer resources for other purposes. Not only do weapons purchases adversely affect the balance-of-payments position of most Third World countries and increase their debt burden, but they also crowd out public and private investment, depriving the economy of vital growth inputs.

Generally, these purchases are thought to preclude productive investments in human capital that can greatly assist development. When resources contract, public services, such as education, housing, and health facilities, are held to be particularly vulnerable to budget cuts.[12]

10. In this connection, the term "opportunity costs" refers to the cost of using resources for defense purposes, measured by the benefits given up by not putting them to their best alternative use in the civilian sector.

11. United Nations, Department for Disarmament Affairs, *Economic and Social Consequences of the Arms Race and of Military Expenditures* (New York: United Nations, 1983), p. 23.

12. Saadet Deger, *Military Expenditure in Third World Countries: The Economic Effects*

On the other hand, some scholars point out that it is not procurement that burdens most less industrialized countries.[13] Whynes asserts, for example, that only a little under 1 percent of the national income in LDCs is devoted to the purchase of major military equipment from abroad; the figure is a little over 1 percent if minor weaponry is included. But arms imports, whether paid for fully or by foreign aid, carry with them hidden costs, such as servicing, training of mechanics, and building infrastructure. Libya, for example, bought 200 Mirage fighters from France at a cost of some $750,000 per plane. Maintaining the squadrons in the air for one hour each week, however, cost several million dollars more per year.[14]

Similarly, a company of tanks entails maintenance, spares, fuel, backup facilities, buildings, administration, and other support likely to cost the LDC about $2 million per annum, in addition to the cost of the tanks themselves. Naval equipment is perhaps the most expensive. A single destroyer, according to Whynes, absorbs over $140,000 each year, excluding the very high costs of docking and harboring. Thus, allowing for such factors as maintenance and training of personnel, and other support, the actual resource commitment for the import of weaponry could easily double the cost of the equipment's purchase price.[15] Whynes concludes that although the purchase of weapons may not have a negative impact, the expenditures related to them do.

Unfavorable political spin-offs. Various analysts also point to other indirect adverse effects of arms transfers and military assistance. First, they allege, spending in general and the importation of weapons in particular increase the influence of the military in society. As Robert S. McNamara declared, "One of the most important effects of military spending, and one that has serious implications for political and economic development, is the degree to which it strengthens the political influence of the armed forces at the expense of civilian groups within society."[16] For those concerned with the role of the military in society, arms transfers help to keep the military or other nondemocratic elites in power, which, in turn, unfavorably affects the basic needs of people and, in the long run, produces domestic instability—all of which are to the further detriment of economic growth. From this perspective, the increased "militarization" stimulated by arms transfers influences public policy in ways that are not conducive to social welfare.[17]

(Boston, MA: Routledge & Kegan Paul, 1986), pp. 121, 246.

13. See David K. Whynes, *The Economics of Third World Military Expenditure* (Austin: University of Texas Press, 1979). See also Nicole Ball, *Security and Economy in the Third World* (Princeton, NJ: Princeton University Press, 1988), app. 1.

14. Whynes, *Third World Military Expenditure*, pp. 96-97.

15. Ibid., p. 97.

16. Robert S. McNamara, "The Post-Cold War World: Implications for Military Expenditure in the Developing Countries," in *Proceedings of the World Bank Annual Conference on Development Economics 1991* (Washington, DC: International Bank for Reconstruction and Development, World Bank, 1992) p. 107.

17. Ruth Sivard, *World Military Expenditures, 1989* (Washington, DC: World Priorities,

A similar argument is offered regarding arms races: arms imports lead to arms races that constantly increase import requirements at an increasing cost. Thus arms races and development are in a competitive relationship for finite resources.[18] Security assistance, in this view, permits states to purchase these expensive weapons, encourages the pursuit of war or its continuation—and therefore encourages insupportable drains on the economy. "The negative implications of the continuation of these conflicts for the economies of the participant nations far outweigh whatever benefits security assistance might bring."[19]

The positive impact

Other researchers have challenged this view. On balance, they maintain, procurement and military assistance have positive rather than negative implications for LDC economies.[20] These analysts have been joined in recent years by a growing number of Third World leaders whose policy decisions reflect their tacit agreement with this position.

Favorable socioeconomic spin-offs. Some believe that arms transfers and military assistance bring unanticipated beneficial socioeconomic spin-offs to the economy. For instance, the Draper Report, issued by the 1959 Presidential Committee, pointed to the educational and civic possibilities associated with military assistance and procurement.[21] The skills gained from learning how to operate and maintain equipment, for example, are deemed to be transferable to the civilian sector. Air force pilots, mechanics, technicians, and health care personnel become valuable human-capital assets for society when they leave military service. Infrastructure built to accommodate weapons and bases is also considered a positive input for society. Roads, bridges, electrical lines, communications systems, housing, and waterworks all provide significant benefits to the civilian population as well.[22]

Security and stability. Others contend that the security and stability benefits to society, although not quantifiable, are overlooked by critics of military assistance and arms transfers. Without security, these analysts argue, there cannot be development. In this view, weapons not only allow for self-defense but deter potential aggressors from attacking and in this way promote peace and stability, which are vital conditions for development.

1989), p. 21; Michael Klare, "Militarism: The Issues Today," in *Problems of Contemporary Militarism*, ed. Asbjorn Eide and Marek Thee (London: Croom-Helm, 1980), p. 39.

18. United Nations, Department for Disarmament Affairs, *Economic and Social Consequences*, p. 63.

19. Ball, *Security and Economy in the Third World*, pp. 292-94.

20. Benoit, for example, acknowledged that defense spending reduces civilian production and "crowds out" civilian investment, but, he concluded, the negative effects are offset by other positive "spin-offs." Benoit, *Defense and Economic Growth*, p. xxi.

21. Whynes, *Third World Military Expenditure*, p. 94.

22. Benoit, *Defense and Economic Growth*, pp. 17-18. See also Stephanie Neuman, "Security, Military Expenditures, and Socioeconomic Development: Reflections on Iran," *Orbis*, 22(3):588-89 (Fall 1978).

George Quester, on the other hand, believes it is not the arms imports per se but the kind of weapons acquired that determines the long-term positive or negative economic burden of arms procurement. Challenging the conventional wisdom regarding the high socioeconomic costs of nuclear weapons proliferation,[23] for example, he points out that nuclear weapons are a direct product of a civilian nuclear program and that both military and civilian nuclear programs have important economic benefits. For those countries with civilian nuclear programs, nuclear weapons programs are cheap force multipliers, since the start-up costs have already been expended. Moreover, nuclear weapons can deter war and thus eliminate its costs. But, he warns,

If nation A wishes fully to reassure nation B that it is not acquiring nuclear weapons, it may thus have to avoid any and all investment in nuclear research and nuclear electrical power production. If nuclear power truly makes economic sense for the countries in question, *avoiding* a weapon, rather than *acquiring* the weapon, could thus become the major economic burden for the country involved, in terms of peacetime outputs.[24]

He presents a similar case for chemical weapons. If both potential enemies have them, he suggests, it reduces the likelihood of war. Furthermore, acquiring chemical weapons is not an economic burden in peacetime. The same chemical plant producing useful pesticides or fertilizers may also be adaptable to weaponry at little cost to the Third World country.

Indeed, given all the difficulties of inspection and safeguards, and the concomitant difficulties of reassuring a neighbor about what one is producing in such plants, it may be possible to "avoid such weapons" only by sacrificing what is good and needed in one's civilian economy.[25]

But, in Quester's view, other kinds of weapons that make aggression more difficult, such as ballistic missiles, cruise missiles, remotely piloted airplanes, smart antitank weapons, and various kinds of air-to-air and surface-to-surface missiles, are expensive and a major economic burden during peacetime, "with any 'spinoff' from military deployment back to civilian life being quite marginal."[26]

Offsets as a motor of development and industrialization. In the Third World, military offset programs are regarded as a way of achieving both security and economic development.[27] Offset requirements and priorities, government officials maintain, are used as a means of luring

23. For a more detailed articulation of this position, see Sivard, *World Military Expenditures, 1989*, p. 10.

24. George H. Quester, "Predicting the Impact of Third World Weapons Spread" (Paper delivered at the conference "Implications of a Changing Third World Military Environment," Washington, DC, 25-26 July, 1989), p. 5.

25. Ibid., p. 10.

26. Ibid., p. 13.

27. An offset program is designed to reduce hard-currency payments for imports through barter, trade, investment by the supplier in the local economy, partial domestic production of the item to be purchased, preferential trade contracts, or increased access to the supplier's commercial market. For a detailed description of different kinds of offset arrangements, see S. Neuman, "Coproduction, Barter, and Countertrade: Offsets in the International Arms Market," *Orbis*, 29(1) (Spring 1985).

developmental investment, creating competitive trade opportunities, promoting industrialization, improving the country's technological capabilities, creating employment, and promoting technology transfer.[28] For example, only 35 percent of the price of 24 Russian SU-27 aircraft sold to the People's Republic of China is being paid for with cash. Chinese running shoes, parkas, canned meat, and other consumer goods are reported to be making up the remaining 65 percent of the value of the aircraft. Similarly, a "secret" enterprise is also said to have signed a $100,000 contract to supply the Chinese with composite materials technology to be used in satellites. One-fifth of the contract price is to be paid in cash, the rest in bartered consumer goods.[29] In Malaysia, Primary Industries Minister Lim Keng Yaik said in March 1993 that Russia is considering the purchase of up to 1 million tons of palm oil in exchange for the delivery of MiG-29 fighter planes to Malaysia.[30] Reportedly, Pakistan was negotiating to buy 320 T-72 tanks from Poland, with only 10 percent of the value to be paid in cash and the remainder in barter.[31]

To ease budget constraints and develop industry, other Asian states are buying arms through offset arrangements that allow them to make the weapons at home rather than buy

them abroad. India,[32] Singapore, South Korea, and Taiwan have successful programs of this kind. Some governments, such as Indonesia's, now demand technology transfer and local assembly for new arms procurements.[33]

For a variety of reasons, successful offset arrangements have been less frequent between industrialized and Third World countries than between the industrialized countries themselves, but this may be changing. Whether successful or not, however, the drive for offsets suggests that increasing numbers of Third World leaders regard military offsets as an important economic policy tool.

Fungibility of foreign aid. Third World leaders as well as some Western analysts also stress the utility of military assistance as an alternate source of development funding. Whether economic or military aid, monies are fungible, they argue. What is not spent in the military sector is freed up for other kinds of spending and vice versa. As one World Bank official notes, some developing countries that have achieved high rates of military spending and dynamic growth—for example, Taiwan, the Republic of Korea, Greece, and Israel—have received substantial military and economic aid. He observes that this assistance was often successful in "transforming military industries

28. Gilbert Nockles and Alan Spence, *Offset: Securing Competitive Advantage and Economic Development in the 1990s* (London: FT Business Information, 1987), pp. 17-22.

29. "Foreign Press Reports" (American League for Exports and Security Assistance), mimeographed, 11 Jan. 1993, p. 2.

30. Hong Kong AFP, 9 Mar. 1993.

31. Reuters Wire Service, 29 Apr. 1992.

32. India's National Aerospace Laboratories, for example, has signed an agreement with a Russian firm to design and produce a 14-seat light-transport aircraft to be used in both countries. *Foreign Press Reports*, 16 Feb. 1994.

33. Reuters Wire Service, 29 Apr. 1992.

TABLE 2
WORLD ARMS DELIVERIES (Billions of 1991 dollars)

Country	1987	1988	1989	1990	1991
China	2.4	3.3	2.5	1.5	0.9
France	3.3	1.9	2.1	4.0	1.1
United Kingdom	5.7	5.3	5.1	4.5	3.7
Soviet Union	25.8	24.6	21.5	14.8	6.6
United States	20.9	16.0	17.2	14.6	13.9
Total	58.1	51.1	48.4	39.4	26.2

SOURCES: For all countries but the United States: U.S., Arms Control and Disarmament Agency, *World Military Expenditures and Arms Transfers, 1991-1992* (Washington, DC: Government Printing Office, 1994). For the United States: U.S., Department of Defense, Defense Security Assistance Agency, Comptroller, Foreign Military Sales Control and Reports Division, *Foreign Military Construction Sales and Military Assistance Facts as of September 30, 1992*, n.d.

NOTES: Included in the U.S. data are Foreign Military Sales deliveries, Foreign Military Construction Sales deliveries, commercial exports, Military Assistance Program deliveries, and International Military Education and Training. Data for the United States are by fiscal year. Most of the data for other countries are by calendar year.

into viable export sectors"[34] and, in so doing, benefited growth.

In the Third World, there is strong support for this position. As sources of both foreign and military aid begin to dwindle, a number of Third World governments are expressing concern.[35] The collapse of communism in Eastern and Central Europe has led to an acute fear of marginalization as Third World governments see themselves competing with these regions for a limited pool of aid, loans, foreign investment, and technology.[36] In their view, foreign assistance, regardless of its form, is vital for economic development and stability.

The situation today

The debate pro and con has been muted by the economic and political realities of a post-Cold War world in which arms exports are in sharp decline (see Table 2). A world recession and the altered political climate have worked to reduce the demand for military equipment. Declining demand has set into motion a cycle whereby shorter production runs raise the unit cost of military equipment.[37] This places an additional

34. Robert Picciotto, "Comment on 'The Post-Cold War World: Implications for Military Expenditure in the Developing Countries,' by McNamara," in *Proceedings of the World Bank Conference 1991*, p. 134.

35. For example, aid to Central America from the United States, with the exception of a $420 million aid package to Panama in 1992, is down. The 1992 allocation of $86 million in economic aid to Honduras is the lowest to that country in 10 years, with the exception of 1989, when aid was frozen over economic policy. Military aid for 1992 came to $6.2 million, a small fraction of the over $80 million Honduras received in the mid-1980s. Lee Hockstader, "Honduras Embattled after Decade of Aid," *Washington Post*, 13 July 1992.

36. Andrew Hurrell, "Latin America in the New World Order: A Regional Bloc of the Americas?" *International Affairs*, 68(1):124 (1992).

37. Francois Heisbourg found that the price indexes of arms, aerospace, and shipbuilding in comparison to other categories of manufactured goods were 26 to 90 percentage

burden on already shrinking budgetary resources, further decreasing the number of weapons the military can afford to buy.

Worldwide, arms imports have declined dramatically since the end of the Iran-Iraq war, dropping 63 percent from 1987 to 1991. Imports fell most precipitously in the Third World (65 percent) and former Warsaw Pact countries (96 percent). In the Third World, the Middle East's arms imports plunged 59 percent; in Latin America, 78 percent; in Africa, 86 percent; in East Asia, 58 percent; and in South Asia, 49 percent.[38]

Muting the fervor of the debate is a form of structural arms control that is now in place. As the growing cost of new-generation weapons limits what many countries can procure, attention is shifting to Third World military production and its implications for the future.

THE DEBATE, PART 2:
DEFENSE INDUSTRIES
AND DEVELOPMENT

Defense production and its impact on economic development have constituted another related and sharply debated issue. Although the substance of the argument differs somewhat, those who attribute negative or positive effects to defense spending and arms procurement tend to adopt

a similar stance regarding defense production for similar reasons.

The negative impact

Defense production is seen by many scholars as yet another socially wasteful military-related activity.

Economic costs. These scholars point to the opportunity costs involved: the diversion of critically scarce inputs—such as capital, technical skills, labor, raw materials, and foreign exchange—from the economy to make weapons. Third World military industries, they note, are largely unprofitable and form an inherently weak sector of the economy that is particularly vulnerable to the swings of the world economy.[39] Considered to be nonproductive, to yield few spinoffs to the civilian sector, and to absorb limited resources, military industries are perceived by these analysts as a drain on the economy.[40]

Technology transfer. Technology transferred from the industrialized world, in this view, constitutes another burden for the economy. The hopes for self-sufficiency have not been borne out, nor have the imported technologies benefited the civilian industrial sector. One scholar concludes, "Although the establishment of a domestic capacity to produce arms is often justified in Third

points higher. Francois Heisbourg, "Public Policy and the Creation of a European Arms Market," in *European Armaments Market and Procurement Cooperation*, ed. Pauline Creasey and Simon May (London: Macmillan, 1988), p. 61.

38. U.S., Arms Control and Disarmament Agency, *World Military Expenditures and Arms Transfers, 1991-1992* (Washington, DC: Government Printing Office, 1994).

39. Amit Gupta, "Third World Militaries: New Suppliers, Deadlier Weapons," *Orbis*, 37(1):59 (Winter 1993). See also Saadet Deger and Ron Smith, "Military Expenditures and Growth in Less Developed Countries," *Journal of Conflict Resolution*, 27:346-48 (June 1983).

40. Nicole Ball, "The Political Economy of Defense Industrialization in the Third World," in *The Political Economy of Defense: Issues and Perspectives*, ed. Andrew L. Ross (Westport, CT: Greenwood Press, 1991), pp. 175-201.

World countries by anticipated technological spin-offs, present experience suggests that it is primarily the military sector that benefits from know-how and other resources already available in civil sector industry."[41]

Research and development. Further, in this view, research and development (R&D) monies expended on defense deprive the civilian economy of important R&D inputs. Because resources are scarce in Third World countries, what is spent on military R&D leads to lower R&D in the public sector.[42] Lower outlays in the civilian sector retard growth by reducing nondefense investment in R&D and indirectly deprive the economy of the new technology that serves as a vehicle for development.

The positive impact

Other observers take a more affirmative view of military industries. Looney and Frederiksen, for example, find that Latin American producers of at least one major weapons system enjoy positive economic benefits from defense expenditures while nonproducers experience declines in growth and investment.[43]

Socioeconomic benefits. Spin-offs from military production are also regarded, by some analysts, as a major benefit to development. Transfers of technology from military to civil industries, for example, are considered a spur to industrialization, particularly in countries where civilian industrialization has lagged. Expenditure on military R&D, in particular, is thought to advantage the larger economy by producing techniques and materials with direct civilian applications. Although these analysts believe it is possible that Third World countries would gain more from commercial industrialization, arms production, in their view, must be considered a plausible alternative way of promoting industrialization, given the sluggish pace of the civilian industrial sector in most LDCs, the political priority accorded defense industries by Third World producer countries, and the positive spin-offs these governments associate with them.[44]

Others claim that foreign exchange savings earned through substitution are another important advantage.[45] When LDCs buy a large proportion of domestically manufactured military items, foreign exchange is saved by reducing the number of imported spares, components, and weapons systems. Military exports, too, in this view, represent a singular source of foreign currency earnings.[46]

41. Ibid., p. 190.

42. United Nations, Department for Disarmament Affairs, *Economic and Social Consequences*, p. 25; Sivard, *World Military Expenditures, 1989*, p. 30.

43. Robert E. Looney and Peter C. Frederiksen, "Impact of Latin American Arms Production on Economic Performance," *Journal of Economic, Social, and Political Studies*, 12:309-20 (Fall 1987).

44. Neuman, "Security, Military Expenditures, and Socioeconomic Development."

45. Jose Encinas del Pando,"Economic, Military and Socio-Political Variables in Argentina, Chile and Peru (1950-1980): A Regional Analysis," mimeographed (Lima: University of Lima, 1983), quoted in Ball, "Defense Industrialization in the Third World," p. 182.

46. Jurgen Brauer, "Military Investments and Economic Growth in Developing Nations," *Economic Development and Cultural Change*, 39:884 (July 1991).

To some, military industries profit the economy by absorbing excess manufacturing capacity. Neither civilian nor military demand alone, they maintain, could sustain an aircraft or shipbuilding industry; together, however, they permit continuous production from an established plant. Governments, they point out, often use military production to manipulate the economy, phasing its own demand to coincide with slack periods within the civilian market, thus averting major slumps and swings.[47]

Military industries are also thought to generate valuable multipliers within the local or regional economy and can, therefore, be used as a tool in regional development programs. As Jurgen Brauer concludes, "relative to LDC [non-arms producers], the mitigated (negative) effect of military expenditures on economic growth in LDC [arms producers] might be due in part to military domestic investments."[48]

Finally, some analysts assert that military industries contribute to stability, an important precondition for economic growth, in that they build domestic political support for the government by creating employment opportunities.

Security benefits. Perhaps most disputed are the self-defense arguments often promulgated by some scholars and the Third World producers themselves. If internal order and tranquillity—for example, freedom from fear of external invasion or domestic upheaval—are essential to development, then military industries make an important contribution to security. In addition, the ability to produce weapons that promise unacceptable casualties to the enemy serves as an important disincentive to regional or Western aggressors.[49] In this view, military industrial production provides an element of self-sufficiency by reducing the state's dependency upon foreign suppliers, leaving it free to build a deterrent force or deal with perceived internal and foreign threats without external interference.[50]

Surprise and secrecy are also mentioned as untouted benefits of indigenous military production. Both India and Israel, for example, have expressed concern that buying equipment from foreign suppliers risks compromising their inventories. One Indian commentator noted that "during the Gulf War a large quantity of Soviet built equipment was seized by the Allied forces, of which Pakistan was a part."[51] The implication is that imported equipment is always less secure than the domestically pro-

47. Carol Evans, "Reappraising Third World Arms Production," *Survival*, 28:101 (1986); Whynes, *Third World Military Expenditure*, pp. 52-53; Brauer, "Military Investments," p. 882.

48. Brauer, "Military Investments," p. 881.

49. Gupta, "Third World Militaries," pp. 67-68.

50. George Tanham, for example, believes that the Chinese-Indian border war provided the impetus for self-sufficiency in weapons production for India. "Indian history had revealed all too clearly that Indian dependence on inferior weapons was disastrous." George Tanham, "Indian Strategic Culture," *Washington Quarterly*, p. 140 (Winter 1992).

51. M. Satish, "Defence Spending: Why It Must Be Increased," *Economic Times* (New Delhi), 11 Apr. 1992, cited in Ian Anthony, "The Conventional Arms Trade in the 1990s," in *Cascade of Arms: Controlling Conventional Weapons Proliferation in the 1990s*, ed. Andrew J. Pierre (Washington, DC: Brookings Institution, 1994).

duced equivalent because a country's enemy may more easily gain access to it and thereby glean sensitive information. Israel has also used this argument as a reason for domestic defense production regardless of its profitability.[52]

The situation today

Economic and political changes are forcing Third World leaders to assess the utility of defense production in a post-Cold War world. Falling defense budgets and contracted demand have had serious negative consequences for Third World exports and military industrial infrastructure. Some military industries are consolidating while others are going out of business. Worldwide, military production of major weapons is falling—some estimate by 20–30 percent during the 1990s,[53] and that figure may underestimate the situation, particularly in the Third World. In an ever reiterative downward spiral, small- and medium-size states' ability to produce sophisticated weapons is dwindling.

In the current world economy, arms production might be seen to have more liabilities than advantages for Third World countries. But

various factors are at work that could make indigenous arms production increasingly attractive to Third World governments in spite of the inhospitable economic environment. Ironically, arms control efforts that emphasize greater transparency in the arms trade may be a catalyst. These initiatives may convince countries with existing defense industries to preserve them and encourage others to establish them in the interests of political independence and autonomy—even if it is uneconomical to do so.[54] Ethan Kapstein comments that

in an anarchic international environment, states must look to their own wherewithal for survival. All other things being equal, states would prefer to be autarkic in the production and deployment of advanced weaponry. Given that no country today can achieve the desired condition of self-sufficiency at politically acceptable costs, governments will still do what they can to maintain at least some defense production at home.[55]

In all probability, then, Third World governments that have the resources to do so will strive to maintain what indigenous military production capability they can. Rather than submit to externally imposed controls, these countries are likely to decide that the additional resource commitment is a necessary price to pay for security. Even those countries with relatively small armies and limited resources seem to take this view. Brazil, for example, sustains a military of about 300,000 and yet sup-

52. Aharon Klieman and Reuven Pedatzur, *Rearming Israel: Defense Procurement in the 1990s*, Jaffee Centre for Strategic Studies, Study no. 17 (Jerusalem: Jerusalem Post Press, 1991), cited in Anthony, "Conventional Arms Trade."

53. Keith Krause, "Trends in the Production and Trade of Conventional Weapons" (Paper prepared for the conference "The Supply-Side Control of Weapons Proliferation," Canadian Institute for International Peace and Security, Ottawa, Ontario, Canada, June 1991), pp. 6-7.

54. Anthony, "Conventional Arms Trade."

55. Ethan B. Kapstein, "Conclusions and Policy Recommendations," in *Global Arms Production: Policy Dilemmas for the 1990s*, ed. Ethan B. Kapstein (Lanham, MD: University Press of America, 1992), p. 240.

ports a diverse, if struggling, military industrial sector. As Raimo Väyrynen observes, Brazil is committed to a policy of "pragmatic antidependency" that strives to increase the autonomy of the nation's infrastructure and Brazil's influence in the Western hemisphere. To Brazil, military industrialization is an important precondition for realizing this policy.[56]

Brazil's commitment to military production is not unique among LDCs. In 1984, there were 28 countries in the Third World that produced major weapons systems,[57] and many more that manufactured small arms and ammunition. States once part of the former Soviet Union must now be added to their number, and others may soon join them. Georgia, for example, according to a senior defense adviser, is planning to build its own defense industry.[58]

56. Raimo Väyrynen, *Military Industrialization and Economic Development: Theory and Historical Case Studies* (New York: United Nations Institute for Disarmament Research; Hampshire, England: Dartmouth, 1992), p. 100.

57. China, India, Israel, South Africa, Brazil, Taiwan, North Korea, Argentina, South Korea, Egypt, countries of the Association of Southeast Asian Nations (Indonesia, Malaysia, Thailand, the Philippines, Singapore), and others (Bangladesh, Burma, Chile, Colombia, the Dominican Republic, Gabon, Madagascar, Mexico, Pakistan, Peru, Senegal, Sri Lanka). The countries are listed in rank order based on data from the Stockholm International Peace Research Institute (SIPRI). See Michael Brzoska and Thomas Ohlson, eds., *Arms Production in the Third World* (London: Taylor & Francis, 1986), p. 10. I added China to the list. SIPRI does not include China as a Third World country and so it is not included in the Brzoska and Ohlson data.

58. Apparently, only an aircraft-producing firm, once part of the old Soviet military industrial complex, is still functioning. "Foreign Press Reports," 11 Jan. 1992, p. 9.

The continuing need for foreign exchange in less developed states and the disappointing results of recent conversion attempts worldwide further encourage domestic arms production. Antoaneta Dimitrova, in her analysis of the Bulgarian experience, describes the problem: the converted former defense industries in Bulgaria use rather than generate hard currency, so they are unable to modernize their equipment. As a result, the new products are uncompetitive, and the factories, unprofitable. Moreover, because Bulgarian arms producers were organized in production chains, when one factory converted, other companies suffered severe input shortages,[59] further aggravating depressed economic conditions in the country as a whole. Similar problems have plagued conversion efforts in other states, making it an economically painful solution that political elites approach with caution.

Privatization is now seen by some as an alternative solution. The intent is to make the military industries more efficient by changing ownership. In many cases, however, it implies the continuation rather than the reduction of arms production. Dimitrova's expressed hope for privatization makes this plain: "As is clear from the interest displayed by would-be foreign investors, there are still hopes that the military industry will revive and help pull the Bulgarian economy out of its current crisis."[60]

Unresolved political disputes in the Third World provide yet another

59. Antoaneta Dimitrova, "The Plight of the Bulgarian Arms Industry," *RFE/RL Research Report*, 12 Feb. 1993, p. 52.

60. Ibid., p. 53.

incentive. For combatants fighting guerrilla wars, insurgencies, and counterinsurgencies, the weapons of choice are not those comprising leading-edge technologies but those most abundantly produced in the Third World, for example, assault rifles, antitank weapons, fixed- and rotary-wing aircraft, cluster bombs, surface-to-air missiles, and antipersonnel weapons. Third World producers may view ongoing ethnic wars and regional rivalries as a ready market for the low- and midlevel military technologies they make for their own troops. The recent wars in the former Yugoslavia serve as an example. In 1993, the Croatian national guard reportedly received arms from Argentina (7.62mm rifles), Hungary, Romania, South Africa (grenade launchers), and Singapore (SAR-80 assault rifles, Ultimax 100 Mk III light machine guns, and Crossbow light antitank weapons).[61]

In short, arms production will, in all likelihood, continue in Third World countries, although what and how much will be manufactured remain unclear. Given the state of the literature, it is difficult to predict what the long-term implications will be for the economic growth and development of these countries. As one scholar concludes,

The relationship between military industrialization and economic development is necessarily complex, historically variable and dependent on the prevailing international context. That is why there is no universally valid answer to the politically perennial question of whether military spending and industrialization, ulti-

mately, promote or prevent economic development.[62]

THE DEBATE IN THE
POST-COLD WAR WORLD

More than thirty years of research on the consequences of various military activities for the civilian economy have failed to yield strong and unambiguous evidence one way or the other. Basudeb Biwas, for example, replicated the empirical part of a study he did with Rati Ram in 1986 that examined the 1960-70 and 1970-77 periods for 58 LDCs. In his recent study, he examined a sample of 74 LDCs for the period 1981-86. He found that, in contrast to the negative effect shown by the earlier research, the more recent data indicated "the positive effect of military outlays on LDC growth."[63] Other studies have come up with similar contradictory findings.[64] Third World leaders and some Western scholars now question whether there is, in fact, a guns-versus-butter trade-off. It is possible, they claim, to do well in defense while doing well in growth and welfare.[65] Others remain more

62. Väyrynen, *Military Industrialization and Economic Development*, p. 101.
63. "Defense Spending and Economic Growth in Developing Countries," in *Defense Spending and Economic Growth*, ed. James E. Payne and Anandi P. Sahu (Boulder, CO: Westview Press, 1993), pp. 225, 230.
64. See Steve Chan, "The Political Economy of Military Spending and Economic Performance: Directions for Future Research," in *Political Economy of Defense*, ed. Ross, pp. 204-22.
65. Davis B. Bobrow, "Eating Your Cake and Having It Too: The Japanese Case," in *Defense, Welfare, and Growth*, ed. Steve Chan and Alex Mintz (New York: Routledge, 1992), pp. 81-98.

61. Gupta, "Third World Militaries," pp. 62-63.

agnostic. As Keith Krause posits, "several of the presumed deleterious consequences of arms transfers and production either do not exist or are more complex than is usually imagined."[66]

In 1978, I surveyed the defense and development field. I queried whether the search for universal patterns applicable to all countries in all time periods could produce useful theory or policy guidelines. I called for an "ideological detoxification" of the research and for longitudinal case studies that would break down military expenditures and analyze their impacts on different sectors of society. I also suggested thinking about culture as a factor in the development process.[67] Today, time and the changing character of the international system have tempered the debate. But innovative methodological approaches and longitudinal case studies remain the exception to the rule.[68] Breakdowns of defense expenditures have proven difficult to obtain for most countries, and cultural differences remain unexamined. In sum, our findings are not more conclusive than they were in 1978. We still do not know whether or when defense has positive, negative, or no impact at all on socioeconomic development and growth. Today, a new generation of scholars is calling for fresh theoretical and meth- odological approaches that do justice to the "complexity of the problem."[69]

It is difficult to assess how the changed balance of power in the post-Cold War world will affect the scholarly debate. But if lessons can be drawn from history, then the interest of the policymaking community—or lack of it—will determine its intensity. The Clinton administration's stress on democratization, and the rising prominence of organizations such as Human Rights Watch and Amnesty International in international affairs, are sending a signal not just to Third World countries but also to the scholars who study them: political development rather than defense and economic development is now center stage as a foreign policy issue. Furthermore, the increasing use of embargoes or the threat of them as a diplomatic tool—in spite of their negative economic impact on the economies of the targeted states—sends a subliminal message to the world that human rights rather than economic growth is the new litmus test for Western aid and

66. Keith Krause, "Arms Imports, Arms Production, and the Quest for Security in the Third World," in *The Insecurity Dilemma: National Security of Third World States*, ed. Brian L. Job (Boulder, CO: Lynne Rienner, 1992), pp. 141-42.

67. "Security, Military Expenditures, and Socioeconomic Development," p. 592.

68. For an important exception, see Steve Chan, "Defense Burden and Economic Growth: Unravelling the Taiwanese Enigma," *American Polit- ical Science Review*, 82(3):913-20 (Sept. 1988).

69. Andrew L. Ross, "The Political Economy of Defense: The Nature and Scope of the Inquiry," in *Political Economy of Defense*, ed. Ross, pp. 15-17; Steve Chan, "The Impact of Defense Spending on Economic Performance: A Survey of Evidence and Problems," *Orbis*, 29:433 (1985). For an excellent discussion of the kinds of research needed, see Richard C. Eichenberg, "Do We Yet Know Who Pays for Defense? Conclusions and Synthesis," in *Defense, Welfare, and Growth*, ed. Chan and Mintz, pp. 231-41; Steve Chan, "Defense, Welfare, and Growth: Introduction," in ibid., pp. 1-20.

trade. If the past can predict the future, then we can expect the scholarly literature to reflect the shift in focus. The number of studies on the relationship between arms and development will probably dwindle, and the intensity of the debate diminish further as analysts turn to issues more central to current policy concerns.

Political and military exigencies will, then, in all likelihood, continue to define defense outlays. Events in the real world will demand a policy response, and with few other guidelines to follow, policymakers will opt for choices they believe to be in their best political interests. As in the past, policy decisions will precede empirical knowledge about the relationship between defense and development, and theory will have only a marginal impact on them.

ANNALS, *AAPSS*, **535**, September 1994

Financing the Arms Trade

By JOEL L. JOHNSON

ABSTRACT: When a government acquires a product from foreign sources, some financial transaction must occur. Countries may pay cash, borrow funds to pay for the goods over time, provide other goods in return, or receive the goods on a grant basis. With respect to commercial goods, such as aircraft, power generation equipment, and telecommunications products, methods of financing are well known, and an international framework disciplining such practices has gradually been established. Financing involving the defense trade is much more opaque, however, and there are no international agreements governing such transactions. With the end of the Cold War, and the sharp decline in military assistance formally available from the superpowers, the issue of how arms sales are financed will become more important for purchasers and vendors. This article will review the means by which arms sales have been and are financed and will discuss the possibility of increasing information and international discipline on financing practices.

Joel L. Johnson is vice president, international, for the Aerospace Industries Association (AIA), the trade association representing the major manufacturers of aerospace products. Previously, he served with the federal government, including as deputy director of the Office of Trade Policy at Treasury, a member of the secretary of state's Policy Planning Staff, and a professional staff member on the Senate Foreign Relations Committee. His work in government centered on economic development and international trade issues. Mr. Johnson received his master's degree from the Woodrow Wilson School of Public and International Affairs at Princeton University.

NOTE: This article is written solely as a personal statement. It should not in any way be interpreted as reflecting official views of the Aerospace Industries Association, where the author is currently employed.

WHEN a government acquires a product from foreign sources, some financial transaction must occur. Countries may pay cash, borrow funds to pay for the goods over time, provide other goods in return, or receive the goods on a grant basis. With respect to commercial goods, such as aircraft, power generation equipment, and telecommunications products, methods of financing are well established, and an international framework disciplining official financing of such transactions has gradually been established.

Financing involving the defense trade, however, is much less publicized, and there are no international agreements governing such transactions. With the end of the Cold War, there is a sharp decline in the military assistance funds previously available from the superpowers for their respective clients. For many developing and middle-income countries, however, the end of the Cold War has not eliminated regional, ethnic, and civil strife. The need to play a greater role in looking after their own interests, plus the normal requirement to replace aging military equipment, means that a number of countries, particularly in the Middle East, the Pacific Rim, and South America, are in the market for new defense equipment.

At the same time, declining defense budgets have increased the importance of exports to most producers of weapons systems. Hence competition is increasing for those foreign markets that do exist, and companies will look for any competitive edge they can use, including financing their products on attractive terms.

The issue of how arms sales are financed will therefore become more important for purchasers and vendors as a commercial issue, rather than as a foreign assistance question. This article will review the means by which arms sales have been and are financed, with particular reference to the United States, and will discuss the possibility of increasing information and international discipline on credit practices.

MILITARY ASSISTANCE

Countries may find it to their advantage to provide military equipment and training to allies on a grant or concessional basis for a variety of reasons. They may wish to gain influence over the recipients, to help a friendly country establish a formidable enough military establishment to dissuade neighboring countries from adventurism, and to enable an ally, if necessary, to fight along with or in lieu of the donor country's own military.

During World War II, the United States was certainly the largest donor of military equipment, primarily through the lend-lease program. Following the war, large amounts of U.S. military hardware were made available to friendly countries, particularly in Europe and Latin America. A more complex program emerged over time that involved both grant aid and concessional and nonconcessional loans, which I will detail later. U.S. assistance focused on poorer countries in the North Atlantic Treaty Organization (NATO) (Turkey, Greece, Portugal, and Spain), the Middle East (Israel, Egypt, Tunisia, and Morocco), and Third World countries facing a direct or indirect threat from Communist-bloc countries or revolutionary movements (for example, South Korea, Iran, South Vietnam, Pakistan, El Salvador, and Honduras).[1]

During the Cold War, this program was more than matched by the Soviet Union in assistance to its ideological allies, including North Korea, Vietnam, China, Cuba, Egypt, Nicaragua, Angola, Ethiopia, and Afghanistan.[2] It is very hard to get a handle on the grant or concessional element of Soviet arms trade, as the Soviets never made such data available. Furthermore, much of the concessional trade involved barter transactions with other nonmarket economies such as Cuba and Vietnam. The Soviets did not know what their military equipment had cost to manufacture; the recipients did not know what it cost to produce the commodities or nonmilitary goods they provided in return. Neither country had a currency that traded freely. It is therefore difficult to know how to place a value on the trade itself, let alone determine the concessional element.

Suffice it to say that with the breakdown of the Soviet Union and the need for cash by its former component parts, we have seen a sharp decline in its exports of military hardware.[3] Of course, much of this decline

relates to the end of conflict for a number of its former client states—Ethiopia, Nicaragua, Vietnam, Afghanistan—international embargoes, such as the one against Iraq, and internal chaos in the production and delivery of weapons systems in the former Soviet bloc. However, it is probably a reasonable conjecture to suggest that over the past twenty years at least two-thirds of Soviet arms exports involved grant or concessional assistance, which is to say that at least $15 billion in arms transfers per year would not have occurred had they not been financed by the Soviets.

With considerably greater authority, we can note that U.S. military assistance tended to hover around the $6 billion level over most of the past two decades, or roughly 40-50 percent of U.S. arms exports. Just as the end of the Cold War and the move toward market economies has brought about a collapse of former Soviet military assistance programs, we have seen a steady decline in U.S. military assistance programs in the past three years.

Furthermore, there has been a narrowing of the focus of the program. For fiscal year 1994, virtually all grant assistance—$3.1 billion—will go to Israel and Egypt. Of that, roughly $500 million of military aid to Israel is allowed to be spent on Israeli military production, and such aid is not reflected in arms transfer statistics, nor does it provide a market for U.S. industry.[4] Unlike the case of Russia, however, U.S. arms ex-

1. U.S., Department of State and Department of Defense, Defense Security Assistance Agency, *Congressional Presentation for Security Assistance, Fiscal Year 1994*, 1993. See also ibid. for previous fiscal years. These documents contain individual-country summaries of the program and objectives.

2. U.S., Arms Control and Disarmament Agency, *World Military Expenditures and Arms Transfers: 1991-92*, March 1993. See also previous volumes in this series.

3. Ibid.

4. U.S., Congress, House, *Conference Report 103-267*, 103d Cong., 1st sess., 28 Sept. 1993, p. 27.

ports per se have not fallen, as cash-paying customers have more than made up for the drop in programs funded via military assistance. Other countries have also had military assistance programs, mostly European nations helping their colonies and former colonies.

The bottom line is that it is perhaps safe to speculate that of the roughly $45 billion per year in arms transfers to developing countries during the 1980s, at least a third was in the form of grant aid, mostly from the Soviet Union. The near disappearance of such Soviet assistance has essentially reduced arms transfers to the Third World by about $15 billion per year in the 1990s, a phenomenon that is not likely to be reversed.

It is probable that there will be a temporary surge of in-kind grant and concessional assistance in the next two or three years as the United States and European countries, including Russia, downsize their own military establishments and look for ways to reduce stocks of older or nonessential hardware. This process was already under way with the signing of the Conventional Forces in Europe Treaty, in which both NATO countries and the Soviet bloc were required to reduce hardware in Europe. In Western Europe, the major beneficiaries of the cascade effect were Turkey and Greece.[5]

OFFICIAL AND CONCESSIONAL LENDING

Large weapons platforms—aircraft, ships, tanks—are essentially capital goods that will remain in inventory for 15 or more years. In this sense, they are not dissimilar from commercial capital goods, particularly transport, power generation, and communications equipment. When countries, particularly developing countries, purchase the latter goods, they often require financing to spread payments over at least part of the life span of the equipment being purchased. This is true whether the purchaser is the national government, a government-owned entity, or a private corporation.

To facilitate such credit needs, exporting industrial countries have established official lending and guarantee facilities that can provide loans directly to the purchasing entity or guarantee all or part of commercial loans for such purchases. In the case of the United States, the Export-Import Bank provided nearly $11 billion in such medium- to long-term loans and guarantees in fiscal year 1993.[6]

The same middle-income developing countries often require similar financing to purchase defense products. For such countries, evaluation of weapons systems offered by foreign contractors will include not only performance, quality, price, and availability of the product in terms of their own defense needs but also the availability and quality of the credit terms. If a country cannot pay for a desired new system without credit

---

5. Edward J. Laurance and Herbert Wulf, *An Evaluation of the First Year of Reporting to the United Nations Register of Conventional Arms* (Monterey, CA: Monterey Institute of International Studies, 1993).

6. Export-Import Bank, *Ex-Im Bank: Jobs through Exports*, Ex-Im Bank annual report, 1993.

terms, then a vendor that does not offer such terms is out of the competition. The terms of the credit offered, such as interest rates, grace period on payments of principal, and duration of the loan, can also make a difference in a country's decision on from whom, or even if, to buy, particularly if commercial interest rates are high, such as during the mid- to late 1970s.

Most of the defense exporters who compete with the United States offer such financing through the same official credit institutions that provide loans and guarantees for purchasers of commercial products. Examples include the British Export Credits Guarantee Department, the French Compagnie Française d'Assurance pour le Commerce Extérieur, the Canadian Export Development Corporation, and the German HERMES Kreditversicherungs AG.[7]

By contrast, the U.S. Export-Import Bank has been prohibited from providing loans or guarantees for the purchase of defense equipment by developing countries since 1968, and it has by its own policy not supported sales of defense equipment to any country since 1974. Exceptions have been made for sales of military equipment to support drug control and eradication efforts of developing countries and for a sale of military helicopters to Turkey.[8]

For at least some purchasing countries, U.S. foreign military sales credits and other forms of military assistance helped fill this gap. In fact, in the early 1970s, the credit program administered by the Department of Defense (DoD) actually provided guarantees to private lenders in much the same way that the Export-Import Bank guarantees loans for commercial products. By the mid-1970s, however, the entire military assistance program consisted of direct government loans and grants to recipients.[9]

These programs were, of course, always structured to meet U.S. national security requirements, not industry commercial concerns. Thus loans and grants tended to be focused on countries involved in Cold War conflict—Southeast Asia and then Central America—as well as on the Middle East—mainly Israel and Egypt. The administration, and often the Congress, set country priorities at the beginning of a fiscal year based on security considerations. This contrasts with official export credit institutions such as the Export-Import Bank, which are designed to assist exporters, generally on a first-come, first-served basis.

Military assistance programs have also been reduced steadily since the mid-1980s; the number of countries served by such programs has also dropped. In fiscal year 1994, 79 percent of the $3.9 billion military assistance program (grants plus loans) will be dedicated to Israel and Egypt, and five countries—Israel,

7. U.S., Office of Management and Budget, *Financing Defense Exports (November 1990)*, 11 Dec. 1990.

8. Export-Import Bank Act of 1945, as amended, sec. (2) (b) (6).

9. For background, see U.S., Congress, General Accounting Office, *Security Assistance: Update of Programs and Related Activities*, GAO/NSIAD-89-78FS, Dec. 1988; Ernest Graves, *U.S. Security Assistance in the 1980's* (Washington, DC: Center for Strategic and International Studies, 1983).

Egypt, Greece, Turkey, and Portugal —account for 99 percent of the program.[10] Hence there is effectively no funding available to support sales in other countries, even if the program did have a commercial dimension.

U.S. industry has argued that without an official credit guarantee program for defense products, it is difficult to obtain financing on reasonable terms in order to bid on contracts in countries that require such finance. U.S. banks have generally been unenthusiastic about making unsecured loans to foreign purchasers. This is partly because, unlike commercial goods, defense exports do not generate a stream of revenue that will help pay for the product. Further, bank management may be concerned that lending for weapons can generate negative publicity and upset stockholders. Finally, just as with commercial products, banks may be reluctant to lend to certain developing countries without some government guarantees regarding repayment.

Lack of finance places U.S. firms at a competitive disadvantage and has resulted in lost contracts. In some instances, U.S. firms have won contracts, but only by using foreign-based production facilities in countries that would provide needed export credits. For example, companies from Germany, the United Kingdom, and the United States were finalists in the late 1980s for a $1 billion Turkish program to build armored personnel carriers. FMC, the U.S. company, won the competition, but because there was no finance available from the United States, the entire program was sourced from Europe, where

10. House, *Conference Report 103-267*, p. 27.

home governments would finance the portions of the program produced in their respective countries.

Over the past three years, some members of Congress, as well as individuals in both the Bush and Clinton administrations, have shown interest in the establishment of a separate government guarantee facility for defense exports that would parallel the Eximbank guarantee program for commercial products. A $1 billion program was authorized by the Congress for fiscal year 1994, but the $25 million in budget authority needed to launch the program was not appropriated.[11]

COUNTERTRADE
AND OFFSETS

In addition to traditional forms of financing, arms sales often involve the seller in a variety of activities that help the purchasing country increase its own economic activity to help pay for the purchase, or at least compensate for the expenditure on a foreign product. These activities are generally known under the rubric of countertrade and offsets.

Countertrade in its simplest form is a barter transaction, in which the

11. In the past, guarantee programs needed only to be authorized, but no budget authority was required. Under the Budget Enforcement Act of 1990, guarantee programs now require budget authority to cover the "subsidy element" of the guarantee. Basically, the subsidy element for guarantees covers the risk element that the government will actually have to provide funds to cover defaulted loans. As the loan guarantee program passed by the Congress covered only NATO countries plus Japan, Australia, Israel, and Korea, the risk element was deemed low by the government, and the subsidy element was thus calculated at $25 million.

seller of a product accepts payment in the form of goods, rather than hard currency, from the buyer. In the defense area, this form of transaction is primarily used when at least one of the parties is a nonmarket economy; in such cases, books can be balanced by trading commodities such as sugar or wheat for arms. There have been a few well-publicized countertrade transactions between market economies, such as the large al-Yamamah I and II sales of arms by Britain to Saudi Arabia, in which Britain is accepting payment in oil,[12] and the recently announced sale of MiG-29s by Russia to Malaysia, in which it is reported that some of the payments will take the form of palm oil exports to Russia.[13]

In most cases, however, governments of market economies do not themselves have products they can directly sell to raise money to pay for defense equipment. Rather, they are interested in stimulating exports that help the overall balance of payments and generate jobs and therefore make using taxpayer revenue for a highly visible purchase of a foreign product more economically and politically acceptable. They may also wish to use the purchase to gain technology that will help the country become less dependent on foreign purchases of defense equipment in the future and/or to stimulate the civilian sector of their economy. Such arrangements are lumped under the general category of offsets.

Offsets have generated considerable political controversy in the United States, with politicians and some industry and labor representatives arguing that offsets give away jobs and create future competitors. There is some truth to these arguments, but on balance, the positive benefits outweigh the negatives. In the first place, while offsets may be inefficient (money and accounting were invented, after all, to allow for commerce without barter), they do not alter the fundamental fact that for every export, there must be, at some time and from some country, an equivalent import. Otherwise, the exporting country is giving away real value for no comparable value in exchange—which, of course, is the case when foreign assistance is involved.

This fundamental fact concerning trade is not understood by most politicians or journalists. There is a tendency to think of exports as good, and imports as bad, even though exports involve giving up goods and services to foreigners, while imports involve getting the results of someone else's work. The problem, of course, is that imports can be identified by displaced workers as the source of their problem and can readily be stopped at the border. When imports are reduced, either exports must also decrease or, more likely, imports are displaced into other sectors. For example, when the United States recently limited the import of flat panel displays from Japan, imports of personal computers containing such screens increased, while U.S. computer manufacturers moved some production out of the United States

12. *Aviation Week & Space Technology*, 8 Feb. 1993, p. 27.

13. Ibid., 5 July 1993, pp. 24-25.

in order to use cheaper flat panel displays in their production.

Offsets face much the same phenomenon. They are identifiable and involve cross-border transactions; hence they are vulnerable to political intervention. Whether they cause much disruption in fact is a matter of conjecture. Several major studies by the federal government have all generally concluded that, on balance, sales of defense equipment with associated offsets produce more benefit to the overall economy than not having the sale in the first place.[14]

Offsets can take many forms and often do within the same transaction. In some cases, the purchasing country demands to produce some portion of the weapons system in question; such an arrangement is generally known as a direct offset. Such a demand is intended to help establish a defense industry, keep some of the jobs involved in producing the system at home, and reduce dependence on external sources of weapons and their components.

There is increased suspicion that direct offsets are poor investments in a climate in which there is global overcapacity in the defense industry and in which there is evidence that, in the future, commercial technology is more likely to drive military technology rather than the other way around. For example, in Operation Desert Storm, commercially available hand-held Global Positioning Satellite units, which are used to pin-

point geographic location, were rushed to U.S. troops both by the military and, in some cases, by parents of troops in the field. Furthermore, given the low volume of production involved in most foreign weapons purchases, the unit cost of domestic production or assembly tends to be considerably higher than an off-the-shelf purchase from the exporting country.

It is therefore possible that so-called indirect offsets will play a larger role in future offset activity. Indirect offsets include any activity by which the exporting company can assist the importing country to increase its export earnings. Such offsets may range from quasi barter, in which a company hires a trading company to move product from the purchasing country on the international market, to joint ventures, in which the exporting company helps start up new industry in the importing country.

For better or for worse, so long as democratic countries find it cost effective to spend their taxpayers' funds for major offshore purchases of defense equipment, offsets are almost certain to provide the political and financial lubrication to allow such deals to go forward. The likely alternative, it might be noted, is not the disappearance of offsets but an increase in demand for outright licensed production. This is essentially what the U.S. government does when it makes any major purchase of a foreign weapons system. While the United States does not demand offsets per se, it has almost invariably demanded a warm production line in

14. U.S., Office of Management and Budget, *Impact of Offsets in Defense-Related Exports*, Dec. 1985; idem, *Offsets in Military Exports*, Dec. 1988.

the United States, as happened, for example, with the AV-8B jump jet, the T-45, the Berreta Pistol, and the Multiple Subscriber System. The Japanese have a similar policy of demanding local production whenever possible. From a European perspective, these policies look very much like a 100 percent direct offset requirement.

THE UNITED STATES AS SELLER AND FINANCIER

The U.S. system of arms sales and official grants and credits, and the terminology used to describe them, have often engendered confusion in the press and in the Congress. Before discussing possible future policy options, it might be useful to summarize briefly how the system currently operates.

Historically, most sales of U.S. weapons have in fact been made by the U.S. government to a foreign government. U.S. firms actively market their products to foreign militaries, but currently 80 percent of all actual sales of defense equipment are handled by government-to-government contracts, known as Foreign Military Sales (FMS). Defense companies in turn are given contracts by the appropriate U.S. military service to provide the equipment for the foreign sale.

Such sales can be financed either through cash payments by the foreign government or through official credits and grants provided by the U.S. government. In recent years, two major programs handled such financing: Military Assistance Program funds, provided on a grant basis, and FMS credits. The FMS credits were generally provided through a mechanism whereby the Department of Defense would provide guarantees to the Federal Finance Bank, which in turn would borrow funds at roughly the same rates obtained by the U.S. Treasury. Those funds would be placed in country accounts to pay for military sales. Countries would have to pay back the loans, but interest rates were well below commercial lending rates. In recent years, the Military Assistance Program was phased out and some FMS credits were provided on a "forgiven" basis—that is, they were grants. In order to reduce confusion, the terminology was changed beginning in fiscal year 1991 to Foreign Military Financing; this category included both grants and official lending.

Government-to-government sales are administered by the DoD's Defense Security Assistance Agency and by comparable offices in each of the services. Given the fact that all FMSs, whether involving official finance or not, are handled by the same DoD and service bureaucracies and are lumped under the generic category of Security Assistance, it is not surprising that people not familiar with the system often assume that all sales through the FMS channels involve some U.S. taxpayer support. In fact, U.S. law precludes cash-financed government-to-government sales from inflicting any cost on the U.S. taxpayer, and hence the government generally imposes surcharges of approximately 3 percent on FMS customers to cover the costs of administering the program.

In many cases, purchasers of U.S. weapons can now also contract directly with U.S. defense contractors, with the only government involvement being the issuing of an export license to the U.S. contractor. Such sales, known as commercial or direct sales, are usually financed directly by the customer, although in some instances, the contractor will help arrange financing if requested. Some countries have been allowed to use official U.S. credits and grants to purchase directly from a U.S. contractor, although DoD has announced that it will generally terminate this practice in mid-1994.[15]

In fiscal year 1992, the United States exported roughly $10.6 billion in defense products. Of these exports, perhaps $9.7 billion, or 92 percent, were government-to-government sales. Of those sales, roughly $4 billion, or 40 percent, involved official U.S. grants or credits.[16] The rest were cash sales, with the purchasing government being required to provide financing. Of the commercial sales, perhaps not more than 20 percent involved official financing. Given the surge of arms agreements in fiscal years 1992 and 1993, exports will almost certainly increase in fiscal

15. Letter from Lieutenant General Teddy Allen, director, Defense Security Assistance Agency, Department of Defense, to Don Fuqua, president, Aerospace Industries Association, 8 June 1993; letter from Lieutenant General Thomas Rhame, director, Defense Security Assistance Agency, to Joel Johnson, vice president, international, Aerospace Industries Association, 3 Dec. 1993. The change in policy relates to several DoD audits that uncovered irregularities in some such contracts.

16. U.S., Department of Defense, Defense Security Assistance Agency, Comptroller, Foreign Military Sales Control and Reports Division, *Foreign Military Sales, Foreign Military Construction Sales and Military Assistance Facts as of September 30, 1992*, n.d.

years 1994-96, with most of that increase in the form of FMS cash sales.

POSSIBLE RULES OF THE
ROAD FOR DEFENSE TRADE

Over the next few years, official military assistance programs are likely to erode further. Russian assistance has already collapsed. Pressure is likely to increase on U.S. and European governments to reduce such programs in favor of increasing domestic social programs. Official financing for defense exports will increasingly be motivated primarily in terms of helping domestic firms compete against other firms in the international market. This will particularly be true over the next four to five years, as the global shakeout in defense production capacity continues, and wins and losses in international markets will play an increasing role in determining which companies survive and which do not.

Given the high stakes, it is possible that governments might find themselves in an official credit competition to help their defense exporters. There are two related issues associated with government involvement in the financing of exports: the availability of credit, and the terms on which credit is made available.

The U.S. or other governments can encourage the private sector to make loans for defense products by providing guarantees to private institutions. Alternatively, governments can lend directly to purchasers of defense products. If such guarantees or direct loans are made at little or no cost to the governments, only availability is deemed to be affected by the government's role.

If, on the other hand, the government makes loans available at a cost to itself—for example, it lends at interest rates below the cost of money it can borrow, provides grace periods on payment of principal or other lending terms considerably more favorable than commercial banks, or lends to countries that involve a high likelihood of major defaults that must be paid by the taxpayer—then such programs are seen as involving concessionality, and hence the government affects the terms as well as the availability of credit.

To avoid a competition between governments in providing taxpayer-subsidized concessional loans for defense products, it is at least possible that governments may also be willing to look at some sort of guidelines or actual limitations on the magnitude and terms of official credit for defense products, just as they have for nondefense products.

All major industrial-country exporters are currently signatories to the Organization of Economic Cooperation and Development's Arrangements on Guidelines for Officially Supported Export Credits, known generally as the OECD Arrangement.[17]

The arrangement basically limits the degree of concessionality of official lending to different classes of countries, prohibiting any concessionality at all in lending to the wealthier industrial states. Currently, credits for agricultural and defense products are not covered by the arrangement.

It might be possible to use the same basic structure of the OECD Arrangement to cover defense exports, at least among OECD members. A separate arrangement might be negotiated, or an understanding to the current arrangement might be added. Such an approach would have the disadvantage of not including such major arms exporters as Russia, China, Taiwan, and Israel. In the case of Russia and China, for the immediate future, credits will be far less important than price and the nature of the technology that those countries will make available to other countries. Israel and Taiwan are still modest players in the international arms trade, and the commercial world will have to find ways to bring such countries into harmony with export credit guidelines for commercial products.

---

17. Organization for Economic Cooperation and Development, *Arrangements on Guidelines for Officially Supported Export Credits*, OCDE/GD (92) 95 (Paris: Organization for Economic Cooperation and Development, 1992). Under the arrangement, all countries are grouped into three categories based on per capita income. Categories I, II, and III basically comprise industrial countries, upper- and middle-income developing countries, and poorer developing countries, respectively. For the first two categories, export credit agencies are not to subsidize interest rates below the market-based rate agreed for their currency by arrangement members. Loans are usually not

to cover more than 85 percent of the cost of the total transaction. For the poorer countries, some subsidization is allowed in the interest rates for high-interest-rate currencies. The arrangement includes understandings for specific sectors, including one known as the Large Aircraft Sector Understanding. Among other provisions, this understanding allows loans and guarantees for industrial countries for up to 12 years, whereas the longest standard term in the arrangement is for 10 years. This recognizes that civil aircraft tend to be in inventory for a longer period of time than other capital goods. An arrangement that included defense equipment might similarly recognize the longer life span of major weapons platforms such as aircraft and ships.

It should be noted that the International Monetary Fund already provides some guidelines on total debt exposure of member countries, which includes debt related to military purchases. The World Bank has also begun looking at expenditures by countries on defense as one factor in evaluating new lending for development purposes. Such reviews may help inhibit overall borrowing by countries for defense purchases, but they do not control competition between selling countries. On the contrary, such scrutiny may increase the pressure on selling countries to provide concessional lending to reduce the economic impact on a purchasing country's overall defense spending.

Informal discussions of some kind of code of conduct on defense trade financing have been held between OECD members, with the United States at least so far being unreceptive to including defense trade under the OECD Arrangement. However, as U.S. military assistance continues to decline, and U.S. industry presses for some form of export finance to counter its foreign competitors, such a discipline may look more interesting to the U.S. government. Meanwhile, export credits will continue to play a role in determining who wins and who loses defense sales among middle- and lower-income countries.

ANNALS, *AAPSS*, **535**, September 1994

Global Trends in
Military Production and Conversion

By DAVID SILVERBERG

ABSTRACT: The end of the Cold War has forced the world's military-industrial complex to concentrate on technological niches rather than broad technological thrusts. The decline in defense budgets and the cutbacks in defense production will erode military capabilities in the developed world, allowing the Third World to catch up in key niches. Defense conversion has not succeeded to date, and is unlikely to succeed on anything like the scale of the previous military production or to absorb significant numbers of unemployed defense workers. The military-industrial complex should be allowed to consolidate and contract while new business formation among former defense workers, researchers, and engineers should be encouraged. In the long run, entrepreneurship will likely prove more beneficial and productive than trying to keep alive the kinds of enterprises that served the needs of the Cold War.

David Silverberg is editor at large at Armed Forces Journal International, *a magazine of military ideas and affairs based in Washington, D.C. He covered the international defense trade for the newspaper* Defense News *beginning in 1986. His work has appeared in numerous publications, and he has written special reports on the militaries and defense industries of Canada, India, Indonesia, Israel, the Philippines, South Africa, South Korea, Thailand, and Turkey.*

Nobody wants a hot war. A hot war is bad for business. The first thing that happens in a hot war is that everyone runs out of money. However, when you have a cold war everyone can plan rationally. The best time for business is a cold war when everyone is insulting each other's mothers.

Jose Luis Whitaker Ribeiro[1]

Jose Luis Whitaker Ribeiro was in a unique position to know about the benefits of cold war and the drawbacks of hot war. From 1976 until 1988, he led his company, Engesa, from the obscurity of a small oil-drilling equipment producer to one of Brazil's major industrial enterprises and one of the Third World's most capable defense manufacturers.[2] The cold war that made Engesa an industrial powerhouse was the one between Iraq and its neighbors. It turned hot in 1980 and ultimately led to Engesa's bankruptcy in 1988 when Iraq refused to pay its bills.[3]

The cold war between the United States and its allies and the Soviet Union and its satellites that chilled international relations between 1948 and 1989 led to a similar industrial buildup throughout the world.

The Cold War was unique in allowing managers, governments, and military planners to rationally plan, budget, and steadily implement industrial policies and programs on a predictable, orderly, and long-term basis. Soviet military defense expenditures followed a steady upward drift. Western expenditures rose and fell with the perception of threat. Neither side ran out of money, and managers could plan ahead.

Today, though ethnic tensions rage and batter the world's equilibrium, the nationalistic and ideological conflicts that rocked the world's nations earlier this century and gave rise to its gigantic, industrialized wars appear to be over for the near future. However laudatory the passing of these ideological conflicts, they nonetheless leave in their wake an immense industrial plant, geared toward conducting massive conflict.

The end of the Cold War has removed the certainty and predictability that governed military production. With the old threats gone and new threats unknown and largely unforeseeable, no industrial manager can predict the military requirements of the future with anything near the certainty he once had.

Further, each side in the Cold War could point to the other to justify research and development, arguing that a technological advance or potential advance by the adversary required an equal and immediate response. Suddenly, the desperate impetus that drove research and development is gone as well. This is not to say that the world's militaries have turned a blind eye to technological advancement. Indeed, the spectacular success of new technologies in Operation Desert Storm have created a revolution in military doctrine, operations, and equipment.[4]

1. Jose Luis Whitaker Ribeiro, Speech to the conference "Third World Defense '88," Washington, DC, 3 Nov. 1988.

2. Jose Luis Whitaker Ribeiro, correspondence with the author, 19 Aug. 1991.

3. Jose Luis Whitaker Ribeiro, correspondence with the author, 22 Aug. 1990.

4. Michael J. Mazaar, Jeffrey Shaffer, and Benjamin Ederington, "The Military Technical Revolution" (Final report of the CSIS Study

The advent of vastly improved surveillance and communications, combined with precision weaponry and a doctrine and structure to tie them all together, have created a new battlefield with new potential for lethality and firepower, dubbed the Military Technical Revolution (MTR). But in terms of what will be needed from the West's industries, "the heart of the MTR is information, and to the extent that new systems or technologies are acquired, priority should be given to the areas of surveillance and command and control."[5] When it comes to the lethal end of the MTR, "within the realm of strike systems, smart weapons should have priority over major platforms."[6]

Here, then, is a clear road map for the world's defense industries. The technologies of the MTR will be the path for military research and development in the developed world of the West and the Commonwealth of Independent States (CIS) for the future.

However, it is also a path that has been seized upon by Third World nations who immediately absorbed the lessons of Operation Desert Storm and are eager for the MTR's capabilities. "Third World countries see the effect of high-tech around them and aspire to induct 'state of the art' equipment," one Indian analyst has written.[7] Lasers, avionics, unmanned aerial vehicles, thermal imaging, missile guidance, surface-to-surface missiles, stand-off air-

launched missiles, precision-guided munitions, and attack helicopters, along with command, control, and communications and a variety of electronic warfare measures, are all technologies that Third World countries will need in order to maintain their military capabilities in light of the lessons of Operation Desert Storm.[8]

The result is a desperate Third World scramble to obtain the needed technologies and equipment, although at lower cost. That scramble is on now, and it is likely to intensify in the future. Indigenous Third World industries are already turning toward production of these items. For the next decade at least, the world's arms industries will likely concentrate on these technological areas, with the developed countries concentrating on refining their leads and Third World countries attempting to catch up.

Israel, as an example of an Asian country[9] with a robust defense industry, is working on a variety of MTR technologies. Israel Aircraft Industries, located near Tel Aviv, was a pioneer in unmanned aerial vehicle technology and has long been selling it on the world market. One of its most successful markets was in the United States, where the Pioneer unmanned aerial vehicle was purchased by the U.S. Navy.[10] Israel Aircraft Industries has also produced the Phalcon, a Boeing 707 airframe fitted with phased-array radar an-

Group on the MTR, Center for Strategic and International Studies, Mar. 1993).

  5. Ibid., p. 57.
  6. Ibid., p. 58.
  7. V. K. Nair, *War in the Gulf: Lessons for the Third World* (New Delhi: Lancer International, 1991), p. 111.

  8. Ibid., pp. 113, 114, 137, 142, 228.
  9. Although whether it is a Third World country is arguable.
  10. Israel, Ministry of Defense, Sibat, *Israel Defense Sales Directory, 1989-1990* (Jerusalem: Sibat, 1989), pp. 249.

tennas that can serve as an inexpensive Airborne Warning and Control System.[11] Elbit Ltd., an Israeli computer company located in Haifa, produces the Opher, a terminal guidance kit that can be fitted on dumb bombs, making them smart.[12]

South Africa, free of the anti-apartheid restraints of the past, is also attempting to branch out into international markets and is using its expertise in artillery, radios, avionics, mine detection, and night vision equipment to do so.[13] India is working on cruise missile technology.[14]

THE CAPABILITY DECLINE

But at the same time that the MTR establishes the technological path for the future, the world's defense industries are scaling down. In the United States, the aerospace industry alone, which had a peak employment of 1.33 million in 1989,[15] by 1992 had experienced a 22 percent employment decline in production workers, a 29 percent decline in administrative workers, a 5 percent decline in scientists and engineers, and a 19 percent decline in technicians.[16]

The Soviet economy was vastly overmilitarized, utilizing about 8 million workers, according to Dr. Igor Khripunov. If their families and dependents are also counted, that number rises to 20 million. Additionally, whole regions were dedicated to production of specific items for the Soviet military machine.[17] The U.S. government estimates Russian defense industry employment at 5-7 million out of a total labor force of 25 million.[18]

11. Israel Aircraft Industries, *Catalog of Main IAI Products and Services* (Tel Aviv: Israel Aircraft Industries, May 1991).

12. "Latest Version of 'Opher,' Elbit's Autonomous IR Terminal Guidance Kit, Will Be Demonstrated during 1993 Paris Air Show" (News bulletin, Elbit, Ltd., June 1993).

13. David Silverberg, "S. Africa Lures Defense Customers," *Defense News*, 30 Nov. 1992.

14. George Leopold and Vivek Raghuvanshi, "India Steps Up Cruise Missile Efforts," *Defense News*, 2 Aug. 1993.

15. Figure includes civil aerospace workers—there is no breakout for defense aerospace workers. Firm figures for workers employed in purely defense-related capacities are, for all intents and purposes, impossible to obtain. "Defense production" or simply "defense" is not an official employment category in any developed country. U.S. government estimates of Russian defense employment cited in this article are precisely that—estimates. To date, reliable figures have not been issued by the Russian government, nor are they likely to be. In the United States, the Aerospace Industries Association has relatively reliable figures for aerospace workers, but they do not take into account naval or ground systems workers. A good discussion of the methodological problems is contained in Herbert Wulf, "Arms Industry Limited: The Turning Point in the 1990s," in *Arms Industry Limited*, ed. Herbert Wulf (New York: Oxford University Press, 1993), pp. 12-15. In the end, Wulf acknowledged that he could only estimate figures for Third World producers like Chile or Brazil. Even in a country as highly developed as the United Kingdom, he could give only an estimate for 1990-92 employment figures. Given these difficulties as well as the impenetrability of closed societies like North Korea's, it seems unlikely that the world will ever know with any precision how many people were employed in making Cold War weaponry.

16. Aerospace Industries Association, "1992 Year-End Review and Forecast: An Analysis" (Paper, Aerospace Industries Association, 1992).

17. Igor Khripunov, "The Three Headed Challenge of Russia's Overmilitarized Economy" (Speech, "Common Defense" [exhibition and conference of international defense producers], Norfolk, VA, 22 Apr. 1993).

18. U.S., Department of Commerce, *Russian Defense Business Directory*, Nov. 1992, p. 2-1.

One estimate, by Herbert Wulf for the Stockholm International Peace Research Institute, puts world defense industry employment at a mid-1980s peak of 16 million.[19] But this seems too conservative, particularly in light of Khripunov's estimates.

Wulf estimates that, of the 15 million jobs in the global arms industry that existed at the beginning of the 1990s, 3-4 million jobs may be lost worldwide between 1993 and the year 2000.[20]

The combination of declining budgets, lack of threats, and dismissal of workers, including scientists, engineers, and designers, inevitably means a loss of capability in the developed world's military technology, with research and development slowing and possibly stagnating except for the few key niches of the MTR. This loss is predicted despite elaborate plans to maintain capability through selective procurements, extensive prototyping, concentration on key technologies, and investment in the defense industrial base.[21] Moreover, this loss comes at a time when the Third World is struggling to catch up to the technological level of the West and Russia.

What is likely to arrest this erosion of capabilities? In the past, technological stagnation has been halted by some startling development or a military defeat, and there seems no reason to expect anything different in

19. Wulf, "Arms Industry Limited," p. 13.
20. Ibid., p. 18.
21. John Deutch, Undersecretary of Defense for Acquisition and Technology, Testimony before U.S., Congress, Senate, Armed Services Committee, Subcommittee on Defense Technology, Acquisition and the Industrial Base, 103d Cong., 2d sess., 18 May 1993.

this case. The battle between the *Monitor* and the *Merrimac* at Hampton Roads in 1862 ushered in the era of ironclads throughout the developed world. When the British introduced the *Dreadnought* in 1905, a new naval era began. Similarly, when tanks first clanked across the battlefield in World War I, a whole new epoch in warfare was begun, and Germany was forced to catch up.

So, too, in our own time, the day will come after a long period of technological stagnation when a third-rate power produces an extraordinary new technology or inflicts a first-rate defeat on an established power and forces the other developed powers to catch up. The Third World does not have to develop the broad spectrum of capabilities and technologies possessed by the developed world—possession of a single, critical, war-stopping technology will do nicely. It will not have to defeat the established powers over a long period of time; a single blow followed by a negotiation will be sufficient. Nor will it necessarily require new hardware. One has visions of an Indian software engineer developing a new algorithm that can jam command and control broadcasts, selling it to Iran, which then uses it to bring the U.S. Navy to a halt in the Strait of Hormuz. Only after a shock as radical and stunning as that will the decline in capability be arrested and reversed—if there is time.

THE CONVERSION MIRAGE

In the immediate wake of the end of the Cold War, the defense industries of the world's largest arms-producing nations—Britain, China, France, Russia, and the United States—as well as minor producers could follow two strategies in order to maintain production levels.

One was to export as much as possible to make up for the shortfall in domestic procurement. The other was to diversify out of defense production. All attempted to follow both strategies, although some gave greater weight to one than the other.

The United States emerged as the dominant exporter to the Third World, largely because of its leading role in Operation Desert Storm and postwar purchases by the Gulf Arab states. The prognosis for future sales is not good, however, with Gulf inventories largely filled and defense budgets going down.[22] Countries of the Pacific Rim are still making purchases, but these are not on the scale of Middle Eastern purchases and are largely efforts to modernize aging fleets of aircraft and ships, while slimming and reshaping conscripted militaries along the lines of the U.S. forces that fought against Iraq.

That leaves diversification and conversion out of defense production as the only alternative.

Russia has been dedicated to wholesale conversion since the administration of Mikhail Gorbachev and is attempting to use its arms exports to finance the effort. As of April 1993, progress was minimal, however. Many large state enterprises were on the brink of collapse, due to cuts in weapons orders and

general inefficiency. Plant managers were attempting to implement vast structural changes amid economic turmoil, unfamiliarity with market mechanisms, and broken supply chains and subcontractor bases. Deep debt was unrelieved by Western investment.[23]

The same has held true for other former Communist countries seeking to convert their defense industries. Czechoslovakia was the most prominent example. In 1990, the postrevolutionary government announced that it would cease arms exports and convert its industries to civilian production. Conversion proved nearly impossible, however, and with the Slovak half of the country dependent on weapons production, the decision to end arms production exacerbated the ethnic tensions that, in 1992, led to the breakup of the country.[24] Ultimately, even the Czech Republic, whose Skoda Pilzen company had begun diversifying out of weaponry as early as the 1960s, found it could not successfully convert on the scale necessary, and the government returned to less restrictive export policies and production of weapons.[25]

In the United States, conversion was invoked in the media and by defense critics as some kind of magic formula, girded by the blithe assumption that the U.S. military-industrial complex was so huge, imper-

22. Francis Tusa, "The Money Mirage: Funds Evaporate From Gulf Programs," *Armed Forces Journal International*, p. 20 (Nov. 1993).

23. U.S., Department of Commerce, *Russian Defense Business Directory*, 2d installment, Apr. 1993, p. 2-2.

24. Stephanie Baker, "Slovak Arms Conversion Falters," *Christian Science Monitor*, 15 July 1992.

25. Brendan McNally, "Czechs Revive Arms Industry, Exports," *Defense News*, 21 June 1993, p. 1.

vious to setbacks, and infinitely flexible that it was capable of any sort of transformation. Further, those who viewed things so optimistically could point to precedent for a wholesale shift from military to civilian production. At the end of World War II, the United States brought down defense spending from nearly 40 percent of gross national product to less than 5 percent.[26]

The difference in 1945 was that there was immense pent-up demand for consumer goods in the U.S. economy, and virtually every other economy in the world had been devastated by the war. Virtually the entire range of civilian production was possible, and the civilian economy was able to absorb both the demobilized veterans and the conversion of industries. Women left the workplace to make room for men and resumed their traditional roles as homemakers.

The post-Cold War build-down, by contrast, has occurred in the midst of a global recession that shows only modest signs of abating. No one is leaving the workplace. Employment for the vast numbers of both uniformed personnel and defense industry workers is far more problematic. In the CIS, where the economy is undergoing the rigors of converting from communism to capitalism, the economic downturn and inflation are even worse and the dislocation far more widespread than in the United States and Western Europe.[27]

The short to medium term appears the most dangerous and volatile period for major weapons-making countries now scaling back their production. It is difficult to discern how these weak economies—either east or west—can absorb the numbers of unemployed defense workers being fed into them. To date, defense conversion success stories are relatively few and far between, and the volume of converted production nowhere approaches the scope or volume of the previous military orders. Further, there appears little prospect that converted production can approach the levels of defense production or answer the problem of defense unemployment, sopping up, for example, the 389,000 aerospace jobs lost in the United States between 1989 and April 1993[28] or Khripunov's estimated 8 million Russian defense workers. These populations of unemployed defense workers, both in the West and in the former Communist countries, already constitute a source of political instability. When combined with the large reduction in the numbers of military personnel, particularly in the CIS, the extent of unemployment appears genuinely frightening.

What is likely is that in the short to medium term a very large number of workers—the lucky ones—will be employed vastly below their capabilities or be employed sporadically. The older ones, those without skills, or those whose skills or knowledge has no civilian application may remain unemployed for the rest of their lives.

26. Loren B. Thompson, "Rethinking National Defense: Mr. Aspin's Roadmap" (Paper, Georgetown University, May 1993).

27. Khripunov, "Three Headed Challenge."

28. Figure derived by subtracting the projected 1994 employment of 942,000 defense and civil aerospace jobs from the 1989 peak of 1,331,000. "Aerospace Employment Dropped Eleven Percent in 1992" (Press release, Aerospace Industries Association, 6 Apr. 1993).

There is, however, some hope for conversion in the long term. It is probable that at least a small stratum of former defense workers will be able to launch their own civilian enterprises and succeed at them. Privatization of state enterprises in Russia offers some promise that robust small businesses can help lift the economy out of its depression and move it toward free enterprise.[29]

The creation of small businesses constitutes conversion at its most successful and holds the greatest hope for the future both in absorbing defense-related unemployment and in turning human talent from military to civilian pursuits.

Most views of conversion tend to see the future through the prism of the huge industrial enterprises that grew up to cope with Cold War demands. However, these enterprises became huge because the demand was huge. The demand is gone now, and attempting to preserve those enterprises in their former size and splendor, whether they are Western corporations or Eastern state-owned design or manufacturing bureaus, is a lost cause. Tailoring conversion programs and funding to turn massive enterprises into equally massive civilian pursuits is a waste of effort and money.

In the West, recognition of the future has led to a round of consolidation through mergers and acquisitions. Those companies that are left are likely to be financially sound and economically healthy without government assistance. In the formerly Communist East, of course, such market mechanisms are not available. Rather than large state handouts, governments hoping to promote conversion would do far better to provide incentives for business creation and maintain or accelerate privatization.

Assisting former defense workers and managers to create their own businesses would encourage economic development, increase the general level of technological innovation, and provide new employment without the need for government direction. Government assistance—for example, low-cost loans, tax breaks, or investment aid to assist former defense workers to start businesses —would go at least some distance toward alleviating the problem of defense-related unemployment.

But large numbers of workers will remain unemployed nonetheless, and the question is whether the discontent of these former defense workers can be contained in established, orderly political channels long enough for civilian production and enterprise to significantly absorb that workforce. Put another way, how long will the dangerous short to medium term last? The answer is, As long as governments permit it to last. In the United States and the West, internal mobility and a rooted political system would make it seem that, no matter how extensive the dislocation, the basic political system remains unthreatened. In the states of the former Warsaw Pact, particularly Russia, whose political system remains volatile and unsettled, unemployed or underemployed defense workers already constitute a serious source of instability.

29. Commerce Department, *Russian Defense Business Directory*, 2d installment, pp. 2-3.

The quicker the pace of privatization and small-business formation, the lower the level of instability caused by the defense drawdown.

CONCLUSION

The prognosis is for a long-term withering of the world's military-industrial complex, in size, scope, and complexity, and for a decline in overall military capability with the exception of a few technological niches until some shock or defeat prompts renewed research and development. There will be deep and widespread problems of unemployment and economic hardship that a shift to civilian production cannot wholly alleviate.

But if free enterprise takes hold in the former Communist world, and if business formation can be encouraged on a sufficient scale, there is some hope for mitigating the hardships of shifting away from large-scale defense production. Richard Grimmett, who analyzes the international defense trade for the U.S. Congressional Research Service, has noted that the "invisible hand" of Adam Smith has imposed more restraint on conventional arms production and trade than have governmental or populist arms control efforts. One hopes that the "invisible hand" can mitigate the effects of downsizing and conversion as well.

ANNALS, *AAPSS*, **535**, September 1994

Constraining Conventional Arms Transfers

By MICHAEL MOODIE

ABSTRACT: Interest in restraining the conventional arms trade has intensified in the aftermath of the collapse of the Soviet Union and the Persian Gulf war as well as in the face of continuing hostilities in Bosnia, Somalia, and elsewhere. Analysts differ considerably, however, over whether the new features of the post-Cold War security landscape create an environment more conducive or more hostile to future arms trade restraint. Developed and developing countries must cooperate on technology transfer and other aspects of the conventional arms trade problem to devise new approaches to replace traditional efforts focused on constraining supply that are virtually doomed to failure in the future. The need for nontraditional approaches is especially strong in the face of the difficulties for both suppliers and recipients in balancing the competing and complex political, economic, and security interests at work in arms transfer decisions. New approaches should be built on the foundations of the initiation of supplier-recipient dialogues, intensified regional arms control efforts, and heightened transparency and confidence building in arms trade transactions.

At the time of writing, Michael Moodie was a senior fellow at the Institute for Foreign Policy Analysis. He is currently president of the Chemical and Biological Arms Control Institute in Washington. Mr. Moodie is a former assistant director for multilateral affairs at the United States Arms Control and Disarmament Agency and a former member of the U.S. Mission to NATO. He has served as a visiting lecturer at Georgetown University's School of Foreign Service and is a member of the editorial board of the Washington Quarterly.

THE nature of conflict in the new international security environment—conflict fostered by regional or local tensions stemming from such diverse sources as historical animosity, ethnic or religious hostility, and attempted regional hegemony—is closely linked to political and technical developments in armaments across a spectrum of capabilities from weapons of mass destruction to conventional weapons of such relative unsophistication as the mortars around Sarajevo. Under such circumstances, arms control and disarmament, far from being an anachronism of the Cold War, will constitute an important instrument for coming to grips with post-Cold War problems. One aspect of arms control that could well receive greater attention in the years ahead is the prospect for increased restraint of the international arms trade.

Edward Laurance points out that historically a heightened public and political sensitivity to the negative consequences of the arms trade has prompted most of the study and research on arms transfer issues and fostered most of the policy initiatives designed to restrain the arms trade.[1]

Interest in restraining conventional arms, including their overseas transfer, has once again intensified in the aftermath of the collapse of the Soviet Union and the Gulf war, as well as in the face of continuing hostilities in places as disparate as Bosnia, Somalia, and Tajikistan.

While traditional arms control issues and approaches will continue to be important in the post-Cold War era, new times demand new approaches. Arms control will have to adapt to the new environment, broadening its scope, increasing its flexibility, simplifying its methods, and enhancing the speed of its accomplishments. Future arms control will become a much more complex endeavor than the large, long bilateral set-piece negotiations of the kind that became so familiar during the Cold War. Such negotiations will not disappear entirely—witness the talks on a Comprehensive Nuclear Test Ban at the Conference on Disarmament (CD)—but they will no longer command center stage in the arms control process.

The need to develop new arms control approaches stems from the nature of the contribution that arms control can make to the post-Cold War security environment. As Brad Roberts points out, arms control agreements have been "influential in changing perceptions about the problems with which [arms control] grapples: national ambitions, the pur-

1. This is a major theme in Edward J. Laurance, *The International Arms Trade* (New York: Lexington Books, 1992). A quick glance at the literature from earlier postwar periods in which greater attention was paid to the arms trade also suggests that such interest stemmed from the strong desire to constrain or control arms transfers. See, for example, John Stanley and Maurice Pearton, *The International Trade in Arms* (New York: Praeger, 1972), especially pt. 2; Anne Hessing Kahn et al., *Controlling Future Arms Trade* (New York: McGraw-Hill, 1977); Andrew Pierre, ed., *Arms Transfers and American Foreign Policy* (New York: New York University Press, 1979), esp. chap. 7; Cindy

Cannizzo, *The Gun Merchants: Politics and Policies of the Major Arms Suppliers* (New York: Pergamon Press, 1980); Andrew J. Pierre, *The Global Politics of Arms Sales* (Princeton, NJ: Princeton University Press, 1982), esp. pt. 4.

poses of armaments, and limits of international cooperation."[2] Arms control also forces states to "make choices about weapons and the purposes to which the military instrument is put."[3] The United States confronts such difficult decisions today. Shortly after the 1992 presidential election, for example, Les Aspin, then chairman of the House Armed Services Committee, contended that " 'what the country faces is a philosophical question about . . . the use of military power in this new era.' "[4] It is a question that not only preoccupies U.S. policymakers but also constitutes the central issue in the global security debate since the collapse of the Soviet Union.

If the role of military power must be redefined, so must the role of arms control. Johann Holst, the late Norwegian foreign minister and noted strategic analyst, gave useful insights to help that redefinition. Rather than stabilizing a fixed set of political relations as it did between the United States and the Soviet Union, arms control in the future, Holst argued, must have as its purpose "directing and framing changing political relations." Furthermore, Holst contended, arms control must be viewed "as an agent of political change," as a management tool in a period of transition and reconstruc-

tion.[5] Holst provided an important reminder that is all too easily forgotten in the arcana of throw weights, weapons types, inspection procedures, and other arms control details: although the currency of arms control is the military instrument, arms control transactions are fundamentally political. At its most basic, arms control is about shaping political relationships, expectations, and behavior.

This is not to argue that arms control need not concern itself with military considerations. Arms control, to serve political purposes, must nevertheless make military sense. It must promote a military balance and stability among participants, especially in situations in which those parties are all worried about being the victim of aggression.[6] By promoting predictability and stability in the military relationship of potential adversaries, arms control alters the context of their political relationship in a positive direction. As Brad Roberts points out regarding the U.S.-Soviet arms control experience, "The bilateral agreements between the United States and the Soviet Union proved significant largely in political effect, by changing over time some of the underlying assumptions about intentions and facilitating a working out of larger ideological conflict."[7] This ma-

---

2. Brad Roberts, "The Chemical Weapons Convention and World Order," in *Shadows and Substance: The Chemical Weapons Convention,* ed. Benoit Morel and Kyle Olson (Boulder, CO: Westview Press, 1993), p. 9.

3. Ibid., p. 11.

4. Quoted in Richard H. P. Sia, "Small Wars to Shape U.S. Military," *Baltimore Sun,* 2 Dec. 1992.

5. Johann Joergen Holst, "Arms Control in the Nineties: A European Perspective," in *The International Practice of Arms Control,* ed. Emanuel Adler (Baltimore: Johns Hopkins University Press, 1992), pp. 87, 114.

6. The author is indebted to Richard Betts of Columbia University for highlighting this point.

7. Roberts, "Chemical Weapons Convention," p. 9.

jor political impact was the product of highly technical agreements focusing on military stability and balance.

Current interest in restraining the international arms trade has surfaced in a very different context from the Cold War environment, a change that could have a significant impact on the choices over the purposes and uses of armaments. Rolf Ekeus, head of the United Nations Special Commission for Iraq, identified one major aspect of the change in context in arguing that the "confrontational dualism of the [Cold War] era became something of an organizing principle for most of the security related developments during the last four decades."[8] The East-West confrontation served as the primary construct underlying virtually everyone's thinking about international security. A state's posture with respect to that confrontation shaped its response in most situations. The Cold War, however, provided more than the prism through which security choices were made; it defined the very parameters for those choices. Today, that construct has disappeared, and a number of factors that have emerged in the post-Cold War context foster both optimism and skepticism about future prospects for restraining the arms trade. Analysts are likely to differ considerably over whether the weight of the respective factors will tip the scales one way or the other regarding future arms trade restraint. It is a judgment whose accuracy only time will determine.

A NORTH-SOUTH CONFRONTATION?

One aspect of the changing arms control context in particular, however, deserves greater attention. The benefits for arms control of the end of the Cold War may prove fleeting if some recent literature is correct in suggesting that the East-West standoff may be replaced by a North-South conflict. This is an oversimplification of Samuel Huntington's thesis of an impending clash of civilizations, but there are elements of such thinking in Huntington's argument. In his *Foreign Affairs* article, for example, Huntington positively quotes Kishore Mahbubani to the effect that the central axis of world politics in the future is likely to be conflict between "the West and the Rest."[9]

Ali Dessouki of Cairo University writes of "two spheres of security" emerging, divided along developmental lines, each having its own values and norms as well as its own way of handling interstate conflict. One sphere exists in the advanced industrial states and is characterized by peace and prosperity, and conflicts in it are more likely to be financial and commercial than military. The other sphere, characterized more by insecurity, encompasses primarily the developing world and is marked by war, poverty, and instability. In this sphere, the use of military power is likely to be a continuing feature.[10]

8. Rolf Ekeus, "Arms Control and the New Security Structure," in *Challenges for Arms Control in the 1990s*, ed. James Brown (Amsterdam: VU University Press, 1992), p. 21.

9. Samuel Huntington, "A Clash of Civilizations?" *Foreign Affairs*, 72(3):41 (Summer 1993).

10. Ali Dessouki, "Globalization and the Two Spheres of Security," *Washington Quarterly*, 16(4):112-15 (Autumn 1993).

These arguments underline a lack of understanding in Washington and elsewhere that the arms control priorities of the industrialized democracies, and of the United States as their leader, are not necessarily shared by much of the rest of the world. Many countries among those that would be labeled "developing," "nonaligned," or "the South" do not perceive or define their security challenges in the same terms as decision makers in Washington. Moreover, these states do not have available to them the same alternatives for dealing with security challenges that the industrialized democracies have. These differences in perceptions, priorities, and available policy alternatives are important because they are significant factors in shaping decisions of developing countries relating to the pursuit and use of military power and the utility of arms control.

For the industrialized nations, especially those most directly involved in the East-West confrontation, arms control has become an accepted tool of policy, albeit with recognized limitations. In the wake of the Cold War, the nonproliferation dimension of arms control in particular has assumed heightened priority; preventing the diffusion of advanced military technology—especially, but not only, weapons of mass destruction—is considered by some policymakers and analysts the single most important international security objective of the post-Cold War era. Arms control is also seen as an essential component of the resolution of political disputes in regions such as the Middle East, South Asia, and the Korean peninsula, which are the most worrisome sources of violent conflict with potentially global impact. Given this perspective, the industrial democracies consider cooperation of the entire international community, including the active participation and support of developing states, vital for achieving arms control objectives.

Developing states have significantly different perspectives. For many nonaligned states, arms control has traditionally been about controlling the arms of others, particularly the nuclear weapons of the superpowers, and it has not been seen necessarily as an integral part of their security environment. Indeed, during most of the post-World War II era, developing states in multilateral forums rather successfully cast the arms control debate in postcolonial rhetoric that served both to deflect global attention away from their security problems and to legitimize to their domestic constituencies and the broader international community potentially contentious national military decisions. Although the South's rhetoric has often addressed the utility of arms control in general terms, the sense has often been conveyed that arms control reflects standards that the West is attempting to impose on the rest of the world. Indeed, some nonaligned states appear to consider arms control when applied beyond the superpower context potentially contrary to their national interests.

This is not to argue that nonaligned nations have opposed global arms control initiatives; the high number of adherents to the nuclear Nonproliferation Treaty (NPT) and the large number of signatories of the

Chemical Weapons Convention (CWC) demonstrate otherwise. To suggest that either their motives in supporting such agreements or their security agendas are the same as those of the industrial democracies, however, is misleading. Many Southern states, for example, emphasize the NPT obligations of the nuclear states to promote the peaceful uses of nuclear energy. Similarly, there were times during the CWC negotiations when participants questioned whether the nonaligned states were more interested in the convention as an arms control accord or as an agreement to promote development of local chemical industries.

Differences over nonproliferation—including the diffusion of advanced conventional military technology—could prove especially troublesome in the future. From the South's perspective, the emphasis and approach of the U.S.-led industrialized states are objectionable for several reasons.

First, the push for nonproliferation is hypocritical. In the view of many Southern states, the developed countries are attempting to deny them legitimate national security instruments that the North already possesses. The NPT is especially criticized in this regard by countries such as India,[11] but efforts by the

United States and others to restrain the diffusion of advanced conventional arms and technology already in weapons inventories of developed states are also considered an attempt to deny them legitimate instruments of self-defense.

Second, the North's nonproliferation approach is perceived as selective. Some Southerners find it difficult to understand why the United States focuses so strongly on stopping weapons programs in some parts of the world while turning a blind eye to others. Israel's nuclear weapons program is most often cited in this regard, but, in the conventional realm, a contradiction is also seen in efforts to constrain arms transfers to the Middle East in the face of Israel's extensive indigenous defense production capabilities.

Third, the South feels a strong sense of discrimination, particularly with regard to restrictions of military and, especially, dual-use technology. As Shahram Chubin points out,

Many states have not had the means to assure their security unilaterally or through access to [conventional] arms or alliances. Nor have they been able to fashion a diplomatic compromise. Moreover, their security has not automatically been improved by the passing of the Cold War.[12]

In response to this situation, developing states see efforts by the United States and others to curb technology transfers as a double standard. In an environment that remains conducive to the use of force, nonproliferation not only denies them needed national

---

11. Given the NPT experience, Southern states have insisted that any future arms control regime be universal and entail equal obligations, and they have been somewhat successful in promoting these principles. It was only when the Bush administration abandoned its position of insisting on retaining a small portion of its chemical weapons stockpile, for example, that the logjam at the CWC negotiations was broken.

12. Shahram Chubin, "The South and the New World Order," *Washington Quarterly*, 16(4):99 (Autumn 1993).

security instruments that other sovereign nations possess but smacks of neo-imperialism.

Regimes such as the Missile Technology Control Regime and the Australia Group are the objects of particularly intense Southern hostility. In the Southern view, these efforts at technology denial—especially because they deal with dual-use technologies—have discriminatory implications well beyond the military realm. They are seen as efforts to deny to the developing world the advanced technologies needed not only for legitimate commercial purposes but as the foundation for sustained development. The guidelines of the Missile Technology Control Regime, for example, are resented on the grounds that they deny nonaligned states the ability to pursue legitimate commercial efforts in the arena of space launch vehicles. Some commentators even describe these regimes as attempts by the developed countries to perpetuate the gap that leaves the South not only militarily disadvantaged but economically incapable of competing with the North. An example of the competing perspectives on this issue was the 1993 session of the U.N. Disarmament Commission, which, after a three-year effort, failed to secure consensus on a study of the role of technology in security and development. The sticking point was the report's language on nonproliferation.

The developing countries' brief on nonproliferation and technology transfer need not be accepted by Washington and its allies. The United States and other developed countries must pursue their interests as they see them, just as developing countries will pursue theirs. At the same time, these very real differences cannot be ignored, and efforts must be made by all sides to find common ground. How well these differences can be accommodated in important upcoming arms control activities such as the Comprehensive Nuclear Test Ban negotiations, the 1995 NPT Review Conference, and development of the U.N. arms transfers register could set the precedent for a considerable time to come.

CONVENTIONAL ARMS TRADE RESTRAINT: CAN NOTHING USEFUL BE DONE?

The need for developed and developing countries to come together on technology transfer and nonproliferation issues is crucial to the success of future arms control efforts, including arms trade restraint. In the past, the United States and other nations interested in such restraints have pursued a singular focus on the supply of arms. Events after the war with Iraq clearly illustrate the shortcomings of such an approach.[13]

The Persian Gulf conflict heightened concern in the broader policy

13. Efforts to restrain conventional arms transfers have also been hampered by the fact that the nonproliferation of weapons of mass destruction has been the primary—indeed, almost the exclusive—focus of interagency policy review. The fact that no one on the Bush administration's National Security Council staff was particularly interested in the United Nations' Transparency in Armaments resolution, which established the arms transfer register, a small step to draw attention to the problem of conventional weapons proliferation, is indicative of broader institutional inattention to the problem. Similar attitudes have characterized the Clinton administration.

community regarding the sale and other forms of transfer of advanced conventional technologies to regions of tension and conflict. The experience of some arms suppliers in Iraq confronting weapons they themselves had sold to Baghdad, and the prospect that the United States could face a similar situation in the future, left many people, including the Congress, distinctly uncomfortable. In 1992, for example, members of Congress introduced more than forty bills pertaining to arms exports, although virtually none were passed into law.

Nevertheless, confronting this situation, the Bush administration felt a strong political need to do something, and it was forced to take action, at least with respect to the Middle East. The simplest route was to focus on the aspect of the problem over which the administration had some control: arms supply. The result was the initiative called Arms Control in the Middle East (ACME), a dialogue between the top five suppliers to the region, who also happened to be the permanent members of the U.N. Security Council. Over a period of several months, these discussions produced guidelines regarding the types of arms transfers to be avoided in the future, prenotification of sales, and a promise to consider concerns about regional stability in deciding any future arms transactions. These guidelines were to be applied not just to the Middle East but globally.

Unfortunately, the ACME process made little real progress. The guidelines are generally perceived as not inhibiting any of the five suppliers from doing something they want to do, a perception reinforced by President George Bush's decision during the election campaign to sell advanced military aircraft to Saudi Arabia and Taiwan, a decision not opposed by candidate Bill Clinton. The Taiwan decision also served as a convenient excuse for China, which had been visibly unhappy with the exercise, to pull out, leaving ACME's future in serious doubt. Those who viewed ACME as a small step in the right direction heard echoes of the Carter administration's ill-fated Conventional Arms Transfers talks with the Soviet Union.

One reason that the issue of constraining the diffusion of advanced conventional technology has received little sustained attention from successive administrations and that those efforts that have been attempted have not yielded much is that the problem has fallen in the too-hard-to-do category. Any administration is obviously reluctant to focus on a problem for which there is no answer. In addressing the question of the proliferation of weapons of mass destruction, "no proliferation" is clearly the best answer and an objective relatively easy to define in operational terms. (Implementation, of course, can be very difficult.) In the conventional realm, however, the complex equation created by the legitimate right of self-defense, with the concomitant implied right to have weapons for that defense; pressures to sell arms in difficult economic times for defense producers; and concerns over introducing advanced military technology into regions of tension does not lend itself to straightforward answers. Specific measures that achieve one objective but do not do injury to another, equally valid, interest are difficult to define.

This dilemma of attempting to balance competing interests at play in conventional arms transfer decisions currently challenges the Clinton administration, which has promised to initiate a major review of arms transfer policy. The dilemma was captured in the statement announcing the review, which, the White House noted, would take into account "national security, arms control, trade, budgetary and economic competitiveness considerations."[14] Devising a policy that effectively meets all of those interests will clearly be no mean feat.

According to reports, the Clinton administration review is likely to build on several other efforts, including

— a Pentagon review to determine how arms exports affect current and future U.S. weapons-buying plans and the importance of arms exports to the defense industrial base;
— State Department efforts to ease Arms Export Control Act restrictions that impede commercial sales when such sales do not conflict with U.S. foreign policy goals;
— ideas offered by Lynn Davis, undersecretary of state for international security affairs, to link easing restrictions of the Coordinating Committee on Export Controls to a requirement that members give advanced notice

when they want to sell to a country on a target list; and
— Commerce Department efforts, led by Secretary Ron Brown, to ease arms export restrictions, and his endorsement of the need for arms exports to bolster the U.S. defense industry.[15]

It would appear that many of these measures could result in increasing arms sales rather than restraining them. This potential points out the difficulty of relying solely on supply-side restraint for stanching the flow of arms around the world.

If balancing competing interests is an acute dilemma for the United States, it is even more so for other major weapons suppliers. The situation is especially severe in the former Soviet Union. According to Andrew Pierre, the arms industries of the former Soviet Union, chiefly located in the Russian Federation (80 percent) and Ukraine (13 percent), are "in a desperate struggle for survival," and the role of the state in the support of the arms industries has become part of the national debate between the economic reformers and conservatives, with the military-industrial complex lining up in the latter's camp.[16] As a result, arms ex-

14. "Fact Sheet: Nonproliferation and Export Control Policy" (U.S., White House, Office of the Press Secretary, 27 Sept. 1993).

15. "White House Braces to Tackle Conventional Arms Export Policy," *Inside the Pentagon,* 30 Sept. 1993, p. 1.

16. Andrew Pierre, "Conventional Arms Proliferation Today: Changed Dimensions, New Responses," in *Science and International Security Anthology 1993: Trends and Implications for Arms Control, Proliferation, and International Security in the Changing Global Environment,* ed. Elizabeth J. Kirk, W. Thomas Wander, and Brian D. Smith (Washington, DC: American Academy for the Advancement of Science, 1993), p. 213.

ports have been viewed as the industries' key to survival. Some Russian officials have indicated that Moscow hopes to generate as much as $20 billion in foreign exchange through overseas weapons sales. Such hopes appear wildly optimistic in light of the fact that, in 1992, Russian arms sales totaled only $1.3 billion.[17] Nevertheless, the Russian government appears willing to sell virtually anything short of weapons of mass destruction to anyone with the money to buy. The variety of weapons that Moscow has exhibited at major international arms shows is staggering; it includes top-of-the-line equipment not yet in service with Russian forces.[18]

Given these realities, is the international community condemned to watch the continued diffusion of advanced military technology that will make regional conflicts not only more destructive but more widespread and globally dangerous? If Washington thinks in terms of a single regime, legally enshrined, the answer is probably yes, especially if that regime is limited to arms suppliers. On the other hand, if the U.S. approach emphasizes multiple actions, many involving the cooperation of suppliers and recipients, chances are increased that something might be accomplished. It must be an approach, however, that does not isolate the issue of the arms trade from other international and domestic considerations.

The need for supplier-recipient dialogues

Three categories of activities suggest themselves as elements of an approach. The first category is that group of measures focusing on the arms trade itself. One suggestion that has been offered, for example, is the revival of the "Perm 5" talks.[19] To give those talks any chance, however, especially to overcome Chinese reservations, they would require a new title, new participants, and a new format. In doing so, they would become incredibly complicated. Moreover, as long as such talks focus only on arms supplies, the competing pressures that cancel out movement toward restraint are likely to be too strong to resist.

Rather than a supplier-only focus, therefore, the U.S. objective should be a supplier-recipient dialogue on a regional or subregional basis. The goal of such a dialogue should be an understanding by all parties of what constitutes the critical military requirements of regional states and their implications for arms acquisitions. Such an understanding, in turn, may foster agreements between regional states to forgo certain weapons systems that they—and not the suppliers—deem to be destabilizing.

No one should be under any illusion that promoting such a regional and subregional dialogue, especially in areas of great tension, will be easy or yield quick results. Such a process of bringing suppliers and recipients together, however, may be the only way to overcome the reservations of

17. David Tanks et al., *Defense Conversion and Arms Transfers: The Legacy of the Soviet-Era Arms Industry* (Washington, DC: Institute for Foreign Policy Analysis, 1993), p. 27.

18. Ibid., pp. 28-29.

19. See, for example, Pierre, "Conventional Arms Proliferation Today," p. 221.

recipients in developing countries toward policies of arms restraint.

The Conference on Disarmament in Geneva provides a forum in which such a dialogue could be conducted, at least on a general level. During the 1993 deliberations of the CD's Ad Hoc Committee on Transparency in Armaments, for example, several participants bemoaned the absence of any criteria for determining an "excessive accumulation of arms." The United States should take such complaints as a rallying cry and challenge CD members to put their usual rhetoric aside and engage in serious discussion of what those criteria might be.

Another vehicle for initiating a broader examination of arms trade restraint might be a focus in the CD or elsewhere on light arms. Certainly, such weapons of relative unsophistication have been responsible for more death and tragedy than any weapon of mass destruction; witness the mortars surrounding Sarajevo or the automatic weapons used to such deadly effect in Somalia. To date, control of light arms has also fallen in the too-hard-to-do category, and the problem has been treated more as a law enforcement issue than an arms control issue. Perhaps it is time to ask whether traditional arms control approaches have something to offer. A starting point might be to build on the U.S.-sponsored U.N. resolution condemning the use of antipersonnel mines.

Finally, the international community might consider whether conditioning economic assistance to developing countries on their cutting weapons acquisitions might be used as an avenue to promote positive supplier-recipient dialogue. The World Bank and the International Monetary Fund have put the conditionality issue on the agenda. If not carefully managed, however, it could feed the resentment of developing countries, as discussed earlier.

Regional arms control

Traditionally, arms control has been pursued either globally, with agreements such as the NPT or the Biological Weapons Convention, or bilaterally, with U.S.-Soviet efforts dominating the process. Although during the Cold War important regional agreements were achieved, such as the Treaty of Tlatelolco, regional arms control, especially outside Europe, was not high on the agenda. One commentator, for example, notes that at the first U.N. Special Session on Disarmament in 1978, regional arms control was mentioned barely en passant.[20]

In the face of heightened regional instability and conflict in the wake of the Cold War, global arms control approaches are not enough to deal with regional problems. A number of important environmental factors, however, must be appreciated in the pursuit of regional arms control. These factors contrast strongly with the situation in Europe, where regional arms control has been somewhat successful. Many developing states, for example, still labor in the shadow of war. Their security perceptions and approaches have been shaped by

20. Jayantha Dhanapala, "Introduction," in *Regional Approaches to Disarmament: Security and Stability*, ed. Jayantha Dhanapala (Aldershot: Dartmouth, 1993), p. 3.

their direct experience with conflict: the several Arab-Israeli and Indo-Pakistan wars, the Iran-Iraq conflict, and the Korean War.

The sources of conflict in these regions are also more varied, including not only interstate war but also intrastate violence. Hypernationalism is intense; fundamentalist movements of a religious, ethnic, and communal nature thrive. Moreover, there is no cooperative security system comparable to the Conference on Security and Cooperation in Europe to provide a framework for the necessary regional dialogue. Finally, one might once have said that the regions beyond Europe gave relatively higher priority to preventing conventional war over nuclear war, but this assertion may no longer be true.

A number of problems will serve as barriers to successful regional arms control. Perhaps the most severe is the skeptical if not negative attitude toward arms control held by many regional states. In some cases, the attitude is shaped by a lack of experience. For many developing countries, there is only a small cadre of arms control experts. Their participation in arms control has been largely limited either to declaratory measures or to adherence to global agreements that limit weapons these nations do not have. Little experience exists with arms control measures related directly to their military situation on the ground or weapons systems in their inventories. In terms of one conceptual scheme that categorizes arms control into preventive and curative measures,[21] most re-

21. Trevor Findlay, "The South Pacific," in *Regional Approaches*, ed. Dhanapala, p. 31.

gional states have concentrated on the former.

Beyond the question of experience, however, is the issue of regional states' perception of the utility of arms control. As mentioned previously, developing countries view their incentives for arms acquisition as no less valid than those of developed countries and in many ways more so. There is also the problem described earlier of arms control being seen as an essentially Western objective. Illustrative descriptions of arms control by regional security analysts have labeled it "alien to the region," "not a high priority," or a "Western concept."

Additional problems could plague regional arms control efforts. These include the need for access to good intelligence that many non-European states do not have, perceptions that arms races were induced or encouraged by the superpowers, the view that defense expenditures and development are not mutually exclusive but complementary, and the importance of bilateral ties to external powers as the means for smaller regional states to ensure their security. All of these will bear heavily on any regional arms control process.

Despite these problems, there is no reason to despair over regional arms control prospects. Indeed, the end of the Cold War has created opportunities that are, at least to some extent, being exploited. Examples include the Arms Control and Regional Security Working Group created as part of the Middle East peace process, the agreement on confidence-building measures between India and Pakistan, the decision of the states of the Association of Southeast Asian Nations to add a security dimension to their dialogue, and a number of developments in Latin America, including last year's unprecedented resolution adopted by the Organization of American States calling on all its members to pursue arms control and disarmament more aggressively.

These kinds of efforts must be strongly supported by the states of the international community. Arms control must be shown to work. Only through such a demonstration will it become a more enduring feature of the security landscape and a means for restraining the flow of advanced military technology into regions of great tension.

Transparency and confidence building

The third category of activities in the U.S. approach relates to measures emphasizing transparency and building confidence. One small but important step has been taken in this regard with the creation of the arms transfer register by the United Nations' Transparency in Armaments resolution, adopted by the General Assembly on 9 December 1991. The goal of the resolution was to draw attention to what in U.N. parlance is called the problem of "destabilizing weapons buildups." Gradually making more information available on the nature of a state's military capabilities is intended to build confidence over time that regional military balances are not upset through the acquisition of new capabilities. The resolution requests member states to provide arms transfer data on a number of categories of weapons—tanks, armored combat vehicles, large caliber artillery, combat aircraft, naval vessels, and missile systems—specifying the supplying nation of any imports and the recipient of any exports.[22]

To date, the positive response has been somewhat surprising, even if the data are not all that some analysts would like.[23] As of October 1993, 79 nations had submitted reports, including all the major suppliers—the United States, Germany, Russia, China, the United Kingdom, and France rank highest—except for North Korea and South Africa. These states account for as much as 98 percent of global arms exports as reported by the Stockholm International Peace Research Institute, the primary source of publicly available data.[24] An important gap in the data exists, however, in that some key arms importers, including Saudi Arabia, Iran, Thailand, and Syria, did

22. For background on the evolution of the resolution, see Michael Moodie, "Transparency in Armaments: A New Item for the New Security Agenda," *Washington Quarterly*, 15(3):75-82 (Summer 1992). See also Edward J. Laurance, "The UN Register of Conventional Arms: Rationales and Prospects for Compliance and Effectiveness," ibid., 16(2):163-72 (Spring 1993); *Study on Ways and Means of Promoting Transparency in International Transfers of Conventional Arms*, Report of the Secretary General, Disarmament Study Series 24 (New York: United Nations, 1992).

23. Natalie J. Goldring, "UN Register Released: Response Favourable, but Questions Remain," *Basic Reports*, 1 Nov. 1993, p. 1.

24. Edward J. Laurance and Herbert Wulf, "An Evaluation of the First Year of Reporting to the United Nations Register of Conventional Arms" (Research report, Monterey Institute of International Studies, Oct. 1993), p. 3.

not report. Still, approximately two-thirds of the imports of major conventional weapons were reported.[25]

The arms trade register was a political response to a particular situation—the experience with Iraq—at a particular point in time. The U.N. resolution that created it was the outcome of intense political negotiation. The U.S. decision to support the creation of the register had at least as much to do with the fact that British Prime Minister John Major had been one of its initial sponsors and the sense that Washington could not let down a key ally as with perceptions of the intrinsic merit of the measure. Expectations about the register in Washington, therefore, have been modest, and the first year's experience would seem to provide a good base on which to build.

Beyond establishing the register, however, the Transparency in Armaments resolution also invites member states to provide information regarding military holdings, procurement through indigenous national production, and relevant arms import and export policies and regulations. It calls for the creation of a group of experts in 1994 to consider how the register might be expanded. The resolution also calls on the CD to address questions related to promoting openness and transparency regarding high technology with military applications and similar questions related to weapons of mass destruction. Pursuant to this call, the CD created the Ad Hoc Committee on Transparency in Armaments, the first new ad hoc committee of the CD in years and the only one focusing on

25. Ibid.

issues related to conventional force. Although some progress was made in elaborating potential future steps, reports that some CD members, especially among the nonaligned group, were hesitant to support the reestablishment of the committee in 1994 were a cause for some dismay. Although the group was finally recreated, its work in 1994 through the first two CD sessions was desultory at best.

CONCLUSION

In the Cold War era, security affairs were fairly simple. The end of the Cold War has made them immeasurably more complicated. The changes to which arms control must respond will force the arms control process to become more complex. The package of activities suggested here is not neat or simple, and it will be difficult to manage. If the arms trade is to be restrained, however, there may be no other workable choice.

There are reasons for optimism about the future but not for complacency. As Ronald F. Lehman II, former director of the U.S. Arms Control and Disarmament Agency, has said,

What is disquieting about [the recent] turn of events is the fact that some of the strongest proponents of arms control—so long as it is restricted to the major powers—are often the most reluctant to engage in meaningful arms control efforts in their regions. These champions of the reduction of weapons of others practice a double standard; they consistently fail to see any value in reducing their own.[26]

26. Ronald F. Lehman, director, U.S. Arms Control and Disarmament Agency, Statement to the First Committee of the United Nations General Assembly, 46th sess., 15 Oct. 1991.

What has been especially disturbing about these attitudes is that they have often been held by countries in regions where tensions are highest, instability greatest, and the prospect for violence never far from the surface.

A wide chasm yawns between what is possible in arms control and what some people might consider desirable in restraining the arms trade. That chasm will be bridged only if there is a rethinking of approaches to restraint. The United States must take a leading role in that effort. The United States virtually created arms control and shaped it as an instrument of national security policy. Although the United States will not always be the central player in arms control activities in the years ahead, no one else can carry the role of conceptual leadership.

ANNALS, *AAPSS*, **535**, September 1994

The Continuing Debate Over U.S. Arms Sales: Strategic Needs and the Quest for Arms Limitations

By GEOFFREY KEMP

ABSTRACT: Arms transfers between sovereign states have become a key and controversial ingredient of international relations. Many historians would argue that American military supplies were instrumental in winning the three critical wars of this century: World War I, World War II, and the Cold War. Critics have advocated increased limits on arms sales on the grounds that they are a cause of war and have led to disastrous, entangling confrontations, including the Vietnam war. The end of the Cold War has witnessed a return to nationalism, not a new world order based on internationalism. The economic pressures to export arms are growing while demand is increasing in the new conflict regions. But many would-be purchasers of advanced arms cannot afford the high costs of modern weaponry. Most regional conflicts today, however, do not use the high-tech wizardry displayed during Desert Storm but rather rely on the traditional instruments of twentieth-century slaughter: small arms, mines, mortars, and artillery.

Geoffrey Kemp is director of the Middle East Arms Control Project of the Carnegie Endowment for International Peace. He received his Ph.D. in political science at the Massachusetts Institute of Technology. He served in the White House during the first Reagan administration and was special assistant to the President for national security affairs. His latest book is Forever Enemies? American Policy and the Islamic Republic of Iran *(1994).*

THIS article argues that, since the late nineteenth century, "armaments"—to use a catchall phrase for all defense matériel and cooperation—have become one of the key elements influencing the nature of international relations; that the global impact of arms transfers has increased steadily over the past sixty years; and that American foreign policy, in particular, has been greatly influenced by decisions to transfer or, equally important, decisions not to transfer arms.

There has been an enduring debate as to the wisdom of this policy. Most American statesmen have traditionally regarded arms transfers as a necessary adjunct of national policy and strategic doctrine. They would argue that, from a long-term historical perspective, arms sales and military assistance programs have been beneficial to American strategic interests. American military supplies were instrumental in winning the three critical wars of this century: World War I, World War II, and the Cold War. Two other obvious examples come to mind. In the case of Israel, American arms have been and remain essential to assure Israel's qualitative edge and to deny the Arab coalitions any prospect of military victory. In the case of Saudi Arabia, vast amounts of American military support during the 1970s and 1980s permitted the United States and the Saudis to develop one of the most elaborate and modern logistical bases in the world, a fact that was crucial to allied victory in Desert Storm.

Critics, including powerful political lobbies, have existed since the late nineteenth century. They have advocated an end to, or limits on, arms sales on the grounds that such activities are a cause of war and have led to disastrous, entangling confrontations, including the Vietnam war and the Iran-contra scandal. In addition, they argue that in peacetime, arms sales to undemocratic countries strengthen corrupt dictators, promote aggressive behavior, and siphon off scarce economic resources that could be used more productively and humanely on other endeavors.

HISTORICAL LANDMARKS IN U.S. ARMS TRANSFER POLICIES

To discuss the key elements of this debate, a strong historical focus is necessary. For, although the contemporary interest in the subject derives from dilemmas over the wisdom and purpose of arms transfers to conflict regions such as the Middle East, the phenomenon we face today must be seen in the context of a long history of arms diplomacy. For example, one cannot understand the full military and diplomatic dimensions of the American Revolution unless attention is paid to the critical role that French arms played in assisting the revolutionaries in the war against the crown. During the American Civil War, foreign arms supplies to the Union and the Confederacy were vital at different stages. The complexities and importance of the Balkan wars preceding World War I make sense only if the role of foreign munitions is fully appreciated. World War I saw the rapid growth of the American munitions industry and exemplified what President Franklin D.

Roosevelt later called the "Arsenal of Democracy." By 1920 the United States dominated the world's arms market, commanding as much as 50 percent of the trade.

It was deep American involvement in the munitions trade that came to be seen, first by scholars and then by politicians, as an important, if not the most important, reason for American involvement in World War I. Hence, during the 1930s, an intensive debate culminating in hearings before the Senate's Nye Committee on the role of the munitions industries resulted in strengthening the case for the neutrality legislation of the late 1930s, which was supposed to insulate the United States from a new European war.

In contrast, one of President Franklin D. Roosevelt's most dramatic initiatives prior to Pearl Harbor was the 1940 arms deal with Britain to provide the Royal Navy with fifty old American destroyers in exchange for important U.S. base rights in British and Commonwealth possessions in the western Atlantic and Caribbean. Roosevelt openly violated the Neutrality Acts and sponsored the open use of American arms to assist Britain and France in the quest for military security at the beginning of World War II. This was followed by the Lend-Lease Program and the entry of America into the war. During World War II, American power within the Allied coalition was strongly influenced by the size and magnitude of its munitions inventories. Without American arms, neither Britain nor Russia could have sustained their respective war efforts. Furthermore, American control of munitions production enabled Roosevelt to determine the nature and direction of Allied grand strategy, especially during the latter years of the war.

In the aftermath of World War II, only the United States retained the economic and military strength to challenge the dual threats posed by the consolidation and expansion of Soviet power in Europe and the Communist struggle for control in China. American military aid to China and later Europe was the ultimate expression of American foreign policy during those years. With the fall of China in 1949 and the outbreak of the Korean War in 1950, the Western world embarked upon a massive rearmament program, much of which was paid for by the United States. Not only did the United States supply thousands of aircraft and armored vehicles to friends and allies at little or no cost, but it also subsidized Europeans, especially Britain, to produce military equipment of their own design—the so-called Offshore Procurement Programs. The 1950s, which witnessed the clearest period of American postwar power, was also the period of maximum American arms aid.

Toward the end of the 1950s, the United States and, to a lesser extent, Britain and France were competing with the Soviet Union for arms sales and aid to the Third World or "nonaligned countries," especially in the Middle East and South and Southeast Asia. Arms diplomacy in the form of aid reached a climax with the war in Vietnam in the mid-1960s. But, before that period, the United States had begun to increase its sales of arms to richer industrial countries in Europe and the Far East.

The Vietnam war led to a new generation of domestic criticism of U.S. arms diplomacy. The critics argued that the reason the United States had become so intimately involved in the future of South Vietnam resulted from the close day-by-day working relationship between the United States Military Advisory Mission and the leaders of South Vietnam. Had U.S. diplomacy in South Vietnam been restricted to economic aid and political support, the quagmire of Southeast Asia might have been avoided, since U.S. prestige would have been less directly and less obviously at stake. The Vietnam war coincided with a bout of wars throughout the Third World, including the Indo-Pakistani war of 1965, the Arab-Israeli war of 1967, the Algerian-Morocco conflict, and the Nigerian civil war. In all cases, foreign arms, or the lack of them, played a central role in determining the fortunes of the adversaries, and this phenomenon, together with Vietnam, reinforced pressures within the Western world to try once more to control the arms trade.

Yet those to whom this control was directed had very different interpretations of what the issues were and argued that the denial of arms was an affront to their sovereignty and an attempt by external powers to retain a neocolonialist control over their destinies. For the more technically advanced Third World countries that were either subject to, or threatened with, restrictive controls, the alternative was to develop their own indigenous arms capabilities. The rela-tively high levels of capabilities found today in countries such as Israel, India, Pakistan, South Africa, Brazil, Argentina, North and South Korea, and Taiwan are not unrelated to the fact that, at periods in their recent histories, these countries have been subject to restraints on arms supplies.

In the early 1970s, another group of recipient countries came to the fore, namely, the very rich oil-producing countries of the Middle East that had purchasing power but were producing few skills. The rapid buildup of arms in certain regions, such as the Middle East, gave rise to simultaneous fears that regional arms races were under way and that the recipients would have difficulty in absorbing, maintaining, and operating their advanced equipment without continuing and intensive support from their suppliers. No better example of this pattern was the relationship that eventually evolved between the United States and Iran during the period 1971-79, culminating in the ouster of the Shah and the attempts by the Khomeini government to sell back military equipment to the United States.[1] The Iranian appetite for sophisticated arms had proven too great for the supporting infrastructure of the country. These so-called back-end problems represented a new phenomenon in the arms relations between states, since in the past, recipients who could afford to buy advanced equipment were usually capable of operating and main-

1. Shahram Chubin, *Iran's National Security Policy: Intentions, Capabilities and Impact* (Washington, DC: Carnegie Endowment for International Peace, 1994).

taining it and those who could not afford to pay either did without or had to rely on tightly controlled supplies in the form of military aid.

American arms transfers have become important tests of U.S. friendship. The reasons are clear. Weapons of war are not like other products traded in the international marketplace, because their end use concerns the most sensitive issue in international relations—the physical security of regimes. Thus the international transfer of military equipment and support material is both a barometer of political relations between states and an active component in influencing those relations. With a few notorious exceptions, sophisticated weapons in service in frontline inventories of the supplier country are usually sold or given only to close allies or, on occasion, to countries that appear to pose no putative threat to the supplier; thus the closer the ally, the fewer the constraints on arms transfers.

Nuclear weapons and their related delivery systems are the most sophisticated weapons. The only recipients of U.S. strategic nuclear delivery systems or support systems and technical know-how have been Britain and France, who have also been the closest U.S. allies. Britain, in particular, has had an extremely close nuclear relationship with the United States. The Nassau Agreement, which was reached on 21 December 1962, was perhaps the arms deal of the century. President Kennedy was prepared to sell Britain its most sophisticated nuclear missile, the submarine-based Polaris A-1. Polaris would be fitted with a British thermonuclear war-head and deployed onboard British-built nuclear-powered submarines. It would allow Britain to remain a global nuclear power into the indefinite future with the putative ability to destroy virtually all the major cities of the world, including American cities.

It is difficult to imagine the circumstances under which the United States would agree to similar arrangements with Japan or Germany. Most recipients of U.S. arms have not been permitted the full array of frontline equipment and key subsystems even if they have been able to pay full market prices. It therefore may be possible to rank the intimacy of relations between states according to the quality of the arms and other military support that have been provided.

American arms sales to close allies such as Britain raise few questions within the arms transfer community because they are seen to be part and parcel of the North Atlantic Treaty Organization (NATO) alliance and the need to integrate military doctrines and force capabilities to serve common goals. Yet transferring nuclear technology and associated delivery systems to a foreign government is surely the ultimate test of friendship in international relations, a fact noted with increasing frequency in countries such as India and Pakistan that bitterly resent the U.S. "double standard" on nuclear weapons.

At the other end of the spectrum, in relations between major powers and minor powers, arms transfers carry equally important messages. The history of U.S.-Soviet rivalry in the Third World was built around competitive arms supply relationships with a long list of countries, large and small. It was the Soviet decision to provide arms to Egypt in 1955 and give Nasser an alternative to the Anglo-American-French arms monopoly that opened the way for more assertive Soviet diplomacy in the region. It was American arms that provided the lure to bring Egypt back into the Western fold when President Sadat finally terminated his military relations with the Russians in 1972. In 1985-86, when Iraq and Iran were desperately fighting for survival in their brutal war, both relied on supplies from the outside to keep them going. The effectiveness of the American arms embargo against Iran was a key reason why Ayatollah Khomeini gave instructions to get hold of American arms even if it meant doing business with the hated Israelis. The White House thought it could use the supply of arms to cajole or tempt Iran into a better relationship and at the same time obtain the release of hostages; the Israelis thought that by supplying arms they could protract the war or, alternatively, ingratiate themselves with those members of the regime who might be favorably disposed to having a relationship with Israel once Khomeini left the scene.

In 1981, the Reagan administration decided to increase U.S. military assistance to Pakistan in view of the latter's support for the Afghan resistance and the need to keep open a supply line to the Afghani fighters. But this raised delicate problems with India. India did not object to some increase in U.S. arms aid to Pakistan, but it drew the line with the F-16 fighter, which was more so-phisticated than any aircraft in the Indian inventory at the time. Some Pakistani air force officers were prepared to compromise and accept the less sophisticated F-5G aircraft, which was also cheaper. But the political elite in Pakistan wanted to put the United States on the line and "test U.S. friendship" by seeing if America would alienate the Indians and go ahead with the F-16 transfer. They won the day, and U.S.-Indian relations entered a very tricky period. Things did not substantively improve until 1987, when, after a lot of internal soul-searching, the United States finally agreed to let India buy high-technology military items including jet engines and advanced gyroscopes. Once more, military items had become the test of intentions.

ANALYTICAL PERSPECTIVES ON U.S. ARMS TRANSFER POLICY

Two distinct perspectives have defined the debate about U.S. arms transfers since the beginning of the century: the realist perspective and the idealist perspective. However, with the escalation of the Third World arms race, and in particular the spread of weapons of mass destruction and long-range delivery systems, a new, more complicated problem has emerged. While there are still strong differences of opinion on the wisdom of arms transfers as an instrument of American foreign policy, there is general agreement that action is necessary to curb the spread of nuclear and chemical weapons and surface-to-surface ballistic missiles. But should curbs be advocated that include U.S. friends and allies such as India, Pakistan, and

Israel in order to rein in other, more maverick countries, such as Iran, Iraq, Libya, and Syria? Or should the United States step up its assistance to friends and allies so that they can better protect themselves against radical states equipped with weapons of mass destruction? This dilemma has new features, but the basic questions are relatively old ones. Before examining the current set of problems, a review of the two basic perspectives is useful since they still condition much of the argument.

The realist perspective assumes that the international system is inherently unstable because of fundamental elements of conflict that have existed since earliest times. This perspective further assumes that states will achieve security in their relations only if they have sufficient power—which, in the last resort, they interpret as military power—to ensure that their interests are protected. Other assumptions of this worldview are that alliances and balancing are necessary for security in an anarchic system; that arms and arms races are usually more a symptom of conflict between nations than a cause for conflict itself; and that, in this context, arms transfers are one of many instruments of diplomacy that nations, especially industrial nations, can use to further their overall national security interests.[2]

Although many politicians and policymakers hold this view of the world, in the case of arms transfer policy, a further distinction should be made between those who see arms transfers as a political instrument of national security policy, whose primary purpose is to provide political and psychological support to friends and allies, and those who regard the primary purpose of arms transfers as improving the military capabilities of friends and allies. These may appear to be fine distinctions, but they have led to heated discussions between those in the U.S. government who have been prepared to sell or give arms to friends and allies almost without regard to their military utility and the capacity of the recipients to use them, and those who want to transfer arms but believe that rigorous analysis is necessary before deciding which arms to transfer. For example, during the Nixon-Ford administrations, there were debates about the level of arms sales to Middle East countries, especially to Iran and Saudi Arabia. Secretary of State Henry Kissinger tended to favor a relatively unrestricted arms sales policy. Thus, from 1972 to 1976, the United States sold highly sophisticated defense articles and services to Iran without thorough analysis of

2. Exponents of the realist perspective are numerous, and only a few can be cited individually. The realists would certainly include most practitioners of international diplomacy in the past hundred years as well as many well-known international relations theorists. The classic study on realist thought is Hans J. Morgenthau, *Politics among Nations*, 6th ed. (New York: Knopf, 1985). See also Kenneth N. Waltz, *Theory of International Politics* (New York: Random House, 1979); Morgenthau's bibliography on political realism in *Politics among Nations*, pp. 625-27; "Theories, Politics, and Practice in International Relations," in *International Relations: Contemporary Theory and Practice*, by George A. Lopez and Michael S. Stahl (Washington, DC: CQ Press, 1989), pp. 3-14. For an example of consistent writing on the arms trade that reflects a realist perspective, see selected writings of Stephanie G. Neuman.

whether or not these particular purchases were appropriate; the arms sales were justified on strategic or balance-of-power grounds, but some critics argued that since Iran was so important to the United States, the arms sales should have been tailored to Iran's capabilities rather than its wishes.

Despite significant disagreements on specific arms policies between policymakers, the realist perspective on arms transfers has been dominant in American diplomacy during most of the postwar period and remains so today.

The idealist perspective is based on a different set of premises about the nature of the international system and the role that arms transfers play in it. Advocates argue that, although war and conflict might have been endemic in the past and therefore assumed to be natural phenomena, the experiences of the twentieth century and, in particular, the development of nuclear weapons have made the realist perspective too dangerous. They take the position that there is nothing inherently unstable in the current international system; conflicts between states and other political groups usually have identifiable causes that, with cooperation and understanding and sound regulatory mechanisms, can be defused. The supporters of this view claim that the emphasis on national military power, rather than on international organizations, as the ultimate arbiter of international relations is one reason why there have been so many extremely violent wars and conflicts; within this context, emphasis on arms production and arms

transfers as important instruments of national policy exacerbates tensions, precipitates arms races, and may, on occasion, trigger wars. Thus industrial powers, especially the United States, whose political traditions commit them to international harmony, should exercise restraint when selling or giving away arms, especially if they are located in regions where the potential for conflict is present. Ultimately, according to the idealist school, the objective of the United States should be to negotiate arms limitation agreements with industrialized and less industrialized countries to reduce both the burden of defense for the world economy and the prospects for open conflict, which might lead to the use of weapons of mass destruction.

There are also different points of view within the idealist school: the unilateralist perspective and the moderate perspective. The unilateralists believe that, in the long run, the only way to remove the risks of war is disarmament, not arms limitations. To achieve disarmament, countries such as the United States should set an example by reducing military expenditures, terminating nuclear and other weapons programs, and, in the context of arms transfers, desisting from selling or giving arms to virtually everyone but especially the developing countries. The moderates, while rejecting this approach as unrealistic and excessively risky, regard arms limitations as useful adjuncts of foreign policy that serve U.S. interests but can be achieved only if the United States shows restraint. This does not mean that arms should not be transferred but, rather, that every effort should be made to use arms transfers sparingly; to enter negotiations with suppliers and recipients to work for constraints; and to make it incumbent upon the advocates of arms transfers to demonstrate the case for providing arms.[3]

During the Carter administration, there was a serious attempt to implement the moderate idealist perspective, in intent if not in practice. The formal guidelines for the Carter policy were announced in May 1977: (1) the annual dollar volume of U.S. arms sales would be reduced; (2) the United States would not be the first to introduce advanced arms into a region; (3) manufacturers would not

3. Examples of supporters of the idealist school would include the many Western nonprofit organizations dedicated to disarmament and arms control goals, peace theorists, many religious groups, and numerous pacifist and socialist political idealists who believe that war can be eliminated from the human condition just as smallpox has been. A recent exponent of this view was Vaclav Havel, the first president of Czechoslovakia after the fall of communism. One of his first edicts directed that all arms exports by his country cease. This proved to be too costly and controversial to implement, and the debate over the dismantlement of the armaments industry helped spur the breakup of Czechoslovakia into the Czech Republic and Slovakia. See also the bibliography on disarmament in Morgenthau, *Politics among Nations*, pp. 644-45. Other examples of the idealist perspective include Ronald V. Dellums with R. H. Miller and H. Lee Halterman, *Defense Sense: The Search for a Rational Military Policy*, ed. Patrick O'Hefferman (Cambridge, MA: Ballinger, 1983); Michael T. Klare and Cynthia Arnson with Delia Miller and Daniel Volman, *Supplying Repression: U.S. Support for Authoritarian Regimes Abroad* (Washington, DC: Institute for Policy Studies, 1981). See also many other writings of Michael Klare for a consistently critical view of U.S. arms sales policies.

be allowed to develop or to modify advanced weapons for export; (4) co-production of U.S. weapons would be severely curtailed; (5) the transfer to third parties of U.S.-supplied weapons would be forbidden; and (6) the promotion of arms sales would require policy-level authorization by the Department of State. Although exceptions were immediately made for the NATO allies, Japan, Australia, and New Zealand, the nominal policy represented a marked contrast to the traditional policies pursued by previous administrations.

During the Reagan and Bush administrations, the United States reverted once more to a realist perspective in determining the basic rationale for arms transfers. This happened for several reasons. First, the U.S. defeat in Vietnam, paralleled by the growth of Soviet military power and the 1973 oil crisis, led to increased concern that the United States and its allies were falling behind in the global struggle against the Soviet Union and its surrogates.

Second, economic and political interests in the United States put considerable pressure on Congress to challenge the Carter administration's more restrictive policies on arms sales on the grounds that they were hurting U.S. exports and leaving the market open to foreign competition, including from the Soviet Union. There was concern in the executive branch itself about losing sales without any parallel economic or political benefits. This economic perspective was not emphasized in the U.S. arms transfer policies in the past because of the enormous sales to the U.S. armed forces and to NATO and the large military assistance program to developing countries. But as the market became more competitive, the old European economic arguments about the need to sell arms overseas in order to maintain a healthy, independent armaments base were heard in the United States.

The U.S. balance-of-payments benefit from overseas sales of arms is important, given the growing deficit caused by increased imports of oil. Programs of arms sales to foreign countries encourage a favorable atmosphere and contracts for sales of other U.S. products, further helping trade and the balance of payments. Moreover, a healthy arms sales program provides jobs. Finally, it has been argued that arms sales to foreign countries extend U.S. production lines, reducing the unit cost of weapons for the armed services, and that keeping U.S. arms production lines open beyond the current requirements for the U.S. forces provides a "warm" production base from which the next generation of weapons can be built.

These arguments have been reinforced with the end of the Cold War. They were highlighted during the 1992 election campaign when both Bush and Clinton endorsed the sale of additional F-15 aircraft to Saudi Arabia.

CONTEMPORARY DILEMMAS:
THE MIDDLE EAST CASE

Which of these perspectives makes the most sense for the United States today? No region of the world better illustrates the complexities of modern arms transfer diplomacy than the contemporary Middle East, including the Persian Gulf. The present article began by noting the great value of U.S. arms sales to Israel and Saudi Arabia in enhancing U.S. strategic interests. It has also been noted that U.S. military assistance programs to Iran during the 1970s created huge problems and helped spur the revolution and, in the end, proved useless in saving the Peacock Throne. Indeed, the case of Iran is frequently cited as a warning that similar catastrophes could happen to other well-armed U.S. clients, most notably Saudi Arabia. To this must be added the arming of Iraq by France, China, and Russia and the provision of nuclear and chemical technology by Germany and other Europeans and the legacy this sowed in Kuwait.

Indeed, one result of the Gulf war was to alert the Arab Gulf countries as to their military weaknesses and the putative power that both Iran and Iraq could wield in the region. They are especially nervous in view of their—and the United States'—huge miscalculations of Saddam Hussein's intentions. They are suspicious of both Iran and Iraq and have no confidence that their Arab allies, Syria and Egypt, are willing or capable of protecting them. They see no option but to rely on American military power to guarantee their survival. The chosen policy of the United States is to strengthen its own military potential in the region and that of the Gulf Arabs while containing the military capabilities of both Iran and Iraq.

As a consequence, the United States has decided to sell more aircraft, tanks, and missiles to the countries of the Gulf Cooperation Council. The reasons are obvious: the Gulf countries can pay hard cash for them; the arms could be useful to U.S. military forces in the event of another Gulf war; and Europe or Russia will sell the matériel to these countries if the United States does not. However, the United States will not sell the very advanced offensive weapons that were so effective in Desert Storm, such as F-117s, Tomahawk cruise missiles, or the U.S. Army's new tactical missile system (ATACMS). It will sell Patriot missiles to friendly countries and will provide new, very sophisticated technologies as compensation for U.S. sales to Arab countries.

Unfortunately, these decisions have made it difficult to persuade other major weapons suppliers to show restraint. Thus, U.S. démarches to Russia over Russia's arms sales to Iran—including submarines—fall on deaf ears. The Russians respond, "What laws are we breaking, and how does this differ from what you yourselves are doing?"

The difference, of course, is that the United States regards Iran as a maverick country capable of upsetting the peace process. Russia, on the other hand, regards Iran as a source of money and as a powerful country on its southern flank that has assumed a fresh importance in view of the challenges that Russia faces around its new borders. Russian foreign policy, in the wake of the breakup of the Soviet Union, has a very different set of priorities from those of American foreign policy; herein lies a real potential for disagreement. Similarly, it is very difficult to imagine the Chinese agreeing to restrict conventional arms sales to the Middle East if they can make

money from the sales and if the United States continues to sell advanced fighter aircraft to Taiwan.

As long as political settlements to the conflicts in the Middle East remain elusive, there is no alternative to strong military preparedness by the United States and its allies. However, if and when Israel and its neighbors make peace, realistic arms control initiatives will be not only relevant but highly desirable and integral to the peace process. At that point, it may be possible to envisage a resolution of the Gulf crises and initiatives to bring Iran and Iraq into the negotiating process.

CONCLUSION

For the foreseeable future, arms transfers will be a key element of U.S. foreign policy, and the debate about arms sales will continue. The problem is that the end of the Cold War has witnessed a return to nationalism rather than a new world order based on internationalism. Until the chaos created by the breakup of the Soviet Union has been given time to settle, wars and war preparedness will remain a prominent feature of the international landscape. The economic pressures on the major arms-manufacturing countries to export their wares are growing at the very time that demand for arms is increasing in those regions most destabilized by the end of the Cold War. It may well be that many would-be purchasers of advanced arms will not be able to afford the high costs of modern weaponry. However, as the crises in Moldova, the Caucasus, Bosnia, Afghanistan, Tajikistan, and Somalia all vividly demonstrate, most protracted and violent conflicts today show little resemblance to Desert Storm and its high-tech wizardry but rather rely on the traditional instruments of twentieth-century slaughter: small arms, mines, mortars, and artillery.

In determining the appropriate types of arms sales that best serve U.S. interests, the basic elements of the realist and the idealist schools do not suffice; what is required is detailed, case-by-case analyses of U.S. interests and the political-military-economic environment in particular regions and particular countries. Sweeping pronouncements about the purpose and goals of U.S. arms transfers can distort and often damage the specific objectives of U.S. policy. General restrictive policies that call for embargoes or moratoriums on weapons sales to certain regions of the world, especially the less developed world or certain classes of countries, can be as harmful to U.S. interests as relatively indiscriminate provision of arms to bolster allies and friends. To talk of less developed countries as a monolith to which a single policy of arms transfers can be applied is no longer appropriate, if it ever was.

Good analysis requires the use of multiple criteria to measure the benefits and costs of particular transfers within a particular period of time. While there are always positive and negative considerations in the transfer of particular numbers of specific weapons, the most important factors influencing U.S. choices will be closely related to American political, economic, and military interests, which vary from one world region to another. More elaborate analysis in the early stages of the transfer process can alert decision makers to future political, social, or even military problems, which, in turn, may influence the magnitude and extent of an initial arms agreement.

In order to establish a conceptual and empirical base from which to analyze the impact of the arms transfer phenomenon on international relations and the reasons why arms sales continue and why sales continue to be opposed, several sets of data are needed. First, it is necessary to have a comprehensive inventory of such transfers over a long period of time. This provides the historical basis for making generalizations about the nature and extent of the activity. Second, it is necessary to establish an inclusive inventory that covers not only all categories of major weapons systems, including nuclear weapons, but support services and training programs as well. Third, it is important to try to estimate the magnitude of cases of arms denial when a supplier, for one reason or another, has turned down a request for arms. Fourth, it is necessary to examine all the data on a global basis and not restrict analysis to particular regions or categories of recipients. Any general theory of the arms trade should include these elements, but they are found only rarely in contemporary analyses of the problem.

ANNALS, *AAPSS*, **535**, September 1994

Will There Be an Arms Trade Intelligence Deficit?

By HENRY SOKOLSKI

ABSTRACT: With the end of the Cold War and superpower rivalry, policymakers will want to know more about more common types of conflict and the transfers of conventional arms needed to fight them. Unfortunately, as interest in arms transfer intelligence increases, the relative amount of money available to track and analyze this trade is likely to remain stable or decline. Improvements in arms trade intelligence are possible, however, if intelligence agencies are willing to risk prioritizing and, arguably, narrowing their focus to those aspects of the trade that have not yet received the attention they deserve. Here key opportunities include defining arms trade intelligence to exclude the proliferation of strategic weapons or the arming of terrorist organizations; substituting unclassified academic analysis for current, less critical classified tasks; and experimenting with market mechanisms to discipline how policymakers task the arms transfer intelligence community.

Henry Sokolski was deputy for nonproliferation policy at the Pentagon from 1989 to 1993. He has served in the Office of Net Assessment in the Office of the Secretary of Defense and as Senator Dan Quayle's senior military legislative aide and point of contact with the Senate Armed Services Committee. He teaches at Boston University's Washington Institute of World Politics and is currently writing a book on proliferation as a National Institute of Public Policy fellow.

A S the prospect of nuclear inter-continental ballistic missile conflict between the United States and Russia recedes, the significance of more common types of war and of the transfers of conventional arms needed to fight them will increase. U.S. policymakers will want to know more about the military, economic, and political consequences of other countries' investments in arms and arms manufacturing. They will have to pay even greater attention to how the integration of new dual-use technologies with existing weapons and the mixing of Warsaw Pact, mainland Chinese, and Western systems will change how wars will be fought.

Unfortunately, what is unlikely to change is the relative amount of money spent by the world's key intelligence agencies to track and analyze the arms trade. Indeed, if anything, the amount is likely to decline. This dilemma and what may be done to avert the trade intelligence deficit that it might generate are the focus of what follows. The premise of this article is simple: whatever improvements are likely to come in the collection and analysis of arms trade intelligence are most likely to result from better use of existing resources. This is possible but only if intelligence agencies are willing to risk prioritizing and, arguably, narrowing their focus to what is most relevant and worrisome.

This may sound like a zero-sum proposition, but it need not be. In fact, the U.S. Intelligence Community Management Staff is currently analyzing how to cope with the prospect of declining budgets.[1] One spe-cific area that they have identified to save money is the classification of information. The staff proposes that the amount of highly classified infor-mation be reduced—that some infor-mation categories no longer be classi-fied—so that contractors working for U.S. intelligence agencies would not have to spend so much money main-taining high levels of security in their companies and could pass these sav-ings on to the government agencies for whom they work

Another area that the staff is ex-amining, which may be of more direct relevance to the future of arms trans-fer intelligence, is how unclassified information and analysis can be used to supplement and, in some cases, substitute for more expensive classi-fied collection and analysis. Finally, the staff is interested in ways to eliminate undesirable duplication of effort and is examining how market mechanisms might be used to disci-pline the way policy and military of-ficials task intelligence collectors and analysts.

Considered properly, each of these areas of possible reform suggests ways in which the collection and analysis of arms transfer intelligence could be enhanced. These enhance-ments include (1) reducing undesir-able duplication of efforts in the ter-rorism and weapons proliferation fields by clarifying what arms trans-fer intelligence is for the policy com-munity; (2) substituting unclassified arms trade analysis and data collec-tion where possible; (3) encouraging

---

1. See Richard Haver, "Collection: Pros-pects and Problems in the Post Cold War World" (Presentation before the Consortium for the Study of Intelligence, Working Group on Intelligence Reform, Washington, DC, 19 Oct. 1993).

additional academic work in the softer, longer-term analytical aspects of the arms trade; and (4) reducing frivolous tasking and eliciting the users' real arms transfer intelligence priorities by having them pay for some of the analysis or collection that they want.

Taken together, these reforms could significantly mitigate the dilemma of falling intelligence budgets and rising interest in arms transfers. The trick will be implementing these reforms properly. Indeed, with not much effort, one can easily compound or create crises by attempting these reforms without proper reflection on what their success requires.

THE DEFINITION OF PROLIFERATION

The need to be thoughtful in any reforms that are attempted is most evident in regard to clarifying what arms trade intelligence is. If the arms trade is defined too broadly, a dilution of focus will be guaranteed, as will a duplication of effort in terrorism and proliferation intelligence efforts. If the trade is defined too narrowly, important aspects of it will go unexamined.

At the low end of the arms trade spectrum—private small arms transfers to terrorists—there is little controversy about having those responsible for intelligence terrorism cover this trade. Nor is there much problem discerning when such trade is being sponsored by one nation to overthrow or destabilize another. When the purpose of such trade is clear and the amounts significant enough to threaten success, as was the case with the transfer of Nicaraguan and Cuban arms to Salvadoran rebels in

the 1980s, it becomes a matter of arms trade concern.

What is becoming more difficult to discern, however, is when a conventional arms transfer is a matter of proliferation concern. The key culprit here is the continuing lack of a prescriptive definition of proliferation. For the longest time, proliferation has been understood to mean the spread of weapons of mass destruction and related technologies. With the advent of high-leverage conventional arms such as conventional submarines and mines that can control confined waters and smart conventional missiles, though, there has been a desire to expand the category of proliferation so that it includes these and other destabilizing types of conventional arms.[2]

The dangers here are fairly clear. But, then, so are the opportunities for a useful division of labor. Obviously, most conventional arms in very large numbers can produce war-winning— that is, destabilizing—results. If this is the only measure of what is meant by "destabilizing," nearly all arms transfer intelligence should properly be done by those covering proliferation matters or, conversely, all proliferation matters should be handled by the arms transfer intelligence community.

A more commonsensical approach would recognize that there are only a handful of weapons systems that in small numbers can produce war-winning or victory-denying results and even fewer systems for which adequate defenses have not yet been de-

2. For a more detailed discussion of these points see Henry Sokolski, "Fighting Proliferation with Intelligence," Orbis (Spring 1984).

vised. Only such weapons systems should be of proliferation concern. The logic here is simple: because strategic results can be inflicted by lower-leverage conventional arms only when these arms are used in large numbers, the acquisition of these arms and the training needed to use them generally are revealed early enough for nations to defend themselves. In contrast, it takes so few weapons of proliferation concern to inflict strategic harm that their acquisition could go unnoticed, and because effective defenses are lacking against these systems, they are much more likely to threaten strategic surprise.[3]

Clearly, the monitoring and warning requirements associated with transfers of common conventional arms are much lower than with weapons of proliferation concern and their related technologies. It therefore would make sense to reduce demands on limited staff time by reducing the attention devoted to such conventional weapons in selected cases.[4] Certainly, for many countries,

the likelihood of war or conflict is sufficiently low to make classified collection and analysis of information on these arms less necessary. This is especially true given the ready availability of publications by Jane's Defense Information Group and the International Institute of Strategic Studies. Assuming that the U.N. arms trade registry is framed properly and implemented with professionalism, it, too, can serve to reduce the current demand on limited intelligence staff resources.[5]

More, however, can be done with the open literature or at low levels of classification than merely updating existing arms balances. Assuming that intelligence agencies are serious about reducing the level of classification and security clearance red tape for private contractors, academics could be used more to analyze some of the less urgent aspects of the arms trade and build a data and analytical base of common interest.

The idea here is not simply to declassify information that might be of interest to academics. In many interesting cases, this simply will not be possible. Yet, even here, intelligence agencies could expand their analytical base by downgrading the classification of some information to a level low enough to allow analysis by visiting professors and students who

3. Examples of weapons of proliferation concern include nuclear, biological, and chemical munitions and high-leverage conventional systems, such as submarines operating in shallow or confined seas, accurate conventional missiles, and advanced command, control, communication, and intelligence systems. For a detailed discussion of what systems should qualify and why, see Henry Sokolski, "Nonapocalyptic Proliferation: A New Strategic Threat?" *Washington Quarterly* (Spring 1994).

4. The problem here is less a matter of monitoring and data collection than it is one of analysis. In this regard, the aim should be not to eliminate all duplication of effort but rather to eliminate duplication that undermines any hope of clarity about why distinctions need to be made between terrorism, proliferation, and conventional arms transfers. On the utility of

duplication of efforts and necessary competition, see James Q. Wilson, "Thinking about Reorganization" (Presentation before the Consortium for the Study of Intelligence, Working Group on Intelligence Reform, Washington, DC, 10 June 1992).

5. Care must be taken, though, to ensure that the U.N. registry does not introduce bad information, thus making it more difficult to know what is going on.

might be granted only a temporary secret clearance for a few months.

The ultimate goal of such short-term contracting would be to encourage more useful unclassified analysis by academics and their students. Of particular interest would be studies that leveraged academics' natural strengths against the weaknesses inherent in intelligence officials' need to meet routine and urgent taskings. Such topics might include analysis of the economic, developmental, and political consequences of particular countries' investments in arms and arms manufacturing, evaluation of the true opportunity costs of such investments, and analysis of how well specific nations have been able to make specific arms imports operational or specific arms manufacturing efforts successful.

CLARIFYING PRIORITIES AND INTERESTS

Arms transfer intelligence would be an appropriate place to experiment with demand-side market mechanisms such as having the military and policy consumers actually pay for some of the nonroutine analysis and collection they want.[6] Such payments, whether by vouchers or

6. This discussion draws heavily from Henry S. Rowen, "Reforming Intelligence: A Market Approach" (Presentation before the Consortium for the Study of Intelligence, Working Group on Intelligence Reform, Washington, DC, 10 June 1993). See also William Harris, "Collection in the Intelligence Process," in *Intelligence Requirements for the 1980's: Clandestine Collection*, ed. Roy Godson (Washington, DC: National Strategy Information Center, 1983).

actual money, would apply to optional analysis and collection; warning and essential monitoring would not be open to such bidding.

Although such experimentation might be tenuous initially, in the long run, it should help clarify what the consumers' intelligence priorities truly are and should reduce the number of distracting, petty, impulsive taskings. It might also help resolve one of the current debates over the extent to which the intelligence agencies should get involved in commercial—as opposed to economic—espionage.[7] This debate has gone on for nearly a year in a consumer vacuum. Presumably, if such information collection and analysis is desirable, requests for it that bore some real opportunity costs would help demonstrate that desire one way or the other.

Such market experimentation could highlight far more than the current system of requesting intelligence does exactly what it is in the arms trade field that the policy and military communities are most interested in—which countries and transactions are of greatest concern and why. Clarity on these points can hardly be overemphasized. Indeed, without it, no quantity of intelligence assets can be put to good purpose. More important, with declining intelligence assets, its absence will be the most likely engine of failure.

7. For a detailed discussion of this debate, see Randall M. Fort, "Economic Espionage: Problems and Prospects" (Presentation before the Consortium for the Study of Intelligence, Working Group on Intelligence Reform, Washington, DC, 8 Apr. 1993).

ANNALS, *AAPSS*, **535**, September 1994

Military Technology and the Arms Trade: Changes and Their Impact

By W. SETH CARUS

ABSTRACT: Revolutionary changes now taking place in the technology of war may have a significant impact on the character of the international trade in arms. Some analysts argue that a Military Technical Revolution is now under way, as military organizations begin exploiting a wide variety of new technologies through organizational adaptation and doctrinal innovation. The result will be fundamental change in the ways wars are fought, just as the blitzkrieg and the aircraft carrier revolutionized warfare following World War I. Among the significant new technologies often identified are information systems, including advanced sensors, communications, and data processing, long-range precision guided weapons, and advanced simulation techniques. If these views are correct, the international trade in arms will undergo a fundamental transformation. While specialized defense hardware will remain, dual-use equipment will become increasingly central to the performance of advanced military forces. As a result, it will become more difficult to track the implications of trade in defense-related hardware simply by monitoring transfers of major weapons systems.

Dr. W. Seth Carus currently works for the deputy for policy planning in the Office of the Under Secretary of Defense for Policy in the U.S. Department of Defense. He has published extensively on the proliferation of weapons technology in the Third World, including Cruise Missile Proliferation in the 1990s. *He is coauthor of* The Future Battlefield and the Arab-Israeli Conflict, *which examined the impact of new technologies on the Arab-Israeli military balance.*

NOTE: The views expressed in this article are those of the author and do not necessarily reflect the policies or positions of the U.S. Department of Defense.

THE international arms trade is primarily a market in equipment, or in items needed to support that equipment, which military forces believe will enhance combat effectiveness. As a result, it seems obvious that there is a connection between the dynamics of the international market for armaments, on the one hand, and the character of the technology used to make them, on the other. From this perspective, developments that have an impact on the technology of war are potentially important to an understanding of future trends in the arms trade.

Many analysts now believe that profound changes in the technology of war may be causing a revolutionary transformation in the conduct of war in general and in the character of conventional military operations in particular. If these views are correct, it seems inevitable that the international trade in arms would be affected in some fundamental ways.

This article will examine the interaction between current trends in the evolution of military technology and possible changes in the arms trade. The starting point for the analysis will be an assessment of the potential impact that changes in the technology of war could have on conventional military war-fighting capabilities. This will be followed by an examination of the possible implications of those changes for the international trade in arms. The objective of this exercise is to take a speculative look into the future of the arms trade in the context of a perspective derived from an equally speculative view of the impact of technology.

THE MILITARY TECHNICAL REVOLUTION

For much of this century, students of war have been aware that the character and conduct of warfare is linked inextricably to technological developments. Hence it is not surprising that analysts have come to pay close attention to the potential impact of changes in technology on military operations. Recently, however, a growing number of analysts have come to believe that recent radical advances in military technology are making possible a truly revolutionary transformation in the character and conduct of warfare.[1] Among the first to articulate this view—more than a decade ago in the former Soviet Union—was Marshall N. V. Ogarkov, who was then chief of the Soviet General Staff. Since the collapse of the Soviet Union, Russian authors have continued to expound these ideas in increasingly sophisticated forms.[2]

1. See Patrick Garrity, *Why the Gulf War Still Matters: Foreign Perspectives on the War and the Future of International Security*, Report no. 16 (Los Alamos, NM: Los Alamos National Laboratory, Center for National Security Studies, 1993), for a discussion of the impact of technological changes on the conduct of war. This study, which summarizes a substantial assessment undertaken by the Center for National Security Studies of Gulf war lessons learned, provides a useful survey of the current state of the debate from an international perspective.

2. This discussion is based on two recent surveys of Russian thinking: C. J. Dick, "Russian Views on Future War" (Research paper AA26, Conflict Studies Research Institute, RMA Sandhurst, 8 June 1993); Mary C. FitzGerald, "The Impact of the Military-Technical Revolution on Russian Military Affairs," vol. 1 (Research paper, Hudson Institute, 20 Aug. 1993).

Russian analysts have identified a variety of types of systems that they believe are essential to the implementation of this revolution in military affairs. They mention advanced conventional weapons with high single-shot kill probabilities, extended-range delivery systems for the munitions (cruise missiles, long-range rocket and tube artillery, and aircraft), electronic warfare systems that can effectively neutralize hostile sensors or equipment without physically destroying anything, sensor systems capable of detecting and identifying targets deep in territory under the control of the adversary, and intelligent command, control, communications, and intelligence (C^3I) systems. The C^3I systems will rely, at least in part, on space-based assets. In addition, many of the delivery systems will rely on low-observable—that is, stealth—technologies to reduce vulnerability to hostile air defenses.

What is significant about the new technology, however, is that it relies heavily on the integration of systems that may be distant from one another. During the Persian Gulf war, Patriot surface-to-air missile batteries were warned about the impending arrival of Iraqi ballistic missiles by satellites hovering thousands of miles over the theater of combat, and the signals from those satellites were processed in the United States before the warning messages were transmitted to the defenders on the other side of the globe. One implication of such developments is the lessened significance of the platforms, such as aircraft and ships, that carry systems into battle areas. At the same time, the systems carried by the platforms will continue to grow in importance. This will be true for a whole range of systems, including combat aircraft, tanks, and naval combatants. To consider but one example, the aerodynamic performance of strike aircraft is becoming considerably less important than the capabilities of the munitions being carried, the effectiveness of the aircraft's integrated navigation and weapons delivery system, and supporting C^3I systems that locate and identify targets for air strikes.

These new systems—no longer based on single platforms—will cause fundamental changes in the conduct of warfare. One consequence often identified by analysts is a profound change in the character of the battlefield. For example, it is thought that the importance of direct-fire weapons—such as tanks and anti-tank missiles—will diminish as weapons capable of striking targets at a distance become dominant. Degrading the effectiveness of an adversary's sensor and C^3I systems will become critical, giving enhanced importance to electronic warfare—what the Russians call radio-electronic combat. Force densities will decline and the depth at which battles are fought will grow dramatically. As a consequence of such developments, control over the forward battle area will decline in importance as the battlefield becomes increasingly fluid. Even this short summary suggests that, if the Russian thinkers are correct, the character and conduct of warfare will undergo a profound and revolutionary transformation.[3]

3. These conclusions draw heavily on Hirsh Goodman and W. Seth Carus, *The Fu-*

The original Soviet ideas have been examined and adapted by Western analysts, who have transformed them in basic ways. These Western analysts argue that we are in the initial stages of what they call a Military Technical Revolution (MTR). This U.S. concept differs in important respects from the original Soviet articulation. While the Soviet view concentrated primarily on the impact of new technologies and on the impact of the changing technology on the theoretical foundations of the battlefield, the U.S. analysts have given greater attention to the organizational and doctrinal changes that are needed to exploit the possibilities offered by that new technology.[4]

According to the U.S. perspectives, the full impact of the revolutionary technologies requires two significant developments beyond the adoption of new hardware: the development of new military doctrines, and the creation of new military organizations designed to fully exploit the new technologies. Without appropriate changes in organizations and doctrines, radically new technologies will be marginalized, perhaps enhancing the effectiveness of traditional ways of conducting war but without necessarily having a revolutionary impact.

The evolution of armored warfare provides a telling example of the critical importance of doctrinal and organizational changes. The tank was widely adopted as a weapon of war during the 1920s and 1930s. However, only the German army fully exploited armored forces at the beginning of World War II, largely because of doctrinal and organizational innovations evident in the German panzer divisions. Most armies relegated their tanks to the infantry support role. The Germans, however, developed a new concept of warfare, the blitzkrieg, which featured a combined arms force, the panzer division, which operated under a new combat doctrine that exploited the potential operational mobility of mechanized forces.[5]

Proponents of the MTR argue that technological changes are making possible yet another revolutionary transformation in military operations. In their view, three trends illustrate this revolution. First, modern command, control, and communications (C^3) systems, along with associated surveillance systems and data fusion capabilities,[6] have radically enhanced the ability of modern

---

ture Battlefield and the Arab-Israeli Conflict (New Brunswick, NJ: Transaction, 1990).

4. The concept of the MTR has been developed in the U.S. defense community by Andrew Marshall, director of net assessment in the Office of the Secretary of Defense. The description of the MTR given here is based on discussions with Mr. Marshall, as well as members of his staff, including Dr. Tom Welsh and Dr. Andrew Krepinevich. However, they are in no way to be held responsible for this account, which reflects the author's own interpretations.

5. The history of the panzer forces is too well known to require much elaboration. The panzer forces adopted a new way of fighting by integrating tanks, mobile infantry, and artillery, along with close support aircraft. The system worked because the Germans gave considerable attention to communications, which enabled the units to react quickly to battlefield developments.

6. Modern military forces can have so many different sensors collecting data that it becomes impossible to assimilate it all in a timely fashion. Data fusion is the integration of these diverse data streams so as to create a coherent picture.

military forces to monitor the battle-field and to target weapons. In part, this reflects the impact of the information revolution on the conduct of war, which is improving our ability to process data rapidly and turn it quickly into useful information and to move data and information from one place to another. At the same time, advances in sensor technology are providing new types of data for these information-processing systems.

A second development is the availability of precision munitions that can be delivered over long ranges. These weapons make it possible to exploit the information capabilities of the new command and control systems. This is not entirely a recent development, since the first generation of effective precision guided munitions appeared two decades ago. However, new generations of weapons are being developed with dramatically enhanced capabilities compared with the munitions previously available.[7]

7. The most commonly employed munitions during the conflict were upgraded versions of weapons first developed during the Vietnam war, including laser-guided bombs and Maverick television-guided missiles. These weapons constituted the bulk of the precision guided munitions used by U.S. forces during the conflict. At present, the United States is in the final stages of developing new generations of fire and forget weapons that can strike targets in all weathers with considerable precision over long ranges. Systems like the Joint Stand-Off Weapon (JSOW) and the Joint Direct Attack Munition (JDAM) will rely on extremely inexpensive integrated inertial and satellite navigation systems to guide weapons to the target. As a result, they will not have to be actively controlled after release, and they will rely on guidance systems considerably less expensive than those found in the current generation of cruise missiles.

A third trend is the spread of advanced simulations that make it possible to provide realistic training for individual soldiers, as well as units of ever increasing size. These same capabilities also can support the development of new equipment and operational methods under peacetime conditions.

An example of how the MTR could transform military forces is a new U.S. program known as War Breaker.[8] Initiated by the U.S. Advanced Research Projects Agency, War Breaker aims to develop technologies needed to find, identify, and destroy time-critical targets, such as mobile ballistic missile launchers. The requirement for such an effort emerged as a high priority based on assessments of U.S. performance during the Persian Gulf war, because of the failure of U.S. forces to target and destroy Iraq's mobile Scud missile launchers.

War Breaker focuses on two key capabilities: surveillance and targeting, on the one hand, and intelligence and planning, on the other. The surveillance and targeting effort will attempt to develop a variety of sensors that can cover a large area in order to detect and identify high-interest targets. The intelligence and planning effort will develop automated systems to process and correlate the massive amounts of information acquired by the sensors. The plan is to reduce significantly the time re-

8. War Breaker is described in William B. Scott, "War Breaker Program Explores New Sensor, Targeting Systems," *Aviation Week & Space Technology*, 31 May 1993, pp. 37-38; William B. Scott, "DARPA System to Find, Kill Mobile Targets Quickly," ibid., 22 Feb. 1993, pp. 59-60.

quired to attack a target from the moment it is detected by a surveillance sensor. According to one calculation, these types of systems could make it possible to transform a process that currently takes eight hours into one that will require no more than one hour. An integral component of the project is a distributed simulation environment to conduct exercises and tests that will assist in the design and development of the system.

War Breaker is really a system of systems, an integrated C^3I system composed of sensors, communications systems, automated data fusion and analysis systems, and mission-planning support systems. The effectiveness of the overall program will depend on the integration of these diverse systems into one cooperative system. Significantly, War Breaker includes no weapons. Yet, if successfully implemented, War Breaker will provide the U.S. military a significantly enhanced ability to destroy missile launchers and other time-critical mobile targets.

Clearly, new technologies, and new applications based on them, are providing military forces with fundamentally new types of capabilities. These changes are likely to have a profound impact on the future conduct of warfare. Essentially, the MTR provides military forces with more information, which is better filtered and organized, and which is obtained and distributed more rapidly than was previously possible.

EXPLOITING THE MILITARY TECHNICAL REVOLUTION

At the very least, exploitation of the MTR will require integration of advanced C^3I systems and precision guided munitions. As important as the technology, however, will be creating a supporting framework, including organizational structures and operational doctrines. Moreover, these efforts must be carefully coordinated, since the effectiveness of much of the new technology derives from the integration of sensors, communications, automated data analysis (to permit near real-time target designation), and delivery of precision munitions. A failure to properly execute any major step in the process will lead to an inevitable collapse of the entire system.

Ultimately, the technology is less important than the system in which it is embedded. The effectiveness of the advanced technology employed by U.S. military forces in the Gulf war owed a great deal to the quality of the personnel and their training and to the organizations, doctrine, and tactics that they employed. Many military forces fail to provide adequate training for their forces or acquire insufficient quantities of spare parts or do not build the infrastructure needed to support their forces.

For various reasons, it seems likely that only a few countries will play a significant part in this MTR. Several factors are likely to constrain efforts to exploit the technological possibilities: lack of access to the required technology, an inability to afford the new military capabilities, and a failure to make necessary adjustments to existing military organizations and doctrines. Even countries capable of the financial expenditures to acquire the systems needed for MTR capabilities may be unable to make the transition. Organizational and doctrinal adaptation will be equally necessary, and it may be more difficult to accomplish than acquisition of systems. Accordingly, it is likely that most countries will only selectively exploit the possibilities offered by the MTR. The tendency will be to acquire discrete capabilities in particular areas, rather than attempting to compete across the spectrum of technological possibilities.

These factors have considerable importance for any assessment of the impact of the MTR on the international trade in arms. Exploiting the MTR will require considerable skill in the implementation of a wide range of such supporting activities. Accordingly, any country trying to buy into the MTR will need to do much more than merely acquire military hardware. This means that arms purchases will be only a minor part of the overall effort. Indeed, because purchases of equipment of any sort constitute only one aspect of an effort to exploit the MTR, it is important to recognize that the character of the arms trade will undergo profound change.

THE ROLE OF DUAL-USE TECHNOLOGY

The reason it will be possible for some countries to buy into the MTR is the growing importance of dual-use technologies for military applications. A fiber optic command and control system, like the one built for Iraq in the 1980s, is essentially identical to a civilian telephone system. Hence any country interested in acquiring a secure communications system with high data transmission rates can ob-

tain it from a large number of companies that supply commercial markets. Similarly, military systems rely increasingly on digital computers, often identical to those sold in the civilian market, to undertake functions that once required specialized analog devices. Thus a modern strapdown inertial navigation system employed in a ballistic missile can provide high-accuracy guidance using computer chips identical to those used in commercial products.

Indeed, it is evident that certain technologies—once the exclusive preserve of the superpowers—are becoming increasingly available. High-quality satellite imagery is one such resource. Several countries intend to provide commercial access to satellite imagery with resolutions of around 1 meter, including France and Russia. Other countries—such as the United Arab Emirates—are seeking to purchase satellites with 1-meter resolution. In addition, other countries are developing systems with 2.5-meter resolution. All of these systems are more capable than the existing 10-meter resolution provided by the French SPOT satellite.[9]

In the future, commercial systems may provide completely new capabilities previously unavailable even to the superpowers. For example, an evaluation of the capabilities inher-

9. Recent trends in the growing accessibility of high-resolution satellite imagery are summarized in Jeffrey M. Lenorovitz, "Industry Presses CIA to Ease Curbs on Imaging Satellites," *Aviation Week & Space Technology*, 21 June 1993, pp. 80-81. For a discussion of South Africa's so-called Greensat reconnaissance satellite, see Craig Covault, "South African Satellite Carries Earth Imaging System," ibid., 21 June 1993, p. 24.

that they may offer interesting capabilities of military interest. Motorola is working to create a global cellular telephone system, known as Iridium. This system will make it possible to communicate with anyone anywhere by using a satellite to transmit signals from the equivalent of a hand-held portable telephone. A system of this type, in theory, could provide the kinds of in-flight communications to aircraft and missiles that U.S. defense planners hypothesized in the late 1970s. One could imagine a Third World country adapting such a capability to put a data link into a missile that could receive over-the-horizon target updates.

Finally, it is evident that the United States and the Soviet Union no longer dominate a growing range of technology. Clearly, Japan and Western Europe possess sophisticated technology and thus can be a source of dual-use technology useful in exploiting the MTR. Even many newly developed countries, such as Taiwan and South Korea, have impressive technological capabilities, which are only likely to be enhanced as time passes. In essence, the technology floor is being raised by the diffusion of military applicable technology. The result is that an increasingly large number of countries have access to many of the technologies needed to exploit the MTR.

ACCESS TO ADVANCED-TECHNOLOGY WEAPONS

Despite the diffusion of technology, however, there is still much technology that is not widely exploited by military forces around the world. A variety of military systems remain available to only a handful of countries, because either access to the technology remains restricted or the cost of acquisition and operation is too high or for both reasons. Nuclear-powered submarines, intercontinental ballistic missiles, strategic cruise missiles, stealth weapons, and strategic bombers are currently in the inventories of only a handful of countries. Because of the high cost associated with the development, production, and operation of such weapons, only the richest countries have been able to afford them.

In addition, because the diffusion of military technology is uneven, there remain some technologies that are dominated by a few countries. The United States, for example, has developed highly sophisticated systems based on military technologies that are unlikely to be commercialized. It seems highly unlikely, for instance, that the United States will sell its stealth technology. This forces other countries that would like to acquire weapons using such technology to expend substantial resources to undertake the research and development needed to permit indigenous acquisition programs. Similarly, press reports suggest that the United States is developing a range of so-called nonlethal weapons, which will disable equipment without necessarily killing people.[10] One assumes that systems providing such capabilities will not be made available on the commercial arms market by the

10. See, for example, David A. Fulgham, "EMP Weapons Lead Race for Non-Lethal Technology," *Aviation Week & Space Technology*, 24 May 1993, p. 61; "Army Prepared for Non-Lethal Combat," ibid., p. 62.

will not be made available on the commercial arms market by the United States. As a result, it seems likely that it will take time before such capabilities become generally available. Certainly, the United States often has no reason to make such capabilities easily accessible to others.

The end of the Cold War also may have important implications for the availability of high-technology weapons. As the East-West armaments competition has reduced in intensity (although it has not necessarily disappeared altogether), pressure to push the military state of the art has declined. In the future, when the United States develops a new capability, it is unlikely that any adversary will devote the level of resources to countermeasures that the Soviet Union could commit to them. Hence countries that relied on the Soviet Union for military capabilities will be at a disadvantage to those with access to Western equipment. Only in cases when countermeasures can be based on the purchase of modified versions of existing systems will it be possible to overcome this deficiency. Thus it will not be possible for countries hostile to the United States to count on the eventual availability of integrated systems designed to counter advanced U.S. capabilities, such as stealth weapons. Clearly, the full range of technologies that might be useful in exploiting the MTR will not be readily available on the international arms market.

However, it may not be necessary for countries to have access to capabilities needed to compete with a major power. Rather, it seems likely that a premium will be placed on capabilities that enable countries to counter the capabilities of the new technology, if not with advanced systems subject to controls, then with other available devices. This can take many forms, some simple and relatively easily achieved, others somewhat more difficult. An example of a relatively easily developed counter for advanced weaponry is increased reliance on underground facilities. The equipment needed to dig tunnels, for example, is inherently civilian in nature and hence can be acquired commercially. An underground facility conceals its contents from prying eyes, thus complicating the intelligence collection process and making target acquisition difficult or impossible; at the same time it makes damage more difficult. Alternatively, some countries might strive to acquire weapons of mass destruction as the most effective means of countering advanced conventional military capabilities.

Moreover, despite constraints on the availability of certain advanced technology systems, on the whole it will be easier to acquire sophisticated military systems in the future than was possible during the Cold War. When advanced systems are already in production, there will be a greater willingness to export that equipment. During the Cold War, the United States and the Soviet Union restricted transfers of their most advanced equipment. The Soviets kept the best systems for their own forces and often exported less capable versions of the equipment that they were willing to supply. In the future, the tighter defense budgets, reduced security concerns, and looser export controls will combine to enhance the availability of many advanced-capability weapons systems.

At the same time, countries that develop new systems or modify existing ones will be able to take advantage of easing access to dual-use technologies. The end of the Cold War has eased access to high-performance computers and to technology needed for optical surveillance satellites, to name but two examples. As a result, it will be possible for many countries to develop systems with sophisticated capabilities that once were available only to the superpowers.

SOME CAVEATS

The relationship between technology and war is at best ambiguous. Technology—and hardware based on it—is only one of many tools required to develop military capabilities needed to fight wars.[11] In other words, for many countries the kinds of capabilities provided by the MTR may have

11. The interaction between technology and military affairs has been the subject of a large and often contentious literature. No attempt was made in the present article either to review that literature or to assess the history of military technology. The author, however, owes a considerable debt to Martin Van Creveld, *Technology and War, from 2000 B.C. to the Present* (New York: Free Press, 1989). This work provides a much richer framework than William H. McNeill's, *The Pursuit of Power* (Chicago: University of Chicago, 1982), which seems dated, given the collapse of command economies and the increasingly important role of dual-use technologies for military applications. For a recent analysis of the history of technology, which puts the process squarely into a social and economic context, see George Basalla, *The Evolution of Technology* (New York: Cambridge University Press, 1988).

limited significance for the military problems they face.

The importance of technology for war fighting depends heavily on the character of the conflict in which it is being used. In many cases, military forces have exploited technological superiority to gain decisive advantages over their adversaries. Yet even in this era of highly sophisticated armaments, most wars are fought using weapons that are by any measure quite unsophisticated. Indeed, it is quite likely that during the past 45 years, more people have been killed in low-intensity conflicts by soldiers or irregulars armed with small arms than by high-technology systems.[12] Clearly, advanced-technology systems have an important role in the generation of military power, but a critical perspective is essential when examining advanced military technology.

The problem arises, as is plainly evident to any student of low-intensity conflict, because sophisticated weaponry may be useless when confronting a technologically unsophisticated, but politically astute adversary. This reflects the inherently political character of war, which may or may not provide an environment where it is possible to rely on the exploitation of technology as a key to military success.

This observation is not intended to downplay the potential importance of technology. However, military hardware is a tool and not an end in itself, and, like any tool, its utility is dependent on whether it is being used

12. Martin Van Creveld, *The Transformation of War* (New York: Free Press, 1991), pp. 18 ff, provides a discussion of the predominance of low-intensity conflict in modern warfare.

appropriately. Under the correct circumstances, technology can be critical. It may be possible to shoot down a helicopter with a blow gun—as allegedly happened during the United Nations' Congo intervention in the early 1960s—but most military forces will rely instead on antiaircraft guns and short-range surface-to-air missiles.

In addition, weapons purchases are not necessarily intended to optimize military effectiveness. Often, purchases of arms are motivated less by military utility than by prestige or the political value of ownership. Even when military considerations dominate acquisition decisions, many countries receive little or no military value from the acquisition of highly capable—and often extremely expensive—weapons systems. The acquiring military force often neglects to obtain sufficient training, adequate levels of spare parts, needed supporting infrastructure, or enabling hardware (such as self-protective electronic warfare pods and guided munitions for advanced combat aircraft).

Finally, the ultimate impact of technology depends heavily on the strategies and operational methods it is intended to support. It is all too easy to ignore the context in which equipment is operated and thus to misunderstand the true significance of particular weapons. A tank in the hands of an army that assigns it to infantry forces for use as an assault gun or mobile antitank platform in support of a strategic defense is very different from that same tank assigned to a mechanized force for deep penetration attacks as part of an offensive strategy. The two tanks may

use the same technology, but the meaning is very different.

These observations suggest that caution is in order when assessing the ultimate impact of technology on the character of the international arms trade. Specifically, they suggest that for most countries—although perhaps not the largest and most powerful—the MTR will have only a limited impact on the character of their military forces. Only countries intent on operating the most advanced technologies—motivated by military, political, or economic considerations—will concentrate on the MTR competition.

CONCLUDING REMARKS

Changing military technology has profound implications for efforts to monitor the size and character of the international arms trade. Traditionally, the international arms trade has been viewed mainly as a market in military hardware. When systems and systems of systems are the critical path to acquisition of military capability, measures that focus exclusively or even primarily on tanks, combat aircraft, or surface-to-air missiles can provide an extremely misleading view of the international arms trade. To an increasing extent, however, military critical trade will be composed of dual-use items, such as communications gear needed for C^3 systems, computers needed to do the analysis for sophisticated detection systems, or electronic sensors of military utility that are produced for commercial purposes.

Consider, for example, two key sources of information on the arms trade. From an MTR perspective, the tables of equipment transfers provided by the U.S. Arms Control and Disarmament Agency are largely superfluous. They provide no insight into MTR developments and, in fact, focus attention on elements of military capability that may be of only marginal importance in the future development of military capabilities. Similarly, the aggregate cost statistics provided by the Stockholm International Peace Research Institute are problematic because of their focus on major weapons systems. To the extent that C^3I systems become central to the development of military power, a focus on weapons becomes at best misleading. This suggests that some effort will be needed to rethink the data sources used to calculate the extent of international arms transactions.

Equally problematic are some of the traditional means at our disposal for assessing military balances of power. Surveys like the annual *Military Balance*, produced by the International Institute for Strategic Studies, provide an extremely misleading perspective on the acquisition of military capabilities under current circumstances. Such works provide detailed orders of battle and equipment inventories in order to give some insight into the military capabilities of various countries. Such data remain useful, but their centrality may be declining. For example, the growing importance of C^3I systems is not captured in such reference works, and for this reason critical information needed to assess balances of military power is not provided. In the future, it may be less important to know about weapons inventories than to have an appreciation of how all the systems fit together. As a result, our ability to assess the implications of particular transactions is being marginalized by the inadequacies of our measurement tools.

ANNALS, *AAPSS*, **535**, September 1994

The Rise of Black and Gray Markets

By AARON KARP

ABSTRACT: Since the mid 1980s, the black and gray arms markets have emerged as major forces in the arms trade. Though they are much smaller than the orthodox trade, covert transfers are of great importance, providing the weapons most likely to actually be used in conflict. The totally illegal black market arises in reaction to embargoes. It is antipolicy, the mirror image of official intentions. The state-sponsored gray market, although it receives less attention, is much larger and more destabilizing. The gray market represents policy in flux as governments experiment with new and risky diplomatic relationships. There is much that can be done to bring the covert arms trade under control, especially through more aggressive law enforcement and radical extension of the United Nations Arms Register. Only collective security mechanisms, though, offer any hope of eradicating the covert arms trade.

Aaron Karp is adjunct professor in the Graduate Program in International Studies at Old Dominion University, Norfolk, Virginia. Previously he has held positions at the Stockholm International Peace Research Institute, the Stiftung Wissenschaft und Politik, and Harvard University. His books include Ballistic Missile Proliferation: The Politics and Technics *(1994) and* Arming Ethnic Conflict *(1994).*

FOR the nonspecialist, reading the formal literature on the arms trade for the first time must be a disappointing experience. Instead of dark tales populated by dangerous conspiracies, shadowy operations, and grave risks, one finds a mature and highly academic field. For almost thirty years, it has been preoccupied with a formal business, dominated by legal transfers of major weapons between governments. The large literature on the arms trade concentrates on statistics and officials, systemic processes and cabinet decisions.

The black and gray markets that fuel romantic literature and the popular imagination are all but ignored in orthodox studies. During the Cold War, there were sound justifications for this schism. Large, formal arms transfers were an essential instrument in the international balance of power. Generated by the superpower confrontation or by regional rivalries, they were the most visible force behind the international spread of military capability. The black and gray markets were trivial by comparison. Today, as the international system becomes more chaotic and ethnic conflict replaces interstate war as the most immediate danger to international peace and security, the black and gray markets cannot be casually overlooked.

Although observers have long acknowledged the intermittent importance of covert arms transfers, systematic assessment has waited. This article tries to outline some of the essential characteristics of the black and gray markets. Although there are serious problems in evaluating any covert phenomenon—in this case, illustrated by the obvious problem that most of the well-known black market deals were failures that ended up in court—enough is known to permit some preliminary conclusions. Why have the black and gray markets become more salient in recent years? How have they evolved from a minor factor in international politics to a leading policy problem? When do they pose their most serious challenges to international security? And what can be done to minimize their threat?

OVERLOOKING THE OBVIOUS

The arms trade is a remarkable phenomenon, situated at the nexus of international politics. Innumerable books and articles have introduced the subject by stressing its uniqueness as a lens through which an immense variety of international processes can be seen and understood, including the full range of political, economic, and military developments. The arms trade is as relevant to discussions of human rights and democratization, and transnational debt and regional industrialization as it is to evaluating military power, geopolitical intentions, and alliance commitments. Its salience was neatly captured by Andrew Pierre's quip a decade ago that "the arms trade is policy writ large," one of the few unquestioned epigrams of modern international relations.[1]

The traditional association between the arms trade, state policy,

1. Andrew J. Pierre, *The Global Politics of Arms Sales* (Princeton, NJ: Princeton University Press, 1982), p. 3.

and military capability make for an exciting, even captivating field of study. But it has the side effect of obscuring some of the most important aspects of the trade. The orthodox approach leads to a natural emphasis on the size of arms deals and to reliance on statistics as a measure of their significance. It also leads to a nearly total fascination with official government-to-government transactions. All too often those of us involved in the arms trade—especially those involved as policymakers and analysts—tend to overlook smaller deals and unofficial transactions that may be far more disruptive than their size might suggest.[2]

Above all, the focus on state policy has discouraged balanced appreciation of the black and gray arms markets. The oversight is not completely unjustified; despite their fearsome public reputation, the black and gray markets are of no more than spasmodic importance to most of the world's 180 countries. Even the most ambitious illegal shenanigans cannot rival the mainstream of officially licensed transfers as a source of military hardware. To offer an extreme example, the largest successful black market deal on record was the sale of 87 Hughes helicopters to North Korea in the mid-1980s. Worth over $80 million, this pales to insignificance compared to the largest conventional arms deal, Saudi Arabia's al-Yamamah purchases of aircraft,

2. Two exceptions to this oversight are Michael T. Klare, "The Thriving Black Market for Weapons," *Bulletin of the Atomic Scientists* (Apr. 1988); Edward J. Laurance, "Political Implications of Illegal Arms Exports from the United States," *Political Science Quarterly* (Fall 1992).

ships, missiles, and infrastructure worth a total of more than $40 billion —500 times as much as the Hughes sale.

The greatest significance of the black market lies not in the overall statistics of the U.N. Arms Register or the divisions and fleets of regional military balances. Its effects are most serious, rather, in contradicting policy and facilitating the most deadly forms of conflict. In stark contrast to orthodox arms transfers, the black market does not represent the policy of any of the states involved. Illegal as sold and illegal as received, black weapons serve no state or government policy. If orthodox transfers are policy writ large, the black market is antipolicy, the mirror image of official intentions. Its significance is greatest for international renegades, be they terrorist cells, ethnic insurgents, or states fenced off by U.N. embargoes.

The black market is disturbing because it threatens to upset policy, to contradict the best intentions of constitutional governments and the international community. What is at issue is not gradual adjustment of the balance of power but rapid and chaotic change. The formal arms trade is a process that can take years or decades to affect regional balances. Saddam Hussein, to offer the most obvious case, emerged as a major challenge to international stability only after cultivating his military capabilities for over 15 years.

The effects of gray and black transactions can be felt much more quickly and with greater certainty. The menace of both the black and gray markets is the danger of weapons that almost certainly will be used to threaten or kill. Their greatest power is felt at the extremes of international conflict, in the small-scale arming of substate actors and in the efforts by pariah states to acquire weapons of mass destruction.

The illegality at its core makes the definition and identification of black market activity relatively simple. The gray market is more obscure. The gray market resembles the covert nature of the black market, but in reality it is very different. Unlike the black market, gray transactions usually are neither entirely legal nor entirely illegal. While the black market constitutes the most wretched aspect of the arms trade, the gray market may be more of a necessary evil. The gray market represents not policy writ large, but policy in flux, as exporting and importing governments experiment with new diplomatic links, cloaking possible policy changes in covert transactions.

By using covert channels, officials on both sides can take greater risks, cultivating new relationships while minimizing the potential embarrassment or danger. Gray processes also enable officials to circumvent or undermine policies they do not like. At its best, gray market activity probably is unavoidable, an unsurprising manifestation of the need for flexibility in international politics. So long as states contemplate major changes in their bilateral security relations, gray market arms deals will remain a tempting first step. Sometimes such efforts are entirely commendable, permitting the rise of new alliances that can check regional aggressors. On other occasions, they only demonstrate high-level frivolousness and contempt for constitutional decision making.

CREATING THE
BLACK MARKET

Contrary to the prevailing wisdom, the black market traditionally was very small, almost trivial. It appears to have reached a peak as recently as the mid-1980s and diminished rapidly to the much smaller size that it is today. Widespread changes in legislation have transformed much of the illegal arms trade, pushing activity out of the wholly illegal black arena into the far more obscure but potentially much larger gray trade.

So long as the trade in military equipment was governed by the laissez-faire rules of the marketplace, there was no opportunity for a black market to emerge. Black markets were created by embargoes. They are the unintended by-product of embargoes prohibiting sales to particular enemies, be they empires like the Turks, class enemies like the peasantry, or felons. As embargoes became more common in the nineteenth century—mostly in efforts to suppress revolution or the slave trade—and often assumed the status of normal policy in the twentieth century—in efforts to isolate conflict and punish unpopular governments—the black market was generated unintentionally but with virtual certainty.

The first studies of the arms trade in the 1920s and 1930s are especially revealing. All of these studies were written to expose the worst aspects of sales of military equipment, yet few went so far as to mention illegal transactions. Their primary themes were the dangers of legal transfers, perceived as a cause of war, and the unethical profits from warfare. With their thinking dominated by the absurdities of one world war and the anticipation of another, observers naturally concentrated their energies on the major armaments firms and their agents. The activities of the black market apparently were too marginal to justify inclusion.[3] Even when writing about arming the enemy, the focus was entirely on the legal but ethically questionable transfers of technology, licenses, and use of subsidiaries by major manufacturers.[4] The most disturbing illegal practice of the time was bribery of government officials to facilitate otherwise legal transactions.[5]

Only as embargoes became normal tools of diplomacy in the 1930s could the black market become more consequential. Most countries already had experience with the problems of banning domestic arms transfers, such as Spain's efforts to contain Carlist forces in the 1870s and American problems controlling sales of rifles to rebellious Indians such as Geronimo's Apache in the 1880s. In the last decade of the century, efforts to halt the slave trade and maintain colonial empires gave the great powers their first international experience in policing illegal arms shipments, mostly by searching vessels at sea. While the number of embargoes grew through the first four decades of this century, it was only with the American Neutral Act of 1937 that governments began to promulgate sweeping legal restrictions on the international arms trade.

The neutrality legislation was short-lived, but the importance of controlling arms transfers was fully established. Led by Washington, Western governments took the initiative by banning transfers of arms and strategic goods to Communist governments through the establishment of the Coordinating Committee (Co-Com) system in 1949.[6] The 1950 Tripartite Declaration showed that America, Britain, and the Soviet Union could cooperate, at least for a while, to halt arms sales to the Middle East. Later, African nations led the United Nations to implement embargoes against South Africa and Rhodesia. The 1970s saw various governments impose their own temporary arms bans, such as the American refusal to sell specific weapons to Pakistan and Zaire. Not until 1983 did the arms embargo reach its greatest prominence, through the establishment of the Western arms embargo on Iran.

In the wake of the Cold War, as the international community gropes for instruments to contain expansionist dictators and ethnic strife, arms embargoes have been a standard instrument. Currently, U.N. arms embar-

3. *Report of the Temporary Mixed Commission on Armaments*, A/81/1921 (Geneva: League of Nations, 1921).

4. For example, Fenner Brockway, *The Bloody Traffic* (London: Victor Gollancz, 1933), chaps. 5-7.

5. H. C. Englebrecht and F. C. Haninghen, *The Merchants of Death* (New York: Dodd, Mead, 1934), chaps. 9-11.

6. Michael Mastanduno, "Trade as a Strategic Weapon: American and Allied Export Control Policy in the Early Postwar Period," *International Organization*, pp. 121-50 (Winter 1988).

goes are in force against Angola, Cam- bodia, Iraq, Haiti, Liberia, Libya, Somalia, South Africa, and the former Yugoslav republics. CoCom restrictions have been relaxed for most Eastern European and ex-Soviet republics, but Western nations and supporters of the CoCom system elsewhere rigorously apply its arms ban on countries like Iran and North Korea.

With each expansion of the international embargo list came new opportunities for black market sales. Most embargoes, however, were fairly porous at first. So long as cooperative governments could be found that were willing to approve sales to an embargoed state, the black market remained inconsequential. For the black market to evolve into a larger force, clients had to learn to purchase technologies that the black market could make available.

This transformation came in the 1970s and early 1980s, as embargoed governments, led by the Soviet Union and South Africa, switched their illicit purchasing away from whole weaponry—which illegal sources rarely could acquire or transfer—to emphasize manufacturing technology. A series of incidents in the 1970s demonstrated the importance of extending controls to cover manufacturing technology and to confirm its final application.[7] Best known is the U.S. export of ball-bearing machines

to the Soviet Union in 1972, which may have led to improved Soviet missile accuracy.[8] While this transfer was completely legal, it showed a change in procurement methods in which illegal transfers also could play a major role.

The result was a large and lucrative market that became the basis for efforts by advanced countries to evade international restrictions. Most of this trade was in legal dualuse technologies. Celebrated cases indicated that these countries and others conducted highly organized efforts to acquire prohibited technologies as well. Intelligence revelations in 1978-80 showed that Soviet-led espionage had evolved to emphasize acquisition of not only weapons designs and data but also ostensibly civilian manufacturing concepts and equipment, an approach subsequently applied by regional weapons proliferators as well.[9]

The black market probably reached its peak in the mid-1980s, reacting to the needs of Iran, Iraq, North Korea, and South Africa. A dramatic series of revelations in 1986-87 showed that Iran had deliberately cultivated illegal and highly questionable sources to acquire the equipment it needed to sustain its war with Iraq. As it became evident that the Iranian web reached into

7. The need to control turnkey or critical technology was the main theme of the Bucy Report, officially known as the Defense Science Board Task Force on Export of U.S. Technology, *An Analysis of Export Control of U.S. Technology: A DoD Perspective* (Washington, DC: Government Printing Office, 1976), p. 24.

8. Donald A. MacKenzie, *Inventing Accuracy: A Historical Sociology of Nuclear Missile Guidance* (Cambridge: MIT Press, 1990), pp. 326-27.

9. *Soviet Acquisition of Military Significant Western Technology: An Update* (Washington, DC: Department of Defense, Sept. 1985). Signe Landgren, *Embargo Disimplemented: South Africa's Military Industry* (New York: Oxford University Press, 1989).

virtually all arms suppliers—at least 40 countries in all—a new transformation of the arms market was set into motion.

In response to the Iranian arms scandals and international pressure, many countries that had never taken arms export controls began to institute serious oversight systems. Other countries greatly tightened their regulations. Notorious suppliers like Italy went so far as to bring their arms exports to a virtual halt. Nations like Belgium, with reputations as permissive transshipment centers, adopted rigorous customs procedures. Exporters everywhere adopted End-User Certificates (EUC) to help ensure that military exports ended up in the proper hands.

The near universalization of the EUC created a quiet revolution in the arms trade. Where only a handful of governments had insisted on EUCs in the past, now export or even transshipment through obscure ports became impossible without it. Previously, arms could be exported from many countries simply by declaring an acceptable destination. The fate of the weapons often was immaterial to the exporting government. After the universalization of the EUC, black marketeers adapted by bribing officials in weak governments to sign false EUCs; Paraguay and Kenya were popular choices in the 1980s, Bolivia in the early 1990s. This ruse, a minimal measure involving little more than a few thousand dollars and a slip of paper, had the effect of eliminating most of the black market. Overnight, black market dealers won the cooperation of governments, transforming black deals into obscure gray ones.

MYTHS OF THE BLACK MARKET

While the black market remains a potentially significant source for some clients, it is never the supplier of choice. The disadvantages of the black market are so pervasive as to make most black deals seem little short of miraculous.

At the most basic level, both black marketeers and their clients would prefer not to deal with each other. For both sides, the risks of such deals are tremendous. Unsuccessful black marketeers do not simply ease out of the business and take up something else; as for clients, they assume the risk of giving money to unknown and untrustworthy characters. Basic business problems inhibit dealing. Black market exporters need immediate payment, which neither embargoed states nor insurgents are in a position to give. They pre- fer that their clients make shipping arrangements, which also is difficult for all but the best-organized groups.

Nor is there much of substance that the black market can offer that holds great interest to most potential clients. States need large numbers of aircraft, tanks, and missiles; insurgents typically require large quantities of prosaic items; but the black market is better suited to small transfers of high-value items. The key to the black market is secrecy, which is difficult to maintain when tanks or aircraft are lifted off a ship. The exorbitant price of illegally transferred equipment—often 3 to 10 times market value—is another serious obstacle, especially for substate actors. Insurgent groups can afford such purchases only intermittently. Only the best-financed groups can afford such prices regularly, but these groups usually have the advantages of state sponsorship and little need for the black market.

One of the most serious disadvantages is the lack of help with financing. Black marketeers have no interest in extending credit. They tend to be cash-on-the-barrel operators. Recipients are expected to complete all financial arrangements themselves. But financing can be especially troublesome for a stateless, impoverished insurgency. Even a financial institution as corrupt as the Bank of Credit and Commerce International (BCCI), which routinely helped countries like Iran and Pakistan with loans and letters of credit for questionable purchases of military technology, apparently balked rather than provide the same facilities to insurgents. Only if they had unambiguous support from a government, which in effect countersigned the arrangement, would BCCI get involved.[10]

A major problem is the inability of illegal deals to include the many services needed to complete an arms transfer and make the equipment operational. An illegal trading network must complete its transactions as rapidly as possible to avoid detection. Illegal arms sales are a serious business, with risks ranging from prosecution to assassination. No black market conspiracy can accept the risk of maintain-

10. *The BCCI Affair: A Report to the Senate Committee on Foreign Relations* (Washington, DC: Government Printing Office, 1992).

ing an open pipeline furnishing training, operating assistance, spare parts, maintenance, and overhaul services.

Some confusion is due to the promiscuous use of the term "black market." Time and again, transactions ascribed to the illegal black market turn out to have been officially sanctioned transactions made under the authority of sympathetic government officials. Although often concealed through covert arrangements, such deals are legal exports. The scope of this problem is illustrated almost daily by the problem of prosecuting the dealers involved in questionable deals; all too often they escape conviction by claiming that they were acting as middlemen in deals that had official backing or acceptance.

This problem clouds the largest gray market operating at this writing, the trade across the Thai border to the Cambodian Khmer Rouge. With much of the western and northern part of the country as well as the profitable timber and gem trade under their control, the Khmer Rouge are well-off financially and can afford to pay black market prices, which are inflated by some 500 percent. Working through Thai intermediaries, they have been able to acquire Western rifles, anti-armor weapons, mortars, and ammunition. But is this an example of the black market or more typical of the covert gray trade in which government officials participate? While the Thai government is unambiguous in its criticism of the Khmer Rouge and the arms trade, it is widely suspected of complicity. Supplies appear to reach the Khmer Rouge only through the collaboration of Thai police and military officers, who receive payoffs.[11] One is led to the conclusion that the Khmer Rouge benefit not from a black market as much as from ambiguous Thai policy.

All too often, complete evidence reveals black market deals to be nothing more than investment schemes or pipe dreams. Real black market transactions tend to be relatively small, involving parts or arms small enough to fit into a suitcase or shipping crate. Occasionally, however, reports emerge of vast black deals worth tens of millions or even billions of dollars. Typically, though, the traders arranging a proposed deal have neither possession nor title to the equipment in question.

This was the case with one of the largest black market deals ever revealed, a conspiracy by 17 American, European, and Israeli businessmen in 1986-87 to supply Iran with the Western equipment it needed most in its prolonged war with Iraq. There actually were two separate deals, the largest involving 39 F-4E fighter aircraft, 5 C-130 transports, 3750 TOW anti-tank missiles and 5000 more for spare parts, millions of shells, and tons of spare parts. A second deal assembled by co-conspirators involved 15 F-4 fighters, 30 M-48 tanks, missiles, and spare parts. Even secondhand, this material had a fair market value of over $2 billion.

In reality, though, there was nothing but paper and promises. The deals were nothing more than an elaborate investment scheme. No one involved had any of the equipment or even a firm idea where it would come from; possibilities included Israel, and Turkey, but the source was never resolved. If the equipment could have been procured, the businessmen undoubtedly would have tried to transfer it, but in lieu of that, the Iranians got only promises. The only thing certain in the conspiracy was greed for Iranian cash.[12] Numerous other less grandiose cases could be cited.

The riddle of drug traffickers on the arms market

Among subnational actors, the black market probably is of greatest importance to drug cartels. They have the financial and organizational resources to acquire large-scale capabilities through numerous small-scale transactions. Over the years, they have developed not only massive financial resources but also wide-reaching contracts throughout official and unofficial society. Most of their equipment has been acquired piecemeal. Latin American narcotics traffickers have acquired much of their firepower from unlicensed purchases on the American private gun market. With over 200 million firearms in private hands, the United States has unlimited potential for illegal diversions.[13]

11. Philip Shenon, "Thai Conduit Reopens for Flow of Illicit Arms," *International Herald Tribune*, 8 Feb. 1992, p. 5.

12. The deals were revealed in Stuart Diamond and Ralph Blumenthal, "Huge Illegal Deal on Arms Was Known to U.S.," *New York Times*, 2 Feb. 1987, based on reporting by Kenneth R. Timmerman. A unique source is the memoir of a participant; see Hermann Moll with Michael Leapman, *Broker of Death: An Insider's Story of the Iranian Arms Deal* (London: Macmillan, 1988).

13. Michael Isikoff, "200 Million and Counting: U.S. Firearms Surge a Sharp 42%," *International Herald Tribune*, 25-26 May 1991.

In the 1980s, it became common practice for smugglers to buy weapons legally in American shops for illegal resale in Latin America.[14] America's permissive ownership and registration requirements do little to inhibit organized smuggling. For many years, the private American gun market was unique as a source of automatic rifles ideally suited to internal conflict. Although the guns sold privately must be semi-automatic (requiring a separate trigger squeeze for each shot), often they can be converted easily to full automatic firing. With the disintegration of the Soviet Union and the collapse of police and military authority, Russia now is in a similar situation, unable to control the trade in small arms.[15] Although most of Russia's illegal gun trade serves organized crime, much also appears to be feeding ethnic strife.

Fears that drug barons would use their funds to systematically arm their own huge private armies have proven to be unfounded.[16] The largest arms sales involving drug marketeers probably are of little use to these marketeers; they avoid conflict with the state through bribery and intimidation, not organized warfare. The most dangerous adversaries with whom drug dealers must contend are their competitors, and this risk seems to be managed through Mafia-style syndicates. Transactions

by drug dealers involving more than a few hundred rifles are more likely to be brokered for third parties, most notably sympathetic insurgents like the Revolutionary Armed Forces of Colombia and Peru's Shining Path.

This unprecedented synergism between drug dealers, insurgents, and the black market is poorly understood. It represents perhaps the most sophisticated development in the market for small and light arms. It apparently is through drug barons that the Shining Path established its largest training camps in Peru's Upper Huallaga Valley in the late 1980s. They supplied the American M-60 machine guns, 81mm mortars, and grenade launchers that arm the Shining Path's heaviest forces. The guerrillas developed their largest fighting units ever, company-sized units of 60 to 120 soldiers.[17] The key question here is who is using whom: did the Shining Path extort weapons from drug growers or did the drug growers buy the guerrillas' services? Were drug economics making it possible for Shining Path to develop in ways previously not feasible, or was cooperation with drug growers leading the group to alter its ideological methods?

Even drug dealers prefer to buy through licensed exporters. While nihilism might lead them to flout the law, basic economics encourage them to work within it when possible. Through legal deals, they receive better-quality equipment at a lower price, and they minimize the risk of prosecution. Cooperation with West-

14. Larry Rohter, "In the Shady World of Illegal Arms, Miami Is Hot," *International Herald Tribune*, 12 Aug. 1991, p. 3.

15. Celestine Bohlen, "Now It's the Turn of Russian Society to Tumble Down," *International Herald Tribune*, 31 Aug. 1992, p. 1.

16. Such a scenario seemed more likely in the late 1980s.

17. Tom Marks, "Making Revolution with Shining Path," in *Shining Path of Peru*, ed. David Scott Palmer (London: Hurst, 1992), p. 200.

ern security and intelligence agencies created opportunities for legal arms acquisition in the 1980s.[18] The greed, disregard, and poor regulation by established exporters creates others.

One of the largest examples of a legal arms sale to organized criminals was a consignment of 500 Israeli rifles and ammunition transferred through the Caribbean island of Antigua to Colombian cocaine traffickers in 1989. Lack of Israeli concern and the cooperation of Antiguan officials allowed the entire transaction to be completed on the books. With the assistance of a member of the Antiguan cabinet (the prime minister's son), an Israeli middleman brokered the deal as part of a larger and fully legal transfer of Israeli weapons to several South American countries. The Antiguan EUC for the equipment should have caught the attention of Israeli officials. With a total constabulary and paramilitary force of 92 men, supplied free of charge by America, Antigua had no possible use for the weapons. Turning a blind eye, the Israeli government permitted the export.

The most difficult part of the deal was arranging letters of credit while concealing the actual source of the money, which never was discovered. The total value of the deal was $324,205 plus commissions, for 100 Uzi automatic guns, 400 Galil automatic rifles, and 200,000 rounds of ammunition. At a price of $609 each for the Galils, this was a very fair transaction by any standard. Rather than pay more, as one might expect, the wealthy drug barons paid far less than any insurgency would on the black market. The weapons were delivered in Antigua in April 1989 by the Danish vessel *Else Thuesen*, which continued to Colombia and other South American destinations with legitimate arms deliveries. How the arms got to Colombia is unknown. The deal was revealed after Colombia police killed the Medellín cocaine dealer José Rodríguez Gacha on 15 December 1989. Subsequent searches of his Colombia properties led police to 232 of the weapons. The rest remain unaccounted for. There have been no prosecutions in the case.[19]

When transactions like this are possible, the black market is irrelevant. As the late Edward Ezell pointed out, the cargo of the *Else Thuesen* was not unique. Similar cargoes recovered in the 1980s include

— 250 British MP5 submachine guns carried by the *SS Bente Folmer* of Denmark, seized off Costa Rica in July 1985, having apparently been transferred from Yugoslavia, en route to an unknown destination;
— 1448 East German AK-47 automatic rifles seized in Balboa, Panama, from the *SS Pia Vesta* of Denmark, en route to an unknown destination;

18. Peter Dale Scott and Jonathan Marshall, *Cocaine Politics: Drugs, Armies and the CIA in Central America* (Berkeley: University of California Press, 1991).

19. U.S., Congress, Senate, Committee on Governmental Affairs, Permanent Subcommittee on Investigations, *Arms Trafficking, Mercenaries, and Drug Cartels: Hearing*, 102d Cong., 2d sess., 27-28 Feb. 1991, pp. 57-148; Louis Bloom-Cooper, *Guns for Antigua: Report of the Commission of Inquiry* (London: Duckworth, 1990).

— 1000 German G3 rifles, 10 60mm mortars, and ammunition discovered in Kingston, Jamaica, on the *SS Copacabana*, a ship of Panamanian registry, on 22 December 1988; a falsified EUC gave Colombia as its final destination, but this was never confirmed; and

— 70 tons of Czechoslovakian rifles, machine guns, and pistols, apparently headed for Colombia, seized in Savona, Italy, from the *SS Jenstar* of Denmark in February 1989.[20]

All of these deals appear to have been legally sanctioned or simply ignored by the authorities in the exporting countries. No laws had been broken, no prosecutions occurred. The weapons were confiscated for lack of proper documentation. But it seems certain that similar shipments reached their final destinations.

What were the intended destinations for these massive shipments? Probably not drug dealers themselves, who do not command forces of sufficient size. A few of these large deals undoubtedly were brokered by drug barons but intended for delivery to cooperative insurgencies like Shining Path.

The most likely recipients for such large arms shipments, however, are not drug dealers or guerrillas at all. Ironically, the most likely buyers are official Latin American armed forces and paramilitary organizations. In countries with histories of political instability, it is not uncommon for the

armed forces to prepare for coups and conflict within the state by maintaining secret stockpiles of weapons. The most likely destinations for the previously specified shipments were such autonomous elements within the state.

This also may explain the riddle of why there have been fewer seizures of illegal arms shipments in the Caribbean in the 1990s despite greatly improved intelligence collection and law enforcement. The evidence—or lack of it—suggests that illegal arms shipments to the region have declined. Yet the demand for arms among drug dealers has changed little, and the requirements of insurgencies probably remain much the same—except in countries like El Salvador and Surinam where guerrillas have surrendered their weapons. The one group in Latin America with much less use for illegal weapons is the military. With the rising strength of democratic principles throughout Latin America, the official demand for illegal weapons may be declining.

Who needs the black market?

The black market is of greatest utility to isolated states, pariahs like Iran, Iraq, North Korea, and Serbia that face international restrictions on their armed forces or military industries. They need the black market to circumvent embargoes, and they have the resources to make good use of the things that it can provide. While the black market is not suited to shipping large quantities of major weapons, it is ideal for transferring

20. All examples are from Edward C. Ezell, testimony in *Arms Trafficking, Mercenaries, and Drug Cartels: Hearing*, pp. 103-16.

inconspicuous components and manufacturing technology. These are less likely to attract the attention of customs authorities. By concentrating on this kind of technology, South Africa was able to use the black market to develop its arms industries and overcome the U.N. embargo. Similarly, Iraq was able to build up its nuclear weapons and ballistic missile capabilities. Through an illegal ruse, North Korea acquired its fleet of 87 American-made helicopters.[21] No substate group ever has been in a position to manipulate the black market as effectively.

THE NATURE OF
THE GRAY MARKET

The rising importance of the gray market directly reflects the chaotic politics of the post-Cold War environment. If the arms trade is policy writ large, the gray market is where policy is being made. The open arms trade is, for the most part, the business of maintaining the status quo by strengthening previously established relationships. It is typified by allies' selling to each other. The gray market, by comparison, serves the needs of diplomatic change and realignment. The gray market is a murky sea of diplomatic innovation, experimentation, and testing. The participants operate in a sensitive environment best served by secrecy, permitting them to enter or exit at minimal risk.

Unlike the orthodox arms market, gray market deals often do not equal

21. Klare, "Thriving Black Market for Weapons"; Laurance, "Political Implications of Illegal Arms Exports."

policy. Instead they are the tangible evidence of policies in flux. In some cases, their secrecy may arise from confusion within a government, as with Britain's controversial exports of dual-use machine tools from Matrix-Churchill in 1988-89, a deal apparently sanctioned by one part of the British government in order to circumvent the restrictions of another part. In other cases, the exporting government may be reorienting policy, waiting to see if the change will succeed before announcing its commitment.

The gray market has its own characteristics and methods, most of them intended to help transfers remain covert and deniable in case they are exposed. These include

— transfer of nonstandard weapons, such as the U.S. furnishing of AK-47 rifles to the Afghan mujahideen or Nicaraguan contras;
— reliance on intermediary suppliers to further disassociate suppliers and recipient governments, such as the 1956 Soviet-Egyptian deal in which most weapons actually came from Czechoslovakia;
— shipping of equipment through private, chartered transportation, preferably vessels or aircraft of foreign registry; an example is the Argentine aircraft used by Israel to transport F-4 fighter parts to Iran in the early stages of the Iran-Iraq war or the use of Danish freighters later in that war and in the Caribbean; and
— rapid completion of transfers, rarely taking more than a few months in contrast to the years

and decades typical of orthodox transactions.

It also should be kept in mind that gray methods are typical of the birth of a new relationship. Over time, successful gray transfers tend to yield to orthodox government-to-government transactions. While the advantages of gray methods are highly persuasive in the experimental phase of a new arms relationships, over time the burdens become harder to bear. The great inconvenience of covert methods, the military complexity of nonstandard equipment, the lack of control that comes with reliance on intermediaries, the high costs of awkward shipping and financial arrangements, and the need for follow-on support are characteristics that push suppliers and clients toward greater openness. Even in those cases where both sides probably would prefer to continue covert cooperation, such as when a state is arming a foreign insurgency or terrorist group, both sides are likely to appreciate that secrecy cannot be fully maintained over time and they prepare for more open arrangements.

These characteristics, of course, are ideal. In practice, reliance on gray market transactions is no guarantee of success or confidentiality. As the veterans of the 1985-86 Iran-contra deals discovered, nothing can save a fundamentally misconceived deal. Even better-prepared arrangements can collapse if accidentally exposed; an example is the Israeli shipments to revolutionary Iran, which were revealed after their chartered Argentine air transport crashed on Soviet soil.

CONTAINING THE BLACK AND GRAY MARKETS

The black market cannot be eliminated so long as its motives exist. As arms embargoes gain popularity as an easily implemented and relatively painless international response to conflict, new opportunities for the black market are certain to be created. It is equally clear, however, that the black market is ever changing and evolving, rising and falling in response to the conditions that make its risks and uncertainties appealing. As a reaction to specific conditions, the black market can be tamed even if it cannot be eliminated.

Tighter national laws and better enforcement already appear to have raised the dangers of black transactions and constrained the freedom to conduct them. Enforcing embargoes through the widest possible U.N. consensus makes them stronger than working through smaller ad hoc groups. The results of these tendencies are increasingly clear. While the chaos created by the collapse of the Soviet Union and Yugoslavia offers enormous new chances for illegal weapons dealers, there is no evidence of a corresponding growth in the black market. Although illegal arms are being caught on the periphery of all these trouble spots and doubtlessly other shipments are getting through, there is no reason to believe that the quantities begin to approach those seen in the Iran-Iraq war of the 1980s.

The difficulties of the gray market are more intractable. The gray market remains as important as ever, allowing states to experiment with new foreign policies and diplomatic arrangements. To eliminate the gray market would require universal acceptance of the political status quo, the end of international politics. Short of world government or a powerful system of collective security, states will continue to find the appeal of the gray market to be irresistible.

One measure to minimize the black market and the worst side effects of the gray market would be to make the U.N. Arms Register far more rigorous than it is today. Based on a weak U.N. consensus, the existing register is an anemic tool that fails even to cover all orthodox government-to-government transfers. Its reporting thresholds are too high to include all major weapons; the questions of production technologies and weapons of mass destruction are allowed no more than gentle debate.

Radical extension of the U.N. register is necessary to bring much of the gray trade into the open, to expose the largest black deals, and to clarify legally licensed from illicit transactions. Instead of tinkering with existing reporting thresholds, searching only for the highest acceptable reporting levels, the United Nations should bring the thresholds down to the lowest levels feasible. With minimal verification, relying primarily on the cooperation of existing customs authorities, it should be possible to include all transactions of military equipment worth at least $100,000. At this level, the U.N. Arms Register would become a serious force inhibiting questionable arms transfers.

If collective security mechanisms cannot be established in the foreseeable future, other international instruments will be needed to head off the black market. If the black market is a direct and inevitable reaction to embargoes, its elimination will be possible only when groups fearing for their survival feel confident that they can turn to legitimate sources for assistance.

The international community must learn to recognize that blanket embargoes do not always serve its interests. The cases of seemingly popular and just rebellions such as those of Eritrea, East Timor, and Bosnia have raised just this issue. Ironically, in such cases, the best alternative to the black market may lie in recognition that embargoes do not always serve our best interests.

ANNALS, *AAPSS*, **535**, September 1994

Main Directions of Research in the Arms Trade

By CHRISTIAN CATRINA

ABSTRACT: Research in arms transfers over the past decades has greatly increased our knowledge, but in a somewhat uneven fashion. With the end of the Cold War, arms transfers take place in a new international system. It appears that the most useful research at this stage—and given the limitations on the quantitative information available—should involve factual description of the different stages of arms transfers, the parties, their interests, the legal aspects, and the mechanics of arms transfers; harder information on the economic aspects of arms transfers, including the effects of offsets, of transfer of technology, and of joint development and production; identification of general trends and of characteristics relevant to more general concepts; and elaboration of ways and means to bring arms transfers under better national and international control. Perhaps most important, researchers should show detachment, devoting their efforts more to establishing facts than to presenting opinions.

Dr. Christian Catrina is the deputy to the representative of the chief of the General Staff for Politico-Military Affairs in the Federal Military Department of Switzerland. Previously, he was a research associate at the United Nations Institute for Disarmament Research and a consultant to the United Nations group of governmental experts established to write the report Ways and Means of Promoting Transparency in the International Transfer of Conventional Arms.

THE accumulated results of the last thirty years of research in the trade of conventional arms are a rich harvest. The community of scientists dealing with this subject has been relatively small, and the interest in arms transfers[1] subject to cyclical swings, but this area has lost some of its mystique. Regular coverage, including systematic and statistical information, of arms transfers has been important in this regard, providing the basis for detailed research, including qualitative aspects and case studies.[2]

Research on the arms trade has at the same time benefited and suffered from the involvement of researchers with strong moral motivation—indeed, in some cases, indignation. The research has benefited because they played a major role in establishing the arms trade as an item on the research agenda and because their findings and opinions—sometimes not entirely separate from each other—sparked discussion and led to additional research, if only to disprove or corroborate their findings. The research has suffered because some of it has been marked by ideological preconceptions resulting in uneven coverage.

This article cannot give an exhaustive view of the research conducted so far.[3] Its main purpose is to address the question of which areas of arms transfers are most deserving of research, taking into account three considerations:

1. What appear to be the most important issues in arms transfers?
2. Where does the present body of knowledge show significant gaps?
3. Which issues are fit for conclusive research using the methods of the social sciences?

Tables 1 and 2 seek to lay out what appear to be the issues most deserving of research.

DEFINITIONS, FORMS, AND COMPONENTS OF ARMS TRANSFERS

Among the scientists in this field, there exists a rough understanding, but no clear agreement, about what constitutes arms and arms transfers. The simplest and least ambiguous case consists of lethal weapons being produced in one country and subsequently sold and physically transferred to another country. The picture gets more complicated

1. Here the terms "arms trade" and "arms transfers" are used synonymously. In a stricter usage, "arms trade" might be used for arms transfers conducted on essentially commercial terms, whereas "arms transfers" denotes all transfers of conventional arms regardless of the contractual conditions under which they take place. Transfers of weapons of mass destruction—nuclear, chemical, biological—are not covered by either term.

2. In this context, the following institutions merit a special acknowledgment: the U.S. Arms Control and Disarmament Agency, for its *World Military Expenditures and Arms Transfers*; the Stockholm International Peace Research Institute, for its seminal publication *Arms Transfers to the Third World* and its regular coverage in the *SIPRI Yearbook*; and the U.S. Congressional Research Service, for its *Trends in Conventional Arms Transfers to the Third World*.

3. The articles in the present volume give a good view of the different facets of research in arms transfers, even though they cannot, of course, review all past research.

TABLE 1

ISSUES RELATED TO THE GENERAL SETTING OF ARMS TRANSFERS

Definition, forms, and components of arms transfers
The structure of the international politicomilitary system
Quantitative information on the development, status, and trends in arms transfers
Supply and demand factors, international and domestic
The impact of technological development on arms transfers
Black and gray markets
Controlling and limiting arms transfers

— when the equipment transferred is designed for use by military forces but is not in itself lethal, or when equipment or goods transferred for use by the military are identical to goods supplied for civilian use, such as transportation equipment (trucks, ships, aircraft), petrol, oil, lubricants, foodstuffs, or medical supplies;

— when technology and components are supplied instead of completed systems, for example, in the case of licensed arms production or technology transfer in all its forms;

— when two countries engage in joint funding for research, development, and production for a weapons system or other system for military use;

— when control and ownership over arms are being transferred without crossing any border, as in the purchase of weapons for forces stationed abroad from the host country; and

— when arms are transferred from one country to another without change of control or ownership, as in the supply of weapons to forces stationed abroad from the home country.

The lack of an agreed definition of arms transfers, taking into account the different forms they may take and the different components they may include, is not the fault of the research community. But researchers should keep track of the evolving forms of arms transfers, as they did in the past, and indicate clearly to which forms their research findings refer.[4]

The definition of arms transfers is of particular importance in the context of systematic collection and publication of data. Two main sources of such data, the United States Arms Control and Disarmament Agency and the Stockholm International Peace Research Institute, have so far been applying quite different definitions, with the result that data from the two sources cannot be merged, and different people wanting to make different points choose their source—and, with it, the definition—arbitrarily.

4. The political and economic implications of different modes of transfers—for example, sales on commercial terms or military assistance, and straight transfers or transfer of technology—can be quite different.

TABLE 2

STAGES OF ARMS TRANSFERS AND RESEARCH DIRECTIONS

Stage	Subjects of Interest at the Current Time	Related Subjects External to Arms Transfers
Production	The economics of arms production	The conversion of military industries
	The situation of the former Soviet military-industrial complex	
	The development of arms production in the Third World	Spin-offs of the development of arms production
	Coproduction and joint development and production	
Marketing		
Evaluation, negotiation, and decision making	Case studies of suppliers and/or recipients	Decision making
	• Export regulations and administration	
	• Evaluation and decision making of recipients	
	• The impact of military doctrine	Military doctrine
	• Decision making on assembly, licensed production	
	• The role of middlemen and multinational corporations	
	• The link between arms transfers and the proliferation of weapons of mass destruction	
Financing	The economics of arms transfers	
	• Costs and benefits to suppliers and recipients	
	• The economics of offset arrangements	
	• The role of military assistance programs	Military assistance
Delivery	Current status of monitoring and control of arms exports	
Operational deployment	Permanent supplier-recipient links	
	• Arrangements for training	
	• Arrangements for maintenance	
	• Arrangements for the supply of spare parts	
	• Resupply in case of armed conflict	
Effects of arms transfers	The link of arms transfers with power, influence, and dependence	Power, influence, and dependence
	The military impact of arms transfers and dependence	
	The economic impact of arms transfers on suppliers and recipients	
Retransfers	Adherence to and enforcement of end-user commitments	The global military stratification

THE STRUCTURE OF
THE INTERNATIONAL
POLITICOMILITARY SYSTEM

The structure of the international system is a major determinant not only of the quantity of arms transfers but also of their main directions, the underlying motivations, and the ways in which they are conducted. It makes a major difference whether the international system is fragmented, bipolar, or unipolar. Few studies have in the past taken such a systemic approach, but those that did contributed profoundly to a better understanding of arms transfers, presenting the big picture.[5] As the structure has changed with the end of the Cold War, the dissolution of the Warsaw Treaty Organization, and the disintegration of the Soviet Union, there is a need for more of this kind of research.

The effect of change in the international system on arms transfers is complicated by the fact that arms are one of the relatively few competitive export goods of some of the states of the former Soviet Union, in particular the Russian Federation. The impression is spreading in Russia that the government has been too accommodating to Western interests—for example, by supporting Western positions in the U.N. Security Council regarding Iraq and Serbia/Montenegro—without getting the expected assistance and that important Russian political interests have been jeopardized needlessly in the process. It is not assured that the changed

5. An important study on this subject is Robert E. Harkavy, *The Arms Trade and International Systems* (Cambridge, MA: Ballinger, 1975).

international scene will not lead back to competition in arms exports between Russia and Western countries. There is therefore a need for future research to take particular account of the policies and practices of the Russian Federation.

Other actors with changing roles in international arms transfers include China, which has become more assertive, and the European Union, which may lead to stronger coordination, as well as cooperation, between France, the United Kingdom, Germany, and Italy, all of them important arms suppliers. Taken in conjunction with the continuing spread of arms production to Third World countries, the shifting international structure of arms transfers is a fertile subject of research.

QUANTITATIVE INFORMATION
ON THE DEVELOPMENT,
STATUS, AND TRENDS
IN ARMS TRANSFERS

The state of information on arms transfers has improved, but it is still far from satisfactory or even complete, and it is fraught with problems. This derives largely from the fact that arms transfers touch on three sensitive issues:

1. National security concerns of recipient states. Full disclosure could, at least in the view of recipient governments or armed forces, be detrimental to national security by giving away military secrets to a potential adversary.

2. Political concerns of recipient governments. In many recipient countries, complete information about the full costs of arms transfers,

including the costs of operation and maintenance, could fan controversy about arms purchases.

3. Commercial secrets of arms-producing companies. Full transparency of the financial conditions of arms transfers could lead to a kind of most-favored-nation debate in the sense that all future buyers would press for the most favorable conditions. On the other hand, full information could also undermine claims about the benefits of arms transfers to the national economy if it pointed to highly subsidized sales.

Authoritative and reliable information is often absent, and data on arms transfers are often just estimates. This refers, in particular, to the price of arms transfers. Information about the number and type of weapons transferred is more easily obtainable, but for some types of research, in particular the economic aspects for producers and recipients, it is insufficient. When estimates of dollar values for arms transfers are published, the methodology used makes it often difficult to relate them to other economic information, be it because some elements of arms transfers are omitted or because the value assigned to individual transfers appears artificial and arbitrary.

Systematically and consistently collected statistical information on arms transfers must continue to be published. This is a very laborious, perhaps not very exciting, but eminently important part of research. It is necessary for getting a comprehensive view of the importance of the subject in military and economic terms, and it allows for the tracing of

the main directions of the arms trade and changes therein. This is a task beyond the capabilities of single researchers. It is important that governmental institutions, such as the U.S. Arms Control and Disarmament Agency, and nongovernmental institutions, such as the Stockholm International Peace Research Institute, continue their work in this field. The register of conventional arms that the United Nations has established may complement these registers of longer standing since it provides information other than that provided by the Arms Control and Disarmament Agency and the Stockholm International Peace Research Institute, information officially acknowledged by states concerning their arms exports and imports. The existence of several sources of systematic information, independent of each other, is very useful—indeed, necessary. To facilitate the identification of trends over time, the registers should not change their rules too often, and if these must be changed to conform to changed realities, it should be ensured that the old and new data can be made compatible.

Some new developments, such as the introduction of the register of conventional arms, contribute to more complete information. But at the same time, there are tendencies in the opposite direction. The trend away from straight arms sales to more complex arrangements involving local assembly, licensed production, coproduction and other offsets, and the proliferation of arms production to countries less subject to political and media scrutiny renders it more difficult to obtain accurate and comprehensive information on arms transfers, especially their financial aspects.

SUPPLY AND DEMAND FACTORS, INTERNATIONAL AND DOMESTIC

Arms transfers often involve substantial amounts of economic and financial resources. Agreements are often concluded for deals worth several billion dollars. Arms transfers also touch directly on political and military matters. Hence strong push and pull factors are involved. The major push, or supply, factors include

— the economic interest of arms-producing companies in sales, in terms of profits, economies of scale, recouping of research and development expenditures, and employment;
— the interest of governments of supplier states in maintaining a viable base of arms production and technology, employment, and tax revenues; and
— the interest of governments in supporting allied or friendly states by increasing their military capabilities and getting some (usually rather intangible) measure of influence over recipient governments.

The major pull, or demand, factors include

— war, when arms are destroyed and the involved countries have the political power or economic wealth to get resupplies during the conflict or rebuild their forces after its termination;

— the interest of recipient governments in maintaining or increasing their states' military capabilities, as long as these are needed for safeguarding perceived national interests;
— the interest of recipient governments in creating or reinforcing friendly politicomilitary relationships with supplier countries by means of arms purchases; and
— the interest of governments in satisfying rival interests of different branches of armed forces (ground forces, air forces, navies).

THE IMPACT OF TECHNOLOGICAL DEVELOPMENT ON ARMS TRANSFERS

The direction and pace of the technological development of conventional arms can have a bearing on several aspects of arms transfers. In cases of major technological advances, the number of producers may shrink, leading to a more concentrated supply side or even to a temporary reluctance of producers to export the most modern technology. Very advanced technology may also surpass the abilities of some states to keep the systems operational without continued foreign assistance. Technological advance is associated with rises in cost. This increases the attraction of upgrades for existing new systems as a temporary alternative to the acquisition of costly newer arms, and it also makes the quantitative reduction of arsenals more attractive as buyers procure ever smaller fleets of more capable, but also more costly, weapons.

In the past, American researchers have shown a greater readiness than those from Europe and the Third World to address this aspect of arms transfers, reflecting, perhaps, a greater willingness to engage in technological and military questions and to take facts for what they are, regardless of ideological color. If research is to promote knowledge, this attitude should be promoted.

BLACK AND GRAY MARKETS

The black market is, in spite of its name, often regarded as the most colorful aspect of arms transfers, involving, as it does, illegal action against the laws of either the country of origin or the country of destination or both and, in cases of international embargoes, also the violation of international law. Much has been written about the black market in arms, most of it rather journalistic, sensational, and anecdotal. The numerous instances in which black market deals have been uncovered give an indication as to the prevailing modes of operation, the actors, and the interests involved. This allows a probably fairly accurate picture of the black market to be painted, but this is always overshadowed by the question of whether knowledge about what has remained black—that is, unknown— would force a major revision of this picture.[6] Research on the black mar-

ket has to rely to a large extent on logical deduction. An exemplary contribution that can serve as a model is Aaron Karp's article in the present volume.

The gray market is, on the supplier side, the domain of those few suppliers who employ arms exports as instruments of their foreign and security policy. If the black market is defined by the violation of national or international law, the gray market is characterized by action counter to stated policy and customary rules. Thus, while the former is illegal, the latter may often be regarded as illegitimate. The reason for engaging in the gray market, for conducting arms trade under the counter, is that open, above-the-counter transfers might raise political problems at home and abroad. This is hardly a tenable basis for a long-term policy, but it may be a method of choice for more delicate periods of policy reorientation. It is mainly this policy relevance that makes research in the gray market worthwhile. Investigative journalism, leading to the uncovering of gray arms transfers, should be left to the journalists; researchers can make a more valuable contribution in the analysis.

CONTROLLING AND
LIMITING ARMS TRANSFERS

To date, international law puts few restraints on the transfer of conven-

6. The United Nations General Assembly resolution requesting the study on "ways and means of promoting transparency in international transfers of conventional arms" (United Nations General Assembly Document A/RES/43/75), the original sponsors of which were Colombia and Italy, made specific reference to the "illicit arms trade," and one chapter of the study (Study on Ways and Means of Promoting Transparency in International Transfers of Conventional Arms, Report of the Secretary-General, United Nations General Assembly Document A/46/301, 9 Sept. 1991), dealt exclusively with this subject, even though it is hardly possible to introduce more transparency into the black market.

tional arms. Except for embargoes imposed by the U.N. Security Council and the provisions of peace treaties forbidding the acquisition of certain categories of weapons, there are no agreements that would directly limit the trade of conventional arms. But proposals to limit the arms trade by way of international agreement have a long tradition. They have in the past foundered on the lack of will for cooperation between arms producers that did not want to rob themselves of flexibility regarding what they consider an important instrument of foreign policy. They have also collapsed on the apprehension, by states with little or no arms production, that limitations on arms transfers would be discriminatory as long as they would not at the same time limit arms procurement from within the state.

Research has in the past served the purpose of describing the attitude of governments toward control or limitation of arms transfers, as well as negotiations undertaken to this end, the reasons why they failed, and the purpose of elaborating proposals for future control or limitation. In this way, the scientific community can and should stimulate official thinking. In doing so, it should lay out not only what should be achieved but also how it could be achieved in the real world.

/   ARMS PRODUCTION

Strictly speaking, arms production is a separate research area. However, an understanding of the essentials of the economics of arms production helps explain changes in the pressure for exports by the arms industries. Such an understanding should include empirically founded information on the benefits of arms transfers to producer companies and to states at different stages of arms projects, from the development stage to the end of the production run.

The main issues include the effect of an increase in the production run, due to arms exports, on recouping fixed costs (costs independent of the number of arms being produced), particularly the costs of research, development, and tooling. This is an area full of claims, with little hard evidence.[7] It must also be taken into consideration that late in the production run, producers may not charge the full share of fixed costs if that helps to sway customers. Another main issue is the effect of foreign orders on production costs. It is frequently being claimed, in support of proposed arms exports, that foreign orders serve to reduce unit costs by making possible economies of scale and other savings resulting from longer production runs, such as a gain in efficiency due to the learning curve of those engaged in manufacturing. Here again the claims are rarely substantiated with hard evi-

7. Notable exceptions providing some empirical findings are Keith Hartley, "The Political Economy of NATO Defense Procurement Policies," in *International Arms Procurement: New Directions*, ed. Martin Edmonds (New York: Pergamon Press, 1981), pp. 98-114; idem, *NATO Arms Co-operation: A Study in Economics and Politics* (London: George Allen & Unwin, 1983); Carl Groth, "The Economics of Weapons Coproduction," in *International Arms Procurement*, ed. Edmonds, pp. 71-83; Trevor Taylor, "Research Note: British Arms Exports and R&D Costs," *Survival*, 22(6):259-62 (1980).

dence, and the findings from one particular project are not necessarily applicable to another. Economies of scale and gains in efficiency by learning are well covered in economics, but are yet to be applied convincingly to arms production and transfers.

When several states and companies in the same states undertake a joint project to research, develop, and produce arms, the picture gets even more complicated, due to the multitude of engaged parties and the difficulties of determining the relative costs and benefits, compared to the alternatives of purchasing arms abroad or starting a national project. Joint projects have their peculiarities in terms of technical characteristics (the tendency is to make the systems more complex in an effort to meet differing national requirements), economics (development and production by a number of companies is usually more expensive than by one company), and politics (the participating countries may have different arms export laws).

Insight into the economics of arms production, which may necessitate close contact of the researchers with these industries, is also a prerequisite for fruitful research into the potential for conversion of military industries to civilian production.

Pure economics is particularly relevant for an analysis of arms production in Western, market-economy countries, but even here economic explanations have their limits, as the state intervenes in various ways, by giving contracts, by bailing out companies at the brink of failure, by helping to promote arms sales abroad, or by vetoing envisaged transfers for po-litical reasons. Research into arms production and its link to arms transfers cannot afford to neglect these factors external to economics. This is even more true for arms production in states that have had, or still have, centrally planned economies.

EVALUATION, NEGOTIATION, AND DECISION MAKING

Except for a few case studies, the decision-making process leading to the conclusion of arms transfer agreements has not been given much attention.[8] Given the economic and political importance of major arms transfers, this is an area in which the key players are reluctant to part with information. Neither winners nor losers of the battle for a contract are eager to go beyond self-serving accounts. This field involves, moreover, a particularly wide variety of aspects, including military, political, and economic aspects.

From the military viewpoint, a supplier might consider whether an envisaged arms transfer presents military risks, such as a loss of priority of the producer states' own armed forces or the risk of compromising advanced technology. A recipient needs to evaluate which arms fit its military requirements in terms of doctrine, threat environment, and terrain. Politically, a supplier needs to determine whether it is likely that a prospective arms transfer will solidify the links with the recipient and provide some influence and whether

---

8. A particularly good example of a case study that does pay attention to this process is Ingemar Dörfer, *Arms Deal: The Selling of the F-16* (New York: Praeger, 1983).

it will be conducive to regional stability. A recipient will consider which suppliers to give preference to on political grounds, for example, because they are members of the same alliance or have offered political support. In terms of economics, a supplier will analyze the impact of an envisaged transfer on the balance of payments, on employment, and on the viability of its arms industries. A recipient will try to structure the transfer so as to minimize adverse economic effects. It will consider the kind of offset arrangements being offered.

Ideally, the researcher should also have a technical understanding, in order to be able to assess whether the evaluation of different weapons systems was conducted equitably and whether the choice was based on technical merits. At the same time, the researcher should have access to the technical specialists and political decision makers who are involved.

PRICING AND FINANCING

The pricing of weapons systems and the packages put together to finance arms transfers are often surrounded by confusion, especially regarding arms transfers to states where the legislative branch does not discuss, much less take a decision on, the proposed deal—or at least not in public session. The pricing of a particular weapons system can appear inconsistent and arbitrary. The ambiguity stems, on the one hand, from the fact that different prices correspond to different things; for example, for aircraft, the fly-away price does not include the associated infrastructure, but the system price does.

On the other hand, different prices may be asked at different times in the production run, due to the write-off of fixed costs and the benefits of an extension of the production run. These differences result in a slanted presentation.

The credit packages put together to finance arms transfers present another difficult field of research that can be quite complex, touching on the involvement of commercial banks, military assistance programs, export credit guarantees by the state, and the intricacies of offset arrangements, that is, arrangements intended to reduce the net capital outflow for the buyer state. Offset arrangements include, for example, commitments by the supplier company to procure contracts for the buyer state's economy amounting to a fixed percentage of the costs of the transfer or agreements to accept part of the price in commodities.

DELIVERY

Since the export of arms is an exercise in foreign policy, states usually try to monitor and control it. The relevant laws, prescribing what conditions have to be met to issue an export license, are, in the final count, only as good as the monitoring and control of the actual exportation of weapons. Full monitoring and control are necessary for the proper exercise by the state of its authority; they are also a prerequisite for the accuracy and usefulness of official information on arms transfers. Research can be directed toward the identification of loopholes and shortcomings in monitoring and control and toward proposals for their improvement.

OPERATIONAL DEPLOYMENT

The back end of arms transfers—what needs to be done so that the recipient country can deploy the arms operationally and keep them operational—is a comparatively neglected field of research in arms transfers.[9] This is not entirely the researchers' fault, however, since military secrecy is involved. Nevertheless, some information is available, mainly in professional journals. Research should go beyond the mere description of the difficulties and bottlenecks. In particular, it should focus on the following questions:

1. What infrastructure—for example, airfields, hangars, maintenance facilities—needs to be built to accommodate arms procured from abroad?

2. In which way does the recipient country or, more particularly, its armed forces acquire the necessary knowledge for operation and maintenance of the weapons?

3. To what extent and in which ways does the recipient state have to rely permanently on services by the producer company, or other foreign companies or states, for the maintenance of the weapons?

4. How is the supply of spare parts organized? To what extent can the recipient produce them in the case of,

for example, licensed production; what is the size of stocks in the recipient country; and how long would they last for peacetime operations and in case of war?

This kind of information is relevant if the dependence of recipient countries on supplier countries or companies is to be assessed, specifically, the dependence that continues after a transfer has taken place.

The resupply of weapons to a recipient engaged in armed conflict is a fruitful field of research because it provides links to several important aspects both internal to and external to arms transfers proper. Recipient dependence is never as high as when resupply of weapons is needed to stave off military defeat. Correspondingly, the power and influence of suppliers should be at a peak in this situation, and so should the temptation for the recipient to tap the black market, too.

EFFECTS OF
ARMS TRANSFERS

The link between arms transfers, the power and influence of the supplier, and the dependence of the recipient has received much attention by the research community,[10] albeit without results that could be generalized beyond the identification of what appear as the most important factors determining the extent of

9. Geoffrey Kemp, "Arms Transfers and the 'Back-End' Problem in Developing Countries," *Arms Transfers in the Modern World*, ed. Stephanie G. Neuman and Robert E. Harkavy (New York: Praeger, 1979), pp. 264-75.

10. See, for example, Christopher C. Shoemaker and John Spanier, *Patron-Client State Relationships: Multilateral Crises in the Nuclear Age* (New York: Praeger, 1984); Lewis W. Snider, "Arms Transfers and Recipient Cooperation with Supplier Policy Preferences," *International Interactions*, 5(2-3):241-66 (1978).

such influence and dependence.[11] It is usually assumed that recipient governments, especially those perceiving a military threat and having no substantial arms production capability of their own, are likely to come under some influence by their major arms suppliers and even more so if they have only one major supplier. However, the search for empirical evidence of such an effect has so far proven difficult and less than wholly conclusive, for several reasons:

1. Only the governments of major supplier countries—the United States, Russia, China, France, and the United Kingdom—have the capability to exert influence. Smaller arms suppliers are hardly sufficiently important to establish a strong base of influence.

2. Governments of supplier states are on the whole reluctant to exert influence, except when important issues are at stake, because a vigorous attempt at influencing a recipient state's government can damage the relationship and is in fact even likely to do so.

3. Influence is more likely to be successful when exerted in silent diplomacy. Heavy-handed exertion of influence is likely to provoke the recipient government to put up resistance, so as not to appear to be a compliant instrument of the supplier government.

11. See Christian Catrina, *Arms Transfers and Dependence* (New York: Taylor & Francis, 1988), in which these factors are dealt with systematically and previous studies on this subject are discussed.

4. A recipient government may adapt its policies to the interests of important supplier states at a very early stage, either before direct influence is brought to bear or at an early point in the process.

Thus the link between supplier influence and recipient behavior is usually elusive, in particular if the researcher is looking for corresponding actions, namely, the clear exertion of influence or even pressure and a recipient behavior unambiguously linked to it. The absence of empirical evidence, however, cannot be taken to imply that there is no causal link between influence and compliance. Rather, it calls for different ways of research, a more narrative approach based on interviews with people directly involved.

The military impact of arms transfers is more difficult to assess than often imagined. As long as the arms are not being used—which is the best outcome for the supplier, the recipient, and the international community—it is difficult to make any judgment on the ability of the recipient to use them in combat. There are recipients unable to ensure the proper maintenance and servicing of the arms or unable to fit them into military planning and doctrine. The fact that arms are not being used in combat does not mean that they have had no military impact, since the increase in military capabilities by a country feeling threatened may have had the desired deterrent effect. This is, in fact, the most preferable outcome. But it presents researchers again with the formidable difficulties of anticipated reactions, the question of what would have happened if an attack had occurred in the absence of a strengthening of the recipient state's military capabilities.

Another issue is the economic effects of arms transfers. A whole literature has been devoted to arguing and proving that arms purchases are economically detrimental to the buyers. This is, of course, the case. Offsets and expected spin-offs for industrial and technological development, when some measure of transfer of technology is involved, can mitigate but not eliminate the economic burden to recipients. What tends to be forgotten—or, if not forgotten, omitted—is the rather trivial fact that arms purchases are neither motivated by economic interests nor designed to stimulate the economy. Arms are procured to enhance security (if we leave aside, for an instant, subordinate reasons such as the need to pacify dissatisfied military officers), and they have to be justified not on economic grounds but on national security grounds. By procuring arms, governments demonstrate that they are willing to accept economic sacrifices for the sake of increased security. Researchers may well second-guess such a decision and point out that a country could have built a hundred hospitals had it not made a specific arms purchase. The fact is that the government, whether legitimately or not, has decided, after consideration of all interests, many of them diverging, that the money has been better invested by procuring arms. This is an area in which the intense and sincere emotional engagement of researchers has in the past been associated with an impressive absence of clear thinking.

As for the economic impact of arms exports on supplier states, one may tend to assume that it is, for the most part, positive. But here again details matter. If arms are provided on very favorable conditions—soft credits, discounted prices—or even free of cost as military assistance, such transfers may be of little economic benefit to the supplier state, perhaps just a straight economic loss, albeit one justified by political interests. On the whole, the economic benefits of arms sales to supplier states (as opposed to supplier companies) are probably exaggerated. Past research has at least raised doubts, and future research should be directed to a clear and comprehensive analysis of the real economic impact of arms transfers. In general, both the economic costs to recipients and the economic benefits to suppliers are probably more limited and certainly more complex than usually assumed.

RETRANSFERS

A somewhat peripheral aspect of arms transfers are retransfers, that is, transfers of weapons acquired by a first recipient to a second recipient. Politically interesting are the motives for such retransfers; examples of motives include support for a friendly state in need, and the obsolescence of the weapons for the purposes of the first recipient but not for a second recipient in a region with a lower degree of armament.

Also of political interest is the question of whether the legal requirements for retransfers are observed or whether their violation goes unpunished. The majority of the major arms-exporting states usually stipulate, as a legally binding condition, that retransfers are subject to their consent.

There has been little research on retransfers so far, and military secrecy poses major obstacles. Additional information on retransfers, the reasons for them, and the reaction by the original suppliers should fill this gap.

METHODOLOGY

Quantitative information on arms transfers is often accompanied by the caveat that the figures given are estimates. The methodology of estimation is in most cases not indicated. The data should often be used only as a device to measure trends, and systematic comparison of these data with economic information is discouraged. This is a pitiful state of affairs for the application of sophisticated quantitative methods. Researchers sometimes apply them, nevertheless, in the hope that the preconditions for their application are not too heavily violated. This practice appears questionable.

Most research is methodologically less ambitious but closer to the subject. In a field as ramified and as affected by secrecy as arms transfers, an objective description without high theoretical ambitions is at this point still useful, particularly if based on hard information instead of on surmises and suspicion. General concepts, such as dependence, can provide direction. We should first estab-

lish what is going on: who does what in the pursuit of which interests and with what kind of consequences. This is the basis required for a successful search for underlying patterns.

CONCLUSION

It appears that the most useful research at this stage—and given the limitations of the quantitative information available—should involve

— factual description of the different stages of arms transfers, the parties, their interests, the legal aspects, and the mechanics of arms transfers;
— harder information on the economic aspects of arms transfers, including the effects of offsets, of transfer of technology, and of joint development and production;
— identification of general trends, and of characteristics—variables—relevant to more general concepts, such as what the important factors for dependence are; and
— elaboration of ways and means to bring arms transfers under better national and international control.

Perhaps most important, researchers should show more detachment, devoting their efforts more to establishing facts than to presenting opinions. The impression has been, over the past decades, that many researchers have had an ax to grind. Those who took such an approach did not have the necessary credibility to have their findings accepted beyond the ranks of those who shared their opinions in the first place. Precisely because arms transfers are eminently political, research must, in order to be taken seriously and have an impact, avoid any impression of being politicized. As in other areas of research, the choice of the subject of research may be, and often is, motivated by value judgments, but the execution of research should be as objective and impartial as possible.

Report of the Board of Directors to the Members of the American Academy of Political and Social Science for the Year 1993

MEMBERSHIPS AND SUBSCRIPTIONS
AS OF DECEMBER 31

Year	Number
1983	8,904
1984	6,564
1985	5,704
1986	5,606
1987	5,151
1988	4,674
1989	4,903
1990	3,932
1991	4,378
1992	3,088
1993	3,243

PUBLICATIONS
NUMBER OF VOLUMES OF *THE ANNALS* PRINTED (6 PER YEAR)

1983	68,236
1984	52,154
1985	52,800
1986	53,201
1987	43,629
1988	53,497
1989	40,269
1990	39,000
1991	37,246
1992	34,900
1993	31,000

FINANCES
SIZE OF SECURITIES PORTFOLIO
MARKET VALUE AS OF DECEMBER 31

1983	485,809
1984	384,312
1985	369,389
1986	373,320
1987	387,997
1988	345,634
1989	284,732
1990	139,451
1991	164,537
1992	150,560
1993	161,117

NUMBER OF VOLUMES OF *THE ANNALS* SOLD
(IN ADDITION TO MEMBERSHIPS AND SUBSCRIPTIONS)

1983	5,877
1984	5,230
1985	5,910
1986	5,119
1987	5,314
1988	13,283
1989	4,802
1990	5,005
1991	3,766
1992	3,681
1993	3,538

STATEMENT OF INCOME AND RETAINED EARNINGS FOR THE YEAR ENDED DECEMBER 31, 1993

Income
Royalty—Sage Publications	$140,000
Sales of review books	1,927
Royalties and reprint permissions	2,503
Miscellaneous	12,175
Total Income	156,605

Operating Expenses
Salaries	86,880
Payroll taxes	8,183
Pension expense	10,423
Employee benefits	4,731
Depreciation	10,643
Insurance	8,827
Postage	2,622
Repairs and maintenance	6,872
Professional and contracted services	11,509
Book review costs	4,260

```
Office expense  . . . . . . . . . . . . . . . . . . . . . . . . . . . . . 5,387
Utilities . . . . . . . . . . . . . . . . . . . . . . . . . . . . . . . . 11,344
Miscellaneous  . . . . . . . . . . . . . . . . . . . . . . . . . . . . . 6,447
        Total Operating Expenses  . . . . . . . . . . . . . . . . . . . 178,130
        Loss from Operations . . . . . . . . . . . . . . . . . . . . . . (21,525)
Other Income (Expenses)
    Investment income (net) . . . . . . . . . . . . . . . . . . . . . . . 8,650
        Net Income (Loss)  . . . . . . . . . . . . . . . . . . . . . . . (12,875)
        Retained Earnings—January 1  . . . . . . . . . . . . . . . . . . 84,597
        Retained Earnings—December 31 . . . . . . . . . . . . . . . . . . 71,727
```

Report of the Board of Directors

During 1993, the six volumes of THE ANNALS dealt with the following subjects:

January   *White-Collar Crime*, edited by Gilbert Geis, Professor Emeritus, and Paul Jesilow, Assistant Professor, University of California, Irvine

March   *Free Trade in the Western Hemisphere*, edited by Sidney Weintraub, Dean Rusk Professor, Lyndon B. Johnson School of Public Affairs, University of Texas at Austin, and Distinguished Visiting Scholar, Americas Program of the Center for Strategic and International Studies, Washington, D.C.

May   *Religion in the Nineties*, edited by Wade Clark Roof, J. F. Rowny Professor of Religion and Society, University of California at Santa Barbara

July   *Citizens, Protest, and Democracy*, edited by Russell J. Dalton, Professor of Political Science and Chair of the Department of Politics and Society, University of California, Irvine

September   *Rural America: Blueprint for Tomorrow*, edited by William E. Gahr, Associate Director, Food and Agriculture Issues, U.S. General Accounting Office, Washington, D.C.

November   *Interminority Affairs in the U.S.: Pluralism at the Crossroads*, edited by Peter I. Rose, Sophia Smith Professor and Director of the American Studies Diploma Program, Smith College, Northampton, Massachusetts

The publication program for 1994 includes the following volumes:

January   *The European Community: To Maastricht and Beyond*, edited by Pierre-Henri Laurent, Professor, Tufts University, Medford, Massachusetts

March   *Foreign Language Policy: An Agenda for Change*, edited by Richard D. Lambert, Director Emeritus, National Foreign Language Center, Johns Hopkins University, Washington, D.C.

May   *Trends in U.S.-Caribbean Relations*, edited by Anthony P. Maingot, Professor, Florida International University, Miami

July   *Strategies for Immigration Control: An International Comparison*, edited by Mark J. Miller, Professor, University of Delaware, Newark

September   *The Arms Trade: Problems and Prospects in the Post-Cold War World*, edited by Robert E. Harkavy, Professor, Pennsylvania State University, University Park, and Stephanie G. Neuman, Senior Research Scholar and Adjunct Professor, Columbia University, New York City

November   *Employee Dismissal: Justice at Work*, edited by Stuart Henry, Professor, Eastern Michigan University, Ypsilanti

During 1993, the Book Department published over 210 reviews. The majority of these were written by professors, but reviewers also included university presidents, members of private and university-sponsored organizations, government and public officials, and business professionals. Over 500 books were listed in the Other Books section.

One hundred and ten requests were granted to reprint material from THE ANNALS. These went to professors and other authors for use in books in preparation and to nonprofit organizations for educational purposes.

OFFICERS AND STAFF

The Board reelected the following officers: Marvin E. Wolfgang, President; Richard D. Lambert, Vice President; Anthony J. Scirica, Secretary; Elmer B. Staats, Treasurer;

Henry W. Sawyer, III, Counsel. Reappointed were: Richard D. Lambert, Editor, and Alan W. Heston, Associate Editor.

Respectfully submitted,
THE BOARD OF DIRECTORS

Elmer B. Staats
Marvin E. Wolfgang
Richard D. Lambert
Lloyd N. Cutler
Henry W. Sawyer, III
Anthony J. Scirica
Frederick Heldring
Lynn Curtis
Mary Ann Meyers
Sara Miller McCune

Philadelphia, Pennsylvania
19 November 1993

Book Department

INTERNATIONAL RELATIONS AND POLITICS

KAEMPFER, WILLIAM H. and ANTON D. LOWENBERG. *International Economic Sanctions: A Public Choice Perspective.* Pp. xiv, 189. Boulder, CO: Westview Press, 1992. $44.00.

In *International Economic Sanctions: A Public Choice Perspective*, William Kaempfer and Anton Lowenberg use the powerful tools of public choice analysis to address puzzles raised by the use of economic sanctions across national borders. Conventional wisdom holds that sanctions have limited impact on the policies of target states. Yet, states continue to use sanctions, and, in fact, the United States is turning to them more frequently than ever before. Kaempfer and Lowenberg suggest that this puzzle, as well as other anomalous characteristics of sanctions episodes, can be understood if we consider the interests of domestic economic groups in the sending and target states.

Kaempfer and Lowenberg rely on the assumption of rational action by self-interested economic actors and the formal techniques common to public choice analysis. Their suggestion that the economic interests of concentrated groups need to be taken into account when analyzing the dynamics of economic sanctions constitutes a genuine theoretical advance. For Kaempfer and Lowenberg, the use of economic sanctions is not an attempt to pursue the national interest, nor is it primarily aimed at gaining policy change in the target country. Instead, groups lobby for sanctions as a redistributive tool, much as they would lobby for protective tariffs or subsidies. Sanctions result when politically powerful interest groups determine that they could achieve a redistribution of wealth in their direction by convincing the government to impose sanctions. Effects on the target country are of no interest to these groups. In fact, sanctions may have analogous redistributive effects in the target country, working to the benefit of some concentrated interests there.

This approach illuminates a dimension of the sanctions problem that is in need of further rigorous analysis. Kaempfer and Lowenberg suggest that they can explain why sanctions continue to be used even if they lead to no policy change and why they are tailored so as to benefit domestic economic interests in the sending state rather than imposing maximum costs on the politically influential in the target state. But this analysis is surely only one part of a complex puzzle. Sanctions are highly inefficient as a redistributive tool, so that the pursuit of redistributive benefits cannot fully explain their use. Governments often act in a way that suggests that they care deeply about the political impact of sanctions, and they devote considerable effort to gaining international cooperation to impose them. Thus the public choice approach is probably best seen as explaining the domestic constraints on the use of sanctions, which governments consider using in the first place for other, more internationally derived, reasons.

LISA L. MARTIN
Harvard University
Cambridge
Massachusetts

TREVERTON, GREGORY F. *America and Germany and the Future of Europe.* Pp. xii, 240. Princeton, NJ: Princeton University Press, 1992. No price.

PETERSON, JOHN. *Europe and America in the 1990s: The Prospects for Partnership.* Pp. xiii, 267. Brookfield, VT: Edward Elgar, 1993. No price.

Gregory Treverton and John Peterson have each written balanced studies of the post-Communist world and the changing shape of relations between America and Europe. They each provide clear, useful discussions of the history of post-World War II international relations before moving to the present and the future.

Peterson's book is a textbook. Each chapter schematically examines an issue in U.S.-European relations—geopolitics, domestic policy, security needs—and then analyzes it in the light of four commonly used international relations theories: liberal trade theory, neorealism, interdependence, and reformism. Explication of these theories, their origins, and present status is clear enough for the average newspaper reader, though a photocopy of the list of abbreviations provided in the front of the book would save the reader much flipping back and forth when deciphering the alphabet soup of agencies and organizations to which the author constantly refers. Peterson uses parenthetical notes rather than standard footnotes, and students might be led to believe that the founders of liberal trade theory, Adam Smith and David Ricardo, wrote their seminal works in 1937 and 1911 because of the editions he consulted. There is no indication in the list of references that these editions are reprints from the late eighteenth and early nineteenth centuries. An expert reader would experience no confusion, but in a textbook, such ambiguity cannot be allowed.

Treverton's book is a more casual, even chatty, study of the possible future relationship between America and Germany. He designates Germany as the center around which Europe has revolved in the past and around which it will revolve in the future. That country is more powerful now, he argues, than it has been for a century. The loose framework he uses to image the future of this powerful state in its relations with its neighbors and America reaches back to the past. Will the future Europe resemble the "loose continental system" installed at the Congress of Vienna in 1815 or the Europe after 1871, when Germany was an ominously rising power? Treverton never presses these analogies too hard, since political conditions are so different now, but they serve to keep the reader's mind on the endlessly changing history of European relations.

Though each author acknowledges that things could change, they both see Europe moving toward greater unity, and America becoming less of a dominant force, as Europe works out its own ways to provide security for itself. Neither predicts the disappearance of the North Atlantic Treaty Organization (NATO), though Peterson sees it developing a closer relationship with the Western European Union, and Treverton says it remains a sensible precaution. However, the "decision-making structures" of NATO must change, according to Peterson. He says that "NATO can no longer operate on the basis of a U.S.-dominated linear command structure, as during the Cold War when NATO's purpose was to defend the German border." Treverton says that the presence of NATO troops in Europe can still be an important deterrent if conditions in Eastern Europe and Russia disintegrate, and their presence will serve to reassure Western Europe that Germany will not resurge as a danger.

Treverton sees America paying much less attention to Germany, and Europe, in the future. He does, however, hope for European and American cooperation in the wider world—on the environment, human rights, and the management of the world economy (though he admits that the latter would have to be trilateral and include Japan). Peterson, on the other hand, hopes for a true partnership between Europe and America that would also concentrate on global affairs and the construction of a New World Order. Nonetheless, he indicates that a true partnership can happen only if Europe becomes truly unified, and such unification, he says, "cannot be taken for granted."

Behind the generally optimistic predictions in both works lurks the possibility of rapid change that could rearrange relations between the United States and Europe. Ethnic wars in the former Soviet Union that might spill over into Eastern Europe preoccupy Treverton and underlie his wish for a continued NATO presence. Peterson is aware of the threat as well.

Each of these books would be an excellent companion for the student or reader interested in current affairs. Their clear analysis demystifies the current state of U.S.-European relations and provides a solid background as the future unwinds.

MARY BETH EMMERICHS

University of Wisconsin
Milwaukee

VAN CREVELD, MARTIN. *Nuclear Proliferation and the Future of Conflict.* Pp. viii, 180. New York: Free Press, 1993. $22.95.

Many observers of the international scene do not believe that the end of the Cold War and the breakup of the Soviet Union, once considered expansionist, have improved the prospects for a peaceful world. They are concerned that, as a result of nuclear proliferation, more countries will acquire nuclear weapons, a most serious development in the case of Third World countries. It is feared that leaders of those countries will be less restrained in using weapons of mass destruction than the political leaderships of the former Soviet Union, the People's Republic of China, and the United States and its nuclear allies. Martin van Creveld rejects the notion that nuclear weapons in Third World countries have a destabilizing effect in contrast to their alleged stabilizing influence in the developed world. He is convinced that the leaders of Third World countries understand the nature and implications of nuclear weapons and "tend to act at least as carefully in handling nuclear weapons as [do the leaders] of the superpowers." These Third World leaders are also aware of various disincentives related to using weapons of mass destruction. Van Creveld, therefore, concludes that the "fear of the consequences of nuclear proliferation has been greatly exaggerated all along."

The author believes that his extensive analysis of nuclear developments in Asia (China, India, and Pakistan) and in the Middle East (Israel, Egypt, Syria, and Iraq) support that conclusion, and he maintains that future conflicts will not resemble pre-1945 warfare, characterized by large armies facing each other in combat. He asserts that the very nature of war has changed as a result of the existence of thermonuclear weapons and that the state monopoly of the use of violence as an instrument of foreign policy—that is, the conduct of large-scale wars—is no longer suited to achieve foreign policy objectives because of the fear of escalation to a full-scale nuclear war. It is difficult to reconcile this view with the fact that quite a number of wars have taken place since 1945 in which countries employed large armies in spite of the existence of weapons of mass destruction.

Van Creveld also draws the conclusion that the fear of nuclear escalation led to the development of tactical nuclear weapons as an alternative to the strategic nuclear forces.

The American nuclear strategy of limited war was based on the operational principle of flexible response. In contrast to the U.S. strategic doctrine, the Soviet Union did not believe that nuclear weapons demanded basic changes of Moscow's military strategy and consequently integrated them into their normal Order of Battle. The Soviet leadership was convinced that any major violent conflict with the United States would escalate to a nuclear exchange.

The nuclear stalemate between the superpowers led eventually to the transformation of the nuclear war-fighting strategy to the strategy of deterrence, and military operation changed to posturing. "The price of peace consisted of enormous expenditures, consistent vigilance, and some tense moments; ultimately that peace held."

According to van Creveld, the disappearance of large-scale warfare had a marked impact upon the role of the state and the very nature of its armed forces. Groups and organizations of greatly varying size became the actors. Some of them, like the Palestine Liberation Organization, are relatively independent, while others, like Hizbollah, are state sponsored. Armies, deprived of their original function, are gradually transformed into police forces, trying to prevent groups and organizations inside their national territories from carrying out provocative acts that might lead to confrontation between states. Nuclear weapons and most other types of heavy modern weapons are of no value in these low-intensity conflicts, which van Creveld characterizes as "the sound tactician's response to nuclear proliferation: If one cannot beat one's enemy in a straightforward contest, one should seek to undermine him." Real or imaginary suppression of ethnic groups in many parts of the world, including the territory of the former Soviet Union, has led to violent fighting with no end in sight.

Van Creveld has succeeded in his effort to provide a better understanding of complex issues. His knowledge of English, Hebrew, Arabic, and Urdu made it possible for him to make use of a wide spectrum of source material. A comprehensive bibliography provides the reader with references for further study of the subject under consideration.

ERIC WALDMAN

University of Calgary
Alberta
Canada

AFRICA, ASIA, AND LATIN AMERICA

BERGER, ELMER. *Peace for Palestine: First Lost Opportunity*. Pp. xv, 287. Gainesville: University Press of Florida, 1993. $39.95.

ASHKENAZI, ABRAHAM. *Palestinian Identities and Preferences: Israel's and Jerusalem's Arabs*. Pp. x, 208. New York: Praeger, 1992. $45.00.

These two books analyze different aspects of the Arab-Israeli dispute. Elmer Berger, longtime president of American Jewish Alternatives to Zionism, Inc., draws on Israeli archives to provide a new account of the negotiations that led to the 1948 armistices between Israel and the Arab states. Abraham Ashkenazi, professor at the Free University of Berlin and the Hebrew University of Jerusalem, presents a study of the attitudes of Israeli and Jerusalem Arabs based primarily on survey research.

In *Peace for Palestine*, Berger makes a genuine effort to write a scholarly, detached diplomatic history despite his career as a critic of Israel and Zionism. His use of recently declassified material from Israeli archives as well as published documents forces students of the period to take his work seriously. Nonetheless, he presents a circular argument, contending that the documents reveal that Zionist aggressiveness prevented a genuine settlement in 1948, if those records are evaluated in the light of Zionist aggressiveness. Despite his detachment, Berger's anti-Zionist commitment leads him to leave much of his case unproven. His notes refer the reader to Simha Flapan's *Birth of Israel: Myths and Realities* and other works for essential components of his argument. His readers must thus accept, at second hand, the assertion that the Irgun and the Stern Gang were effectively controlled by the Hagana and that the massacre in Deir Yassin was a delib-

erate act of Israeli policy, in order to embrace Berger's main thrust. These issues are not Berger's subject, but they are prerequisites for his point.

The impact of Berger's findings will depend entirely upon his readers. To a naive Zionist, the notion that Israeli negotiators did not seek immediate peace at any cost, sought to preempt diplomatic processes by establishing facts on the ground, employed contradictory arguments in different circumstances, sought to hold territory not assigned to Israel in the partition plan, and did not slavishly obey United Nations resolutions may come as a shocking revelation. For me, however, it is difficult to regard this demonstration that the new Israel acted like a state rather than a band of saints as an epiphany.

As Don Peretz states in his brief introduction, Berger's work deserves attention as serious scholarship. It is not, however, above reproach on scholarly grounds. For example, he repeatedly refers to the 1919 Zionist Organization memorandum to explain Israeli behavior three decades later without showing that anyone referred to the document in 1948. More generally, one must question whether Berger's sources or his preconceptions determined his findings.

Ashkenazi, who has written on nationalism as a historian as well as a sociologist, analyzes Israeli Arab and Jerusalem Arab societies, working in the universe defined by the studies of Ian Lustick and Sammy Smooha. His work depends primarily on opinion surveys of Jerusalem Arabs, with most polling and interviews conducted between 1987 and 1990. His preliminary chapters, including an extremely interesting discussion of the structure of ethnic conflict, provide context for the opinion research. The early chapters demonstrate Ashkenazi's broad insights into nationalism in general and the divisions between Palestinians. These chapters are more satisfying to the reader than the core of the book, but this is not Ashkenazi's fault. The opinion surveys reveal such extreme fractionation among Jerusalem Arabs that any analyst would be hard put to draw clear conclusions. There is indeed only one, that the vast majority of Jerusalem Arabs are Palestinian nationalists, for whom a Palestinian state matters more than their religions or economic well-being. The extraordinary detail of Ashkenazi's research may lose general readers, but it offers much useful material for specialists on Jerusalem.

DOUGLAS E. STREUSAND

North Potomac
Maryland

NAFZIGER, E. WAYNE. *The Debt Crisis in Africa.* Pp. xxiv, 287. Baltimore, MD: Johns Hopkins University Press, 1993. $38.50.

SARRIS, ALEXANDER H. and ROGIER VAN DEN BRINIC. *Economic Policy and Household Welfare during Crisis and Adjustment in Tanzania.* Pp. xvi, 215. New York: New York University Press, 1993. $35.00.

Scholars have engaged in a lively debate on the effects of the structural adjustment policy of the International Monetary Fund (IMF) and World Bank (WB) concerning national economies. The volumes by Nafziger and by Sarris and Van Den Brinic continue that debate, each coming to a different conclusion.

Nafziger presents a fundamental critique of WB and IMF policies, arguing that these policies have exacerbated the decline in economic welfare. Blame for the situation is shared with African elites who continuously subordinate national interests to the needs of the international capitalist system; they have misused borrowed resources, invested in projects with low rates of return, and kept overvalued exchange rates.

Nafziger is at his best in the presentation of the debt crisis, critiques of the WB and IMF policies from different theoretical perspectives, and his discussion of alternative plans for alleviating the conditions, such as the Baker and Brady plans, debt rescheduling, debt-equity swaps, and so on. Nafziger is weakest in the case studies. By comparing the experience of so many countries—Nigeria, Côte d'Ivoire, Zaire, Zambia, Senegal, and Ghana—he offers necessarily only a broad-brush overview. Only in the case of Ghana does he find that stabilization policies have led to an economic turnaround.

Where Nafziger generalizes, Sarris and Van Den Brinic examine the specifics of the Tanzanian case, concluding that during that country's adjustment period, the only groups to experience real income decline were the rural middle-income and richer households and the urban rich. Contrary to the studies of many IMF critics, these authors find that the rural and urban poor have hardly been affected. While poverty may have been greater than reported, there has been a relatively equitable distribution of income.

The strength of the Sarris and Van Den Brinic volume is in the meticulous attention to statistics. Using excellent household budget surveys from several time periods and calculations from the Bank of Tanzania, the authors profile income across classes and geographic location, consumption patterns, as well as the performance of the agricultural sector. In addition to providing a rich examination of the implications of the data, Sarris and Van Den Brinic suggest innovative ways to reexamine data, including ways to measure household incomes and different measures of the second economy. Thus the book can be read at two levels:

as an example of technical economic research at its best and as an empirical examination of the effects of changes in macroeconomic policies.

Together, these books suggest that the debate over the effects of IMF and WB policies will remain a contentious one in the years ahead.

KAREN MINGST

University of Kentucky
Lexington

EUROPE

SCHWARZ, L. D. *London in the Age of Industrialisation: Entrepreneurs, Labour Force and Living Conditions, 1700-1850.* Pp. xv, 285. Cambridge: Cambridge University Press, 1992. $54.95.

Based on an impressive array of statistical evidence, L. D. Schwarz's *London in the Age of Industrialisation* is an essential supplement to the two classic studies of London in this period, Dorothy George's *London Life in the Eighteenth Century* and George Rude's *Hanoverian London.* Those classic histories are broader and, along with social histories like Earle's *Making of the English Middle Class* or Linebaugh's *London Hanged,* still provide a feeling for the experience of life in the metropolis that is largely lacking in Schwarz's often dry study. But no other work matches Schwarz's thorough anatomization of London's changing economy, demography, and living standards.

London in the Age of Industrialisation is in part revisionist. Where George pictured an era of steady improvement, Schwarz sees a more complex pattern. The second quarters of both the eighteenth and nineteenth centuries were pe-

riods of depression. Even at the best of times, the London economy was seasonal, limited by the weather, port activity, and the social season. London also faced an increasing challenge from the growth of mass manufacturing in the provinces that undermined a number of trades. Some of these responded by leaving. More of them adapted through an expansion of sweating, increasing exploitation of the capital's always large reserve army of labor. Schwarz's London is not "the Athens of the artisan," as E. P. Thompson called it, but a fragmented urban economy in which a small minority of the work force, largely employed in trades catering to the rich, maintained their skills and social position, while the vast majority were proletarianized, confined to trades that relied on casual or sweated labor. This pattern became more pronounced in the nineteenth century, as many established trades adapted to the changing market, but was already present in the eighteenth century. Unlike many recent commentators, Schwarz also sees no fundamental change in women's work. Instead of increasing degradation and economic exclusion, Schwarz depicts women's confinement to certain trades as already well established by the eighteenth century. Women's economic position therefore did not worsen, because it was already limited to begin with.

As a statistical analysis of London's changing demography and economy, Schwarz's study is likely to be unsurpassed for some time. But it leaves considerable room for further consideration of the way these changes affected the people who lived through them and how they made sense of them.

PETER WEILER

Boston College
Chestnut Hill
Massachusetts

UNITED STATES

CHAPLIN, JOYCE E. *An Anxious Pursuit: Agricultural Innovation and Modernity in the Lower South, 1730-1815.* Pp. xiv, 411. Chapel Hill: University of North Carolina Press, 1993. $45.00.

Joyce E. Chaplin's intention in *An Anxious Pursuit* is to write a "cultural history of the early Lower South that uses changes in agriculture to trace the extent to which white inhabitants redefined themselves as a modern people." The result of her endeavors is an innovative work that expands our understanding of the meaning of the term "agricultural history" and that shows many aspects of Southern history in a new and revealing light.

In the first half of the book, Chaplin outlines the way in which the South fitted into the eighteenth-century scheme of things. Individual chapters explicate the role the South played in what we would call political economy; the way in which outsiders, particularly travelers, labeled the region as "exotic" and the consequent gnawing feelings of inadequacy that this instilled in the locals; and the way in which white Southerners created their own work ethic, one that was carefully constructed around the fact that the work was actually done by black slaves. The final chapter in this section looks at the history of agricultural improvements and their complex relationship to expectations about slavery.

Having outlined the context, Chaplin proceeds, in the second part of the book, to analyze the agricultural innovations that transformed the region. Chapters examine the introduction of indigo and cotton, tidal rice cultivation, and the creation of the Cotton South. For me at least, this was the best part of the book. Among other things, Chaplin's accounts of the way tidal cultivation worked, her careful demonstration of the manner in which the Revolution affected the autonomy of the slaves, and even her rewriting of the familiar story of the introduction of cotton are all, in their different ways, substantial contributions to our understanding of Southern history.

A bare summary such as this does very little justice to this book. What impresses most about *An Anxious Pursuit* is both the depth and breadth of Chaplin's understanding, her mastery of material ranging from the thought of relatively obscure Scottish thinkers to the mechanics of flooding a rice field. The book bristles with sharp observations and penetrating insights not only about Southern agriculture but also about the region's culture, the effect and impact of the Revolutionary struggle, and the nature of slavery. It deserves the widest possible readership among those interested in the social, cultural, and intellectual history of the South. Both the author and the press—the book is a very handsome production with a particularly eye-catching dust jacket—are to be congratulated on their achievement.

SHANE WHITE

University of Sydney
New South Wales
Australia

ELY, JOHN HART. *War and Responsibility: Constitutional Lessons of Vietnam and Its Aftermath.* Pp. viii, 244. Princeton, NJ: Princeton University Press, 1993. $24.95.

The war in Vietnam sparked a national debate both over the intent of the framers of the Constitution as to who controlled the war powers in the United States and over who should control the war powers in a cold war era. This debate resulted in the passage, over the veto of

President Nixon, of the War Powers Resolution in 1973, which was designed to reclaim for the Congress some of its war-declaring power, which had eroded, been taken, or been given over time to the presidency.

In this short but compellingly reasoned book, John Hart Ely argues that the congressional effort to regain its constitutional power has essentially failed, in part because the Congress is content to stay in the background and avoid responsibility. The Congress and the courts have, Ely argues, "conceded the ground without a fight. In fact . . . the legislative surrender was a self-interested one: Accountability is pretty frightening stuff."

This, of course, is not what the Founders envisioned. Seeking to "clog" the road to combat, "hoping to slow the process down, to insure that there would be a pause, a 'sober second thought,' before the nation was plunged into anything as momentous as war," the Founders gave the power to declare war to the most deliberative body of government: the Congress. The intent, according to Ely, was very clear: "The debates, and early practice, establish that this meant that all wars, big or small, 'declared' in so many words or not—most weren't, even then—had to be legislatively authorized." Only then was the president, as commander in chief, granted the right to engage in war. In short, "the constitutional strategy was to require more than one set of keys to open the Pandora's box of war."

Did the War Powers Resolution return the United States to the framers' vision? No, argues Ely, and "thanks to a combination of presidential defiance, congressional irresolution, and judicial abstention, the War Powers Resolution has not worked," Ely writes. Ely blames the Congress more than anyone for this failure of law and nerve.

Perhaps Ely's most compelling chapter deals with covert wars (chapter 6). With clarity and sophistication, Ely walks us through a mine field of legal and political nuances, concluding that the same requirements of congressional authorization that apply to war apply to almost all covert operations. Since very few covert operations are, in fact, covert—most are widely known to everyone but the American people because the secrecy enforced is, as Ely comments, "intended to keep *us* in the dark" and not the victim—Ely concludes that "the Constitution requires that 'covert' wars that aren't in fact secret receive congressional authorization."

Ely's fine book should be seen as part of a revival of scholarly commitment to the separation of powers and to the theory of governing that undergirds it. After years of divided government, deadlocked government, and executive branch abuses of power, the scholarly community has rallied to embrace a model of shared, cooperative, and consensus government that has been absent since the Vietnam era. In this sense, Ely's work is quite compatible with other excellent books, such as Harold Koh's *National Security Constitution* and Robert Spitzer's *President and Congress*.

What of the war powers in a post-Cold War world? Ely suggests that we have an opportunity to recommit to the constitutional principles of requiring several keys to open the door to war, and he concludes his book with a revised version of the War Powers Resolution, a version that attempts to correct the many shortcomings of the current resolution.

MICHAEL A. GENOVESE
Loyola Marymount University
Los Angeles
California

GUSTAINIS, J. JUSTIN. *American Rhetoric and the Vietnam War.* Pp. xvii, 169. New York: Praeger, 1993. $45.00.

This book is one of the most recent contributions to the Praeger Series in Political Communication. Established in 1988, the series is currently producing a new book every sixty days. It shows. The research in *American Rhetoric and the Vietnam War* is drawn almost entirely from secondary sources, the analysis often fails to transcend the mundane and intuitively obvious, and the work as a whole is flawed by numerous errors of historical fact and questionable leaps of logical inference.

The book is divided into three separate but unequal sections: "Prowar Rhetoric," "Antiwar Rhetoric," and "The Rhetoric of the Media." In the first section, Justin Gustainis discusses "the domino theory as condensation symbol," "the rhetorical use of the hero myth," "rhetorical dimensions of the Tet offensive," and "Nixon and the silent majority." While all of these topics could conceivably provide interesting starting points for rhetorical analysis, Gustainis damages his credibility by making numerous errors of historical fact. For example, the reader is told that the Truman Doctrine was first articulated "in an April 1947 address." The speech was delivered on 12 March 1947. The reader is further advised that "during the 1950s, China, the most populous nation on Earth, had become a Communist country." Mao prevailed in 1949. We are told that "the Special Forces were in fact organized in 1952 by order of President Eisenhower," which, of course, overlooks the minor detail that Eisenhower was not president in 1952. Such errors of fact—and there are others—seriously undermine not only the credibility of the author but the integrity of an editorial process that allows such blatant errors to survive.

Fortunately, the errors of fact are limited to section 1. Section 2 deals with antiwar rhetoric and is the strongest part of the book, with short chapters on the rhetoric of Daniel Berrigan, *The Port Huron Statement*, the Weathermen, and a concluding chapter, "The Rhetorical Failures of Antiwar Protest." The chapters are so short, however, that Gustainis can give only the briefest sketch of the rhetoric under study. In the Berrigan chapter, for example, he finds "the presence of five consistently recurring rhetorical strategies: support for nonviolence as a protest tactic, a call for others to resist, disdain for the government, disdain for corporations, and religious references." The chapter then provides examples of each strategy. Leaving aside the question of whether "disdain" constitutes a strategy, the chapter is a perfect illustration of the central problem that plagues the work as a whole: the tendency to operate at a very low level of categorization and description, with little effort made to analyze or interpret the rhetoric in light of some overarching theory or paradigm of persuasion. A related problem is the tendency to oversimplify, as when the author conflates anticommunism with McCarthyism.

Section 3 is composed of three chapters, each of which is six or seven pages long. These brief excursions examine the rhetoric of the media as found in *Doonesbury*, four Vietnam war films, and the film *Apocalypse Now*. Since *Apocalypse Now* is also one of the four films discussed in the middle chapter, it is not surprising that the final chapter is highly repetitious, even to the point of repeating whole paragraphs verbatim. The section contributes little to our understanding of mediated rhetoric during the war.

Rhetoric was an important aspect of the Vietnam war. Unfortunately, the reader learns very little about that aspect from this book.

MARTIN J. MEDHURST

Texas A&M University
College Station

HING, BILL ONG. *Making and Remaking Asian America through Immigration Policy, 1850-1990*. Pp. xiv, 340. Stanford, CA: Stanford University Press, 1993. $45.00.

This book is not easy reading, but it is solid and useful. Written by an immigration lawyer turned associate professor of law at Stanford University, it emphasizes the legal side of Asian American history and its social effects from 1850 to 1990. This is a long time to be covered in only 191 pages of actual text, the rest of the book's 390 pages consisting of appendices, footnotes, bibliography, and index. Actually, as the chapter titles reveal, the entire period is by no means covered in the historical time frame indicated in the title. Thus chapter 1, "Two Contrasting Schemes: Understanding Immigration Policies Affecting Asians before and after 1965," sets a chronological framework. Chapter 2 discusses "Asian America prior to 1965." This subdivides into Chinese, Japanese, Filipinos, Koreans, and Asian Indians, with 5-10 pages devoted to each and emphasizing "population, gender ratio, and family formation." The chapter concludes that during this period, Asian Americans "survived the worst [prejudice, exclusion, relocation, and so on] largely through what some might label a decidedly American ingenuity and resilience."

Chapter 3 takes up "social forces unleashed after 1965." This should be read with Appendix B, "How the Immigration System Worked after 1965." Taken together, these show that "Kennedy-inspired" immigration egalitarianism was included in the 1965 immigration law with "unexpected support" from President Johnson, propelled by Johnson's "keen political strategizing."

Whatever the political reasons for the 1965 law, it definitely helped reunite and enlarge Asian American families in the United States by enabling relatives to enter under preference numbers 1, 2, 4, and 5 and to bring in professional, skilled,

and even unskilled Asians working in fields in which there might be a labor shortage in the United States, this under preference numbers 3 and 6. China (Taiwan), Korea, India, and the Philippines quickly filled their immigration quotas, and Japan, though lagging somewhat on immigrants, sent thousands of "temporaries"—businessmen and students.

Chapter 4 is titled "Shaping the Vietnamese American Community: Refugee Law and Policy." In 1975, when the United States withdrew its troops from Vietnam, the number of Vietnamese Americans was negligible. By 1990, there were 614,547. This increase was the result of the U.S. tradition of separating political refugees from immigration quotas and of a so-called seventh preference in the 1965 law whereby "persons fleeing from a Communist dominated country, a country of the Middle East or who were uprooted by a natural catastrophe" could enter without regard to immigration quotas. By 1980, over 400,000 refugees from Southeast Asia had been admitted. In 1980, the seventh preference was replaced by a new refugee act, which somewhat slowed the refugee immigration.

The main message of chapter 5, "Immigration Policy and Asian American Life: Educational Performance, Political Participation, and Identity," is that the Asian American population of the United States is now so diverse that the traditional stereotypes no longer apply. There are rich and poor, educated and uneducated, hardworking and the opposite, and much more inclination for political participation than in earlier history.

Appendix A presents a historical chronology; B, the 1965 law; C, "excerpts from laws and cases" to the 1920s. The appendices are followed by footnotes and a bibliography, both of which are well done.

HILARY CONROY

University of Pennsylvania
Philadelphia

JASSO, GUILLERMINA and MARK R. ROSENZWEIG. *The New Chosen People: Immigrants in the United States.* Pp. xxxv, 460. New York: Russell Sage Foundation, 1991. $49.95.

This excellent study of immigrants in the United States is one of an ambitious, competent, and very sophisticated series, The Population of the United States in the 1980's. It revives a long tradition of scholarship going back to 1930, when "teams of social scientists worked with the U.S. Bureau of the Census to investigate significant social, economic and demographic developments revealed by the decennial censuses."

The Jasso and Rosenzweig monograph uses historical data on immigration and employs highly sophisticated social science methodologies in its analyses. The monograph comes at a particularly appropriate time to examine closely the foreign-born population of the United States, which in 1980 stood at 14.1 million, just a shade below the peak foreign-born population of 14.2 million recorded by the 1930 census. (The United States has continued to have a rapid increase in its immigrant population since 1980.) The foreign-born population in the United States constituted just over 6 percent of the country's population in 1980. The increase in the foreign-born population from 1970 to 1980 was 4.46 million persons, the largest decadal increase since the middle of the nineteenth century. "Moreover, the growth in the foreign-born population accounted for 19.1 percent of the total increase in the U.S. population as a whole between 1970 and 1980, the highest share since the 1900-1910 decade, when the proportion was 19.9 percent."

The focus of this study of the foreign-born in the United States is on the 1960-80 decades. Some attention is paid, however, to comparing this group to the foreign-born of 1900 and 1910 and to the native-born population in both time periods. The study is organized as follows. In chapters 1 through 3, Jasso and Rosenzweig begin with analyzing the relationship between the selection of immigrants and U.S. immigration policy. They briefly review changes in immigration laws and rules in operation since 1965 that affect actual and potential immigrants. They go on to "examine the changes in the educational attainment of the foreign-born population between 1960 and 1980 as manifestations of the selectivity associated with the interactions between immigration law and the decisions of the foreign-born." Next, they examine the ways that changes in immigration laws and origin-country conditions affect the decision of immigrants to naturalize or not. The authors then study the emigration of the foreign-born from the United States and its determinants over time, across country-of-origin groups and observed characteristics of entry cohorts, to study the "polar extremes of immigration, one signifying the ultimate absorption of immigrants into the body of U.S. citizens and the other choice of immigrants not to 'take root.' "

Chapters 4 through 6 are devoted to studying the implications of U.S. immigration law's provisions concerning the family. First, Jasso and Rosenzweig examine their impact on marital migration, that is, immigration made possible when a foreign national marries a U.S. citizen and is successful in obtaining an immigrant visa under the family provisions. This type of admission currently accounts for the largest number of immigrant visas granted by the United States. Then the authors examine the effects of the law's provisions on assimilation, the sex ratios among immigrants, and divorce rates among the foreign-born and among those who are in mixed marriages, that is, marriages between U.S. citizens and the foreign-born. This section of the study also devotes a chapter to family provisions and their implications for the composition of the households of the foreign-born population. Another chapter investigates the ways in which these provisions of the law influence the characteristics, size, and national composition of immigration flows and examines the characteristics of the U.S. citizen sponsors of these immigrants.

The study proceeds to discuss the roles of the immigrants, legal and illegal, in the U.S. economy and the impact immigrants have on the well-being of native-born citizens as workers, consumers, and investors. A chapter is devoted to the English language ability and locational choices of the foreign-born. A special chapter focuses on two major refugee groups, the Cubans and the Indochinese, who were allowed to enter the country under criteria very different from those used for most of the other immigrants. The next chapter of this monograph looks at fertility and schooling among the foreign-born as compared with those among the native-born. The study concludes with an assessment of the impact of the reforms of the immigration law that were enacted from 1965 to 1980 on the 6.3 million immigrants who were admitted as permanent residents to the United States between 1978 and 1988.

The thesis and some of the findings of this excellent monograph are extremely well captured in the authors' own words on the last two pages of their text:

For now, it would appear that current policies represent a particular balancing of objectives. Permitting the numerically unrestricted immigration of immediate relatives simultaneously achieves the goal of unification of immediate families of U.S. citizens and honors the tradition of the country's first 150 years. . . . However, the family-reunification emphasis in selection criteria makes immigration difficult or impossible for many foreign-born persons who might greatly benefit themselves and the United States but who do not possess the requisite U.S. relatives.

. . . Finally, the current immigrant-selection system produces illegal immigrants. However,

so long as more persons wish to immigrate than the United States is officially prepared to accept—an extraordinary acknowledgment of the primordial attractiveness of the political and economic freedoms that characterize this country—there will be illegal immigrants. Indeed, there may be no better testimonial to the relative attractiveness of the United States than the fact that numerous persons prefer life as an illegal alien in the United States to life as a citizen in another country.

As for the specific criteria by which the United States selects its immigrants, it may be that their effect is far outweighed by that of the chief characteristic of immigrants—their above-average willingness to invest in themselves and in their children. The long-run contributions and effects of immigration may be more influenced by the choices made by the foreign-born than by the selection criteria embodied in U.S. immigration laws. (pp. 427-28)

SURINDER K. MEHTA

University of Massachusetts
Amherst

MULLIN, MICHAEL. *Africa in America: Slave Acculturation and Resistance in the American South and the British Caribbean, 1736-1831.* Pp. 412. Champaign: University of Illinois Press, 1992. $37.50.

This book on American slavery focuses on the topic of slave resistance. Michael Mullin's approach is comparative—the book includes the British colonies in North America and the Caribbean—and his conclusions, which reflect considerable research in manuscript sources, attempt a synthesis of knowledge about a phenomenon that has usually been examined in case studies. Most analyses of slave resistance have examined specific plantations, provinces, or episodes of rebellion. Mullin's more ambitious strategy has yielded a curiously disjointed story, but its flaws may be intrinsic to its very subject.

The book describes chronologically the main phases of slave resistance; each stage is correlated with a different phase of African acculturation to British and Anglo-American culture. Slaves' strategies to defy whites' authority altered as the proportion of tribal Africans declined relative to assimilated and Christian slaves. Indeed, Mullin might have titled his book *The Waning of Africa in America*, as his three-part analysis traces the diminishment of African culture—and modes of revolt—and the emergence of a Creole community. Each stage of resistance is well established, but the transition from one to the next is unclear. Mullin fails to analyze the historical development of slave resistance, the processes that lay beneath the visible but perplexing artifacts of slavery.

Two main problems are apparent. First, Mullin emphasizes unity over division, describing how different African tribal groups metamorphosed into Christian Creoles. But the focus on similarity leaves behind nagging evidence of crucial antagonisms within the slave community. The reader wonders why the unities meant more than the divisions, and Mullin never explains this. Second, Mullin tends to use facile dualities in his analysis even as he realizes that his topic defies such simplicity. At the end of one chapter, he denounces "either-or" suppositions (p. 114), yet he takes up such a distinction in the opening sentence of the very next chapter: "Were planters capitalists or medieval seigneurs . . . ?" (p. 115).

Planters were both and neither, just as slaves were both African and American, yet not always similar enough to each other to erase divisions within their ranks. New World slavery was a bewildering pattern of fragmentation and tentative regrouping. Mullin's tentative and fragmented study is, therefore, a metalogue on slavery: the narrative takes on the form of that which it documents. Mullin's insightful portrayal of stages of slave resistance will reward readers; his reluctance to assess slavery's larger contradictions and to posit a method of analyzing them point to areas for future research.

JOYCE E. CHAPLIN

Vanderbilt University
Nashville
Tennessee

WALSH, JOHN R. and GARTH MANGUM. *Labor Struggle in the Post Office: From Selective Lobbying to Collective Bargaining*. Pp. xvi, 271. Armonk, NY: M. E. Sharpe, 1992. $39.95. Paperbound, $19.95.

This labor union history by Walsh and Mangum traces the rise of the American Postal Workers Union and its allies from its origins in the closing days of the 1960s—actually 1970 and 1971—to its present struggles with alternative carriers (like United Parcel Service), alternative communications technologies (fax, electronic mail), and a changing political environment. The success of the American Postal Workers Union and its allies compares favorably to the failure of another public sector union, the Professional Air Traffic Controllers Organization; this theme is mentioned without being systematically explored by the authors.

Instead, Walsh and Mangum present a chronological account of the intra-union struggles, the interunion alliances, and the complex union-government maneuverings that shaped the employment practices of the United States Postal Service. Most of the energy of the union was focused on bread-and-butter wage and benefit issues. Walsh and Mangum mention in passing the relatively highly educated profile of postal workers and, later, the absorption of large numbers of Vietnam veterans into their ranks. They do not examine the race and gender politics of the union, although the selection of photographs that accompanies the text suggests that the integration of women and people from communities of color must have been significant issues at some time. Nor do the authors make much mention of the academic literature about union behavior and union efficacy (beginning with Seymour Martin Lipset's *Union Democracy* and continuing from there). This is primarily a descriptive history, told from the point of view of union leaders.

In order to tell their story, Walsh and Mangum gained access to union officials and to documents, memos, minutes, and photos in the union's possession. The book performs the valuable service of making these documents available to a wider public. In general, the book's strength is to rescue the story of the American Postal Workers Union from the backroom files and fading memories in which it would otherwise have been entombed. It is perhaps both a strength and a weakness that the narrative is presented almost without any authorial agenda beyond recording the facts. The lack of even a policy framework hobbles some of the discussion. For example, the attempt by Bush's postmaster general to transfer postal work from postal workers to Sears employees is lamented but not analyzed. Nevertheless, Walsh and Mangum make a useful contribution to the history of public sector labor unions.

EVE SPANGLER

Boston College
Chestnut Hill
Massachusetts

SOCIOLOGY

BAUM, ALICE S. and DONALD W. BURNES. *A Nation in Denial: The Truth about Homelessness.* Pp. vii, 247. Boulder, CO: Westview Press, 1993. $49.95. Paperbound, $16.95.

In this very readable and provocative book, Alice Baum and Donald Burnes seek to redefine the problem of homelessness. For them, it is not, as the media and some homeless advocates portray, merely a problem of lack of affordable housing. Instead, Baum and Burnes argue that homelessness is rooted in the problems of alcoholism, substance abuse, and mental illness. Most homeless people are not "just like us," the authors assert, and providing shelter does little to solve their basic problems. While the authors present their material in an academic style, they are practitioners, combining the experience of directing a homeless program with that of counseling substance abusers. They reinforce their ideas and arguments with stories of the homeless people they have encountered, and they dedicated this book to them.

Chapter 1 uses statistical evidence to make the point that alcoholism, drug abuse, and mental illness are the real problems of the homeless. America's unwillingness to "blame the victim," according to the authors, is the blinding lens preventing us from seeing that these are the real problems. America, they assert, is in a state of denial (hence the title of the book). In their second chapter, Baum and Burnes use the demographic impact of the post-World War II baby-boom generation to partially explain the dramatic burst of homelessness in the 1980s. In chapter 3, they use the development of an urban underclass also to partially explain the rise in the numbers of homeless. Chapter 4 allows the reader to share a day with a homeless man, and chapter 5 explains the system he has encountered. Chapter 6 gives a short but very interesting review of the history of American homelessness; chapter 7 reviews the politics of homelessness and argues that the philosophy of the 1960s and the mass media were the villains that shifted our view about the homeless problem and caused us, according to the authors, to misdefine it as a problem of lack of housing. In chapter 8, "Causes and Solutions," and chapter 9, titled "The Truth about Homelessness," the authors reject some of the traditional approaches to the homelessness problem and offer their own. Finally, in chapter 10, Baum and Burnes are very specific and provide a practical outline to practitioners in their "call to action," briefly describing some successful programs; they even include cost estimates.

The authors raise an important point, namely, that at least 70 percent of homeless people suffer from problems that shelter alone will not cure, and they are quick to point out that shelters often turn away the needy who suffer the most with behavioral and substance abuse problems. But while it is true that lack of shelter is not the only problem that needs addressing, Baum and Burnes seem to turn this insight, conceptually, into a forced choice for policymakers—either give them a place to sleep or address their real problems.

The authors consider an emphasis on the housing problem to be part of a liberal agenda. In their eagerness to discredit that emphasis, Baum and Burnes seem to be ignoring the seriousness of the shelter problem for the half million or more people who currently live on the streets. Furthermore, their denying that the problem is lack of shelter is, in fact, inconsistent with other parts of their book. Baum and Burnes do an excellent job of explaining how a series of demographic changes, market circumstances, and gov-

ernment policies reduced the number of places to sleep for those who are now homeless. Following are some of their examples. Because of gentrification and urban renewal, skid rows across the country disappeared, and with them, flophouses; also because of urban renewal, there has been, during the last decades, a dramatic decline in the number of single-room occupancy hotels. Furthermore, decriminalizing alcohol removed the jail as a place of shelter for alcoholics, and deinstitutionalizing the mentally ill, without adequately funding mental health centers, dramatically reduced the number of beds for them. All this, coupled with the post-World War II baby boom, created an unmet demand for shelter for the homeless population whom Baum and Burnes describe and with whom they work.

It is the strength of this book that the authors demonstrate that the demand for shelter comes from a heterogeneous group who have a variety of problems and service needs. The book is well documented and well enough written to qualify it as a basic and very readable text on homelessness. It could easily be assigned in an undergraduate public policy course.

ROBERTA ANN JOHNSON

University of San Francisco
California

BOUVIER, LEON F. *Peaceful Invasions: Immigration and Changing America.* Pp. 218. New York: Center for Immigration Studies, 1992. $45.00. Paperbound, $17.50.

Bouvier's volume is bound to spark controversy and reflection as he analyzes the impact on the United States of the renewed massive flow of immigration since 1965. This volume is not merely one more look at the changes brought about by the law of 1965, which opened the door to renewed massive immigration; rather, Bouvier describes the implications, now and into the future, of what he believes to be a series of unanticipated developments—many of them negative.

Bouvier treads a rational middle ground between the liberal scholars and demographers who see the renewed wave of mass immigration as largely an unmitigated success and the neo-Nativists who see the largely non-European immigrant population as a threat to the melting-pot ideal or even a challenge to the basic institutions of American society. He suggests that the United States must recognize the shortcomings of the 1965 legislation while adopting a policy that clearly meets the needs of the country and its native-born citizenry, especially the needs of the unskilled minority populations that increasingly must compete with low-wage immigrant populations. Moreover, he sees an implied threat to America's resolve to retool and prepare for the inevitable needs of a high-tech future in the mass immigration of low-skilled and low-wage immigrants who he believes merely prolong the agony of declining and noncompetitive low-tech industries that inevitably will be displaced. When these are displaced, Bouvier notes, there will be the question of pools of additional low-skilled unemployed left behind.

Bouvier cites a need to view the very real question of recent immigration from a "Nonelite" perspective, which he implies has been largely ignored. He voices special concern that opportunities for upward mobility by native-born Americans—especially blacks—may be lost as they are forced to compete with low-wage immigrants. The example of Los Angeles, where the number of "unionized Black janitors . . . fell from 2,500 in 1977 to 600 in 1985 even though janitorial employment rose 50% because of a boom," is worth assessing. Competing janitorial services "that offered to clean buildings for 25% to 35% less and [that] paid their immigrant workers up to two-thirds less than the prevailing union wages" were a direct and irrefutable cause for the drop in the number of unionized black janitors. Bouvier cites a similar impact on the job situation in luxury hotels in San Francisco, where wage scales remained low and increased only slowly even though hotel facilities expanded rapidly. Given the historical reality that the cessation of mass European migration to the United States in 1914 set the stage for the first great movement of blacks northward and toward upward economic mobility, is there a possibility that renewal of mass immigration, now Asian and Hispanic, likewise has dramatic implications for black America? This needs to be considered seriously.

I am sure that this volume has added a significant dimension to the ongoing discussion of the implications of recent currents in U.S. immigration history. Leon Bouvier's contentions will undoubtedly provoke discussion among advocates of liberal as well as conservative immigration policies.

ROBERT J. YOUNG

West Chester University
Pennsylvania

ECKSTEIN, MAX A. and HAROLD J. NOAH. *Secondary School Examinations: International Perspectives on Policies and Practice.* Pp. xi, 283. New Haven, CT: Yale University Press, 1993. $32.50.

Is it possible to create an examination that offers a final, unimpeachable assessment of a student's academic accomplishments? Educational measurement technology and a call for accountability seem to support a common belief that it is possible to create an examination or a series of examinations to evaluate what a student knows upon exiting secondary school. This kind of examination is called an external examination, the topic of *Secondary School Examinations: International Perspectives on Policies and Practice*. Max A. Eckstein and Harold J. Noah have written a book that will be of interest to a wide audience of policymakers in and out of education as well as K-16 teachers and administrators interested in this controversial issue.

The authors' international comparison focuses on England, Wales, France, the Federal Republic of Germany, Japan, China, the Soviet Union, Sweden, and the United States. They analyze examination politics in each country, offering concluding recommendations that cautiously favor the adoption of external examinations in the United States.

A strength of the book is Eckstein and Noah's portrayal of each country's sociocultural context. They offer evidence as to why the American system of external examinations is weak. In contrast, they show why external examination systems are strong in China, England, Wales, France, Germany, and Japan. Threaded throughout the book is a caveat that each country is different and that, in fact, an examination in national language and literature is more than inert knowledge, more than a representation of a country's beliefs and values. It is curious that, despite their caveat, Eckstein and Noah recommend the implementation of external examinations in the United States. They clearly show that external examinations are not valueless artifacts easily exported across national boundaries. Contrary to their recommendations, it is this very point that signals a warning against adopting external examinations in the United States based on external examination practices elsewhere.

Readers tending to favor the notion of external examinations are likely to argue that this book supports their case: external examinations work reasonably well in countries such as England, Wales, France, Germany, and Japan. Conversely, opponents will be able to cite evidence from the book that would not support implementing external examinations in America: the external examinations in most of these countries are for a small number of elite students, students sorted and selected out throughout their educational experiences. The American school system selects in, a major philosophical difference.

That proponents and opponents of external examinations will be able to utilize this book to undergird their positions speaks to the comprehensiveness and thoughtfulness of Eckstein and Noah's work. The authors conclude with a series of sticky dilemmas sure to provoke continued debate.

AUDREY M. KLEINSASSER
University of Wyoming
Laramie

FUCHS, ESTER R. *Mayors and Money: Fiscal Policy in New York and Chicago*. Pp. xiv, 361. Chicago: University of Chicago Press, 1992. $42.00. Paperbound, $15.95.

STEIN, LANA. *Holding Bureaucrats Accountable: Politicians and Professionals in St. Louis*. Pp. xi, 133. Tuscaloosa: University of Alabama Press, 1991. Paperbound, $19.95.

Mayors and Money examines the causes of urban fiscal problems and the consequences of different remedies by comparing fiscal policymaking processes in Chicago and New York from the 1930s through the 1980s. *Holding Bureaucrats Accountable* explores circumstances that enable elected officials to hold bureaucrats accountable, as the title indicates, by examining personnel practices, basic service delivery, and selected policy areas in St. Louis. Thematically, the two works are similar. Ester R. Fuchs and Lana Stein argue that political explanations are central. Generalizing from their case studies, they criticize progressive reform legacies and public management practices. These erode political parties, strengthen expert administration, enhance interest group power—both special interest and bureaucratic—and weaken political control by elected officials.

Stein's chief hypothesis is that bureaucratic autonomy is relative and its accountability contingent upon factors that vary from city to city. These include the city's size, economic conditions, and workforce; the form of government, its legal authority, and intergovernmental constraints; local political culture and participatory traditions, including race and ethnic relations; and so on. Politicians and bureaucrats can exploit these factors with different degrees of success. For example, disarray among health professionals, unorganized support staff, and a racial divide in St. Louis—two public hospitals serving constituents defined chiefly by race—enabled two mayors facing fiscal constraints to close first one hospital and then the other as well and engineer the privatization of public health services through a nonprofit corporation. On the other hand, willful mayors and aldermen have had difficulty constraining the public safety departments. Since the Civil War era, the state legislature has controlled police funding levels, which the city must meet, and appointments to the Police Board, which selects the chief. This reduces local political accountability and shifts the politics to the state level, where the police union and local business elites exert their influence. Political control over the fire department is problematic due to its politically active union. Fire fighters successfully mobilized grassroots support to secure pay parity with the police, thereby transferring effective control over sala-

ries to the state capital. Stein finds some evidence of local control over police and fire department hiring and promotion practices, but chiefly to the extent mandated by federal courts and federal law.

Beginning with the responses of Chicago and New York to the Great Depression, Ester Fuchs describes their expenditure and revenue trends and their roles vis-à-vis intergovernmental aid and state and federal constraints. Chicago is more fiscally "stable" over time, whereas New York lurches from fiscal instability to fiscal "crisis," with periods of presumed normalcy being merely interludes before instability or crisis returns. Traditional public administration and fiscal management remedies—improved management, balanced budgets, pared debt, cut expenditures, and so forth—provide short-term relief but not long-term fiscal stability; indeed, they may lead to counterproductive decisions in deferring necessary social service and capital expenditures to the future.

Fuchs's principal hypothesis is that fiscal stability is a function of the mayor's ability to centralize and control the budget process. Decisions either to restructure fiscal policy processes or to retain faulty processes and impose fiscal management solutions have cumulative impacts. Stable cities focus on common function or essential services—streets, solid waste, police and fire protection—and effectively divest noncommon function services—education, welfare, public health, mass transit—to state and federal agencies or to quasi-independent authorities. These distinctions reflect constituency differences within the urban area. Essential services are paid through property tax revenues, and costs and revenues are generally in balance. Middle- and upper-middle-class homeowners and business owners—who are the more politically active and influential members of the community—have disproportionate stakes in having these services provided efficiently. On the other hand, noncommon functions, which often produce deficits, tend to benefit lower-income groups, who are less politically active and influential. In periods of fiscal instability or crisis, either these services are cut or alternative sources of revenues are sought. For alternative revenue sources, cities may follow the Chicago model and divest such services to other taxing authorities. Alternatively, they may follow the New York model and expand such services while seeking other revenue sources, among which intergovernmental transfers increase the city's dependency on state and national politics.

The relative success or failure of mayors to control fiscal policy is also a function of inverse relationships between political parties and interest groups. Fuchs's penultimate chapter underscores the significance of responsible political parties, although the theme is implicit throughout. And on this theme, the Fuchs and Stein books converge. Competitive, responsible political parties can enable political leaders to aggregate potentially conflicting interests and resolve budgetary problems or exert leverage over bureaucracies. Conversely, weak parties enable narrow interest groups to exert centrifugal forces on the budget and exert influence through functional bureaucracies. Also, when the local party system is relatively weak, politicians require interest group support to win election and thus they attempt to accommodate interest group demands. In most urban environments today, the latter conditions, not the former, predominate.

One should not conclude that Fuchs and Stein prefer corrupt machines or believe national party models can be superimposed on urban politics. But they do assert that fiscal responsibility and political accountability cannot be achieved if the costs of reform and the limitations of good-management panaceas are not

understood. Reform that weakens parties and unleashes interest group demands sets the stage for fiscal instability and the absence of public accountability. Stein goes so far as to say that accountability is more likely to be present "the more unreformed the city." Perhaps that overstates the matter, but it is in keeping with Fuchs, who concludes, "If fiscal stability is the desired policy objective, then 'bad' machine government appears preferable to 'bad' reform government."

ROBERT C. GRADY

Eastern Michigan University
Ypsilanti

GLICK, HENRY R. *The Right to Die: Policy Innovation and Its Consequences.* New York: Columbia University Press, 1992. Pp. 238. $32.50.

This timely work should be read with interest by professionals in medicine and law and by members of legislative and judicial bodies. The book is based on a careful study of court and legislative proceedings, public opinion polls, and documentation of scientific and mass media articles. Henry Glick's goal is to describe the development of the right-to-die issue from its beginnings in the 1940s, its movement through social and governmental agencies, and the transformation of the right to die into policy.

The book is based on data from case studies of three states considered innovative in their passage of right-to-die and related legislation: California, Florida, and Massachusetts. In addition, selected data on court decisions for all states were examined.

The research compared all 50 states on these issues and looked closely at the politics of the three state cases. Glick was concerned with how agenda setting and innovation occurred in the development of right-to-die issues as well as how national trends influenced states into becoming late adopters.

The book begins with the problem in modern medicine of new technology that enables the sustaining of life for terminally ill and comatose patients but creates a dilemma for health workers who become confused about their roles and targets of liability. Glick traces the origins of this dilemma and provides a helpful overview of the elements of the issue for the benefit of both legal and medical readers. An excellent feature of this book is the clarification of all important concepts associated with right-to-die issues.

The second chapter is basically an explanation of Glick's theoretical approach, consisting of models of agenda setting and innovation. The chapter contains a valuable discussion—especially for lay readers—about "outside and inside" forces that explain how issues move through a process that leads to a government agenda.

In the following chapter, Glick examines the role of publications in medicine. He also reviews legal, religious, and social science journals and mass literature to find the trends from the 1950s to the onset of the right to die as a topic of interest to the wider public. Glick shows how public opinion changed dramatically during the 1980s, a period of widely publicized cases. The publicity is attributed to the Quinlan case and to a rise in political action by the American Medical Association and the President's Commission for the Study of Ethical Problems in Medicine. As a consequence of media effects, there was dramatic change in public support for the right to die, with approval approaching 80 percent by the mid-1980s. In his fourth and fifth chapters, Glick examines judicial innovation at the state level and stresses that right-to-die legislation benefited from the persistence of the courts that made innovative decisions.

Glick concludes with some observations about the right-to-die issue at the national level. What is clear is that there is no agreement between states on right-to-die policy and that federal action has not unified the law. As of 1990, some limited federal policy on the right to die exists, but the federal institutions lag far behind the policies developed by states. The U.S. Supreme Court approved the Missouri Supreme Court's requirement that a patient's wishes regarding medical treatment must be clear and convincing in its decision in the 1990 Cruzan case. In this way, a limited national right-to-die policy was established. The Congress entered the right-to-die issue by its creation of the Patient Self-Determination Act of 1991. This law affects all medical facilities and medical workers; it states that patients have the right to refuse treatment, an issue at the heart of the right-to-die movement.

To Glick, the result of these changes is not a national right-to-die policy; rather, they "will make . . . medical directives more visible and available to many people." Glick notes that, while there are still unsolved problems surrounding this issue, there is a growing consensus on policies that allow patients and their families to participate in decisions on discontinuing treatment and the use of living wills and proxy instruments.

THOMAS S. KORLLOS

Kent State University
Ohio

HANSON, F. ALLAN. *Testing Testing: Social Consequences of the Examined Life*. Pp. ix, 378. Berkeley: University of California Press, 1993. $28.00.

Are you applying for a job? Take a battery of tests. Do you want your daughter to enter kindergarten? Arrange for her to take a test. Do the state police have reason to believe you have been driving and drinking? Take a test. Tests of every description are part of everyday life. Testing is big business in America.

F. Allan Hanson, professor of anthropology at the University of Kansas, emphasizes the pervasiveness of testing for aptitudes, intelligence, academic achievement, truthfulness, and drug use. He documents the origins of these different kinds of tests, describes testing procedures, and shows how tests have acquired a superior, almost magical, prophetic status in our society. Parents come to believe that a Scholastic Aptitude Test result measures in some important way the worth of their child, what can be expected of him or her; employers come to rely on lie detector tests to determine whether a potential employee is likely to be an honest steward of the company's till and stock-in-trade.

A large literature already exists pointing out the fallibility of tests as accurate reporters of our personal characteristics, innate or acquired. This book goes beyond these critiques to claim in persuasive terms that, even if tests report reliably, they are not just passive measuring instruments but, rather, shape and create the very characteristics they are supposed to measure. This is a well-known phenomenon in schooling, where teaching to the test is frequently cited as a danger to be avoided—or, because it may be inevitable, as a challenge to create pedagogically useful tests. Tests, according to Hanson, move remorselessly from measurement of past performance toward attempting to predict future behavior or characteristics.

The power of tests to select, and therefore to create that which they profess to measure, is so great that they sometimes determine life chances in the most literal sense. Parents use

amniocentesis to identify the gender of fetuses, and in some cases, they couple the procedure with abortion if the gender is not to their liking. . . . There can be no more vivid or disturbing example than this of how future-oriented tests, as gate-keepers, may exercise a determining effect on those who are allowed to pass through (p. 291).

Together with a mass of highly relevant information about tests and testing, this book presents a strong, yet always well-controlled, warning about the social consequences of our love affair with tests. The volume can be highly recommended to the lay as well as the professional reader.

HAROLD J. NOAH

Columbia University
New York City

MATSUDA, MARI J., CHARLES R. LAWRENCE III, RICHARD DELGADO, AND KIMBERLÈ WILLIAMS CRENSHAW. *Words That Wound: Critical Race Theory, Assaultive Speech, and the First Amendment.* Pp. viii, 160. Boulder, CO: Westview Press, 1993. $46.50. Paperbound, $15.95.

This book of essays includes three classic contributions from critical race theory to contemporary free-speech debates. The authors, Mari Matsuda, Richard Delgado, and Charles Lawrence III, are major developers of that theory. A previously unpublished essay by Kimberlè Williams Crenshaw adds a gender perspective by challenging hate-speech analyses attentive to race alone. There is a useful introduction by all the authors jointly describing the history and aims of critical race theory, and a brief epilogue by Matsuda and Lawrence on the recent unanimous Supreme Court decision in *R.A.V.* v. *Minnesota*, which overturned a St. Paul ordinance forbidding cross burning and other forms of hate speech.

These essays offer all that is most powerful in recent arguments advocating public regulation of hate speech. They also provide an example of the capacity of every system of belief, including the system entertained by critical race theorists, to defend itself from challenge by becoming logically closed. The authors describe themselves as "outsider law teachers who work at the margins of institutions dominated by white men." But what outsiders—law professors with tenure at Stanford, the University of California at Los Angeles, and the University of Colorado. Moreover, the influential and much cited articles reprinted here were originally published in the *Michigan Law Review*, the *Duke Law Journal*, and the *Harvard Civil Rights-Civil Liberties Law Review*, not in struggling underground rags. There are no coal miners here, no street sweepers, only members in good standing of an elite higher education establishment, claiming warrant not only to speak on behalf of the excluded, as elites often do, but defining themselves as seriously marginalized, their positions of real social and cultural privilege notwithstanding. Why is this important? Because the authors wish to assign or withdraw expressive rights in relation to their definition of social power.

The ambiguity of their notions of social insiderness and outsiderness might be interpreted as suggesting both the flexibility of symbols and the indeterminacy of power, issues at the heart of the problems of race and gender conflict that this collection addresses. Rejecting the traditional philosophical and legal distinction between action and speech as constructed rather than real, these essayists substitute the no less constructed distinction between power and powerlessness. The analyses are often grandly compelling, and many readers who have not previously encountered these arguments will be excited and exhilarated. Others will be more skeptical, for these analyses are not without analytical and moral problems at least as serious as those accorded by their authors to speech-action distinctions.

CAROLYN MARVIN

University of Pennsylvania
Philadelphia

SCHOENHERR, RICHARD A. and LAWRENCE A. YOUNG. *Full Pews, Empty Altars*. Pp. xxii, 437. Madison: University of Wisconsin Press, 1993. $65.00. Paperbound, $19.95.

Schoenherr and Young use standard demographic techniques to examine the decline in the number of Catholic priests as well as a graying of the Catholic clergy. They use a census of priests in 86 dioceses across the United States to document the changes between 1966 and 1984 and to forecast trends to the year 2005.

The basic facts are well known. This study contributes by analyzing the components of population change: recruitment (ordination), migration, resignation ("leaving the priesthood"), retirement, and death. It pays close attention to regional and age-specific differences in these factors and explores how the components have evolved over time.

The authors conclude that the shortage of priests in the United States is due to a continual decrease in the number of ordinations and a high number of resignations. Their forecasts indicate that by 2005, the number of priests in the United States will be about 40 percent lower than it was in 1966, while the Catholic population will have grown about 65 percent.

In light of the authors' demonstration that ordination and resignation rates, in particular, are very different between regions and over time, these forecasts might seem tenuous. Even their optimistic variant, however, shows 26 percent fewer priests. They certainly have shown that without some dramatic change, the shortage of priests will be much more severe in the future.

Schoenherr and Young provide new evidence for a number of well-known phenomena, such as low ordination rates in dioceses with large Hispanic populations. They also uncover a number of statistical regularities with intriguing implications; for instance, they note that dioceses with low rates of recruitment also tend to have high resignation rates. However, they use only demographic variables, such as growth rates of the Catholic population, so they cannot test whether these statistical regularities are due to differences in governance between dioceses.

Most of the book shies away from the big question about the future of the Catholic Church's rule that all ordained priests be celibate males. The latter chapters address the issue briefly and promise us another book with a more thorough examination. The answer is not found in this volume. Instead, this study shows that the Catholic Church cannot maintain its current system. The data show that the staff simply will not exist, and wishful thinking will not produce more priests.

DANIEL A. NUXOLL

Virginia Polytechnic Institute
and State University
Blacksburg

SIEGEL, JACOB S. *A Generation of Change: A Profile of America's Older Population*. Pp. xxxvi, 647. New York: Russell Sage Foundation, 1993. $65.00.

With *A Generation of Change*, Jacob Siegel has developed an invaluable handbook documenting the demographic, social, and economic conditions of the aged from the 1950s to the late 1980s. Drawing from hundreds of sources and data sets, including but not limited to U.S. census data, Siegel systematically examines the changing characteristics of the aged over time, the occasionally stark differences between the aged and other age groups, and the widespread diversity among the aged as a group. In addition to basic demographic reports on race, sex, mobility, morbidity, and mortality, Siegel examines broader issues related to work and retirement, income and wealth, health and longevity, and living arrangements. Each table is carefully documented and clearly articulated; the wraparound text includes concise interpretations of the various trends and characteristics. Siegel and his assistants delve far enough into the literature to provide readers with adequate, albeit brief, summaries of the various explanations for differences related to age, cohort, gender, race, and so on.

As is often the case with demographic data, the material in the handbook is already somewhat dated. Though published in 1993, most of the descriptive data stop with the mid-1980s. Readers may also feel somewhat shortchanged by the final chapter's discussion of the implications of these data. For example, Siegel's passing suggestion that older workers be trained and encouraged to remain vigorous in the labor force well beyond current retirement ages demonstrates an unfamiliarity with studies showing that while much early retirement is voluntary, a significant portion is due to company closings, relocations, or other managerial efforts to forestall recession. Within that context, Siegel's proposal that Social Security benefits be delayed even beyond age 67 may seem unthinkable for marginalized workers who already find waiting until age 65 for benefits problematic.

In any case, *A Generation of Change* is the sort of reference book chock-full of statistics that professors, policymakers, and analysts concerned with old age dream of having at their fingertips. It represents years of conscientious analysis; it is unsurpassed in the literature on aging.

MADONNA HARRINGTON
MEYER

University of Illinois
Urbana-Champaign

ECONOMICS

ENCARNATION, DENNIS J. *Rivals beyond Trade: America versus Japan in Global Competition.* Pp. xviii, 222. Ithaca, NY: Cornell University Press, 1992. $24.95.

HART, JEFFREY A. *Rival Capitalists: International Competitiveness in the United States, Japan, and Western Europe.* Pp. x, 305. Ithaca, NY: Cornell University Press, 1993. $32.95. Paperbound, $16.95.

Despite the similarity in their titles, these two studies approach the issue of international economic competition from quite different perspectives. Jeffrey Hart seeks to identify sources of international competitiveness in the institutional linkages between business, labor, and government, while Dennis Encarnation examines direct foreign investment as a means of market access.

Jeffrey Hart's study, *Rival Capitalists,* seeks to link "state-societal arrangements"—interaction between business, labor, and government institutions—with the level of international competitiveness in Japan, France, the United Kingdom, Germany, and the United States. He compares the role of these institutions from country to country in formulating industrial policies and other government measures to improve the performance of the steel, automobile, and semiconductor industries, which are used as bellwethers of competitiveness. Ger-

many and Japan emerge as the "winners" because of their ability to harness labor-business and state-business partnerships, respectively, as a means of promoting the efficient diffusion of new technologies. Hart concludes that state-societal arrangements in the other countries are largely unsuccessful, due in part to the domination of one group's influence over the others. For example, business has the greatest influence in economic policy in the United States, labor in the United Kingdom, and the state in France, and in each case these countries suffer from the absence of joint commitments to innovation and technological change among societal groups.

Hart provides a useful account of industrial and trade policies in the three industries, as well as the institutional channels and linkages of policymaking in the countries under study. In addition, he rightly emphasizes receptiveness to technological change as a major determinant of international performance in these industries. His conceptual framework suffers, however, from an attempt to link industrial competitiveness in certain products with national competitiveness. In this regard, his choice of steel, automobiles, and semiconductors introduces problems into the analysis. In Europe and the United States at least, steel and automobiles suffered as much from mismanagement as from deficient state-societal arrangements, and their failure to adapt to new technologies can be traced to their insulation from international competition, aided and abetted by trade restrictions.

Furthermore, there is a basic conflict between Hart's approach and an economic analysis of the gains from trade. National competitiveness as an economic concept should properly be measured as the ability of a country to improve its standard of living in a global economy, and in this sense, it is actually improved by allowing industries such as steel to contract, shifting resources to more internationally competitive industries. Steel is in fact declining in each of the countries in Hart's study, indicating a market-driven, welfare-enhancing adjustment to shifting comparative advantage rather than declining national competitiveness.

In *Rivals beyond Trade*, Dennis Encarnation is concerned less with national competitiveness than with the impact of a country's foreign investment environment on market access. His well-documented research shows that local sales by multinationals in a foreign country are typically much higher than the volume of imports from these companies' home country—as long as the control of local operations through majority ownership by the multinational is not restricted. In addition, there is a linkage between trade flows and the presence in the host country of majority-owned subsidiaries, which will engage in intracompany trade with home country suppliers and distributors. The ability to establish a controlling interest in foreign operations thereby emerges as an important means of market access in the host country.

Encarnation focuses on the inability of U.S.-based multinationals to establish majority-owned subsidiaries in Japan. He argues persuasively that there are systematic barriers to foreign majority ownership of Japanese firms, although the barriers are no longer a matter of government policy. Whereas in the early postwar period, capital controls limited foreign ownership, since the late 1960s private restrictions in the form of cross-share holdings, contractual constraints on foreign equity holdings, and keiretsu arrangements have achieved the same result.

Encarnation's hypothesis invites comparison with allegations of informal Japanese trade barriers, and he draws directly from the strategic trade policy literature to suggest that Japan has pursued a conscious "strategic investment policy." However, the notion that Japan has thereby captured economic rents at the expense of foreign countries, as predicted by the strategic trade literature, is dubious at best. If any rents have been transferred, they have probably gone from Japanese consumers to domestic oligopolies, which have taken advantage of a restrictive investment environment to reduce competition.

In light of the private, often informal nature of these investment restrictions, policy recommendations are difficult to formulate. Strategic investment screening by the United States or other countries would be counterproductive, and bilateral dispute settlement would have difficulty addressing unofficial barriers. A more productive path for reform may lie in more aggressive antitrust enforcement and an opening of distribution systems in Japan.

KENT JONES

Babson College
Babson Park
Massachusetts

LEADER, SHELDON. *Freedom of Association: A Study in Labor Law and Political Theory.* Pp. x, 325. New Haven, CT: Yale University Press, 1992. $32.50.

Sheldon Leader, barrister and professor of law at the University of Essex, has written a book that is intellectually challenging and that is concerned with significant issues, such as the rights of workers to associate and to dissociate, the right to strike and the right to refuse to strike, the right of unions to take collective political action and the right of members to refuse to be associated with such action. It displays a familiarity with political theory and labor law in a number of societies—for example, the United Kingdom, France, and the United

States—and a familiarity with supranational arrangements, including the Freedom of Association Committee of the International Labor Organization and the European Court of Human Rights. Despite these commendable qualities, however, I am afraid that all but specialists in labor theory and law will find the book less than satisfactory.

That conclusion is based both on the costs that the nonspecialist reader must pay in terms of closely reading and rereading Leader's arguments and on the payoff in terms of Leader's moderate positions on the dualities he poses and analyzes. It is my experience that when political and social scientists invest much time and thought in following a sophisticated argument, they are most likely to feel rewarded when they are presented with an extreme viewpoint. Leader is the reconciler of viewpoints rather than the defender of extreme positions. This, of course, is not a criticism of Leader but rather of other political and social scientists.

Leader's approach is to look beyond the particulars of labor law in time and space and to, in his phrase, "look at fundamentals." A listing of the variety of opinions on identical issues among national court systems, among courts within national systems, and among judges on the same court supports the fundamentals approach.

For Leader, the problem of the right to freedom of association is at the core of all the other issues reviewed. To begin, freedom of association may be viewed as a derivative right or as an independent right. In the latter case, "it attaches to anything we are permitted singly to do, giving individuals the right to do together what each of them is at liberty to do alone." Although Leader views this right as an independent right, he argues that "it is not best understood as either a purely individual right or a purely collective right."

Almost lost in Leader's argument are a number of exciting insights. For instance, he points out that changes in the nature of work and in the nature of the workforce in industrialized societies have resulted in situations in which sexual, racial, ethnic, and age minority groups as well as part-time and temporary workers find themselves represented by unions that may give priority to the interests of others. It is in this context that Leader raises his qualification on the independent nature of the fundamental right of freedom of association itself. This qualification is that "it cannot be adequately understood or deployed in particular cases save in the light of the more global right to equal treatment."

MARK OROMANER

Hudson County Community
  College
Jersey City
New Jersey

MARTIN, LISA L. *Coercive Cooperation: Explaining Multilateral Economic Sanctions.* Pp. xiii, 299. Princeton, NJ: Princeton University Press, 1992. $39.50.

Lisa Martin's purpose is to identify the conditions under which states are most likely to cooperate in imposing sanctions on a target nation. She uses a two-player model of strategic behavior in which three alternative paths to cooperation are defined. The first is a "coincidence game," in which the dominant strategy for both players is to impose sanctions. This fits the liberal conception of international relations (IR), in which cooperation is viewed as mutually advantageous. A second type of cooperation problem is a "coercion game," in which the equilibrium outcome is unilateral sanctions. To elicit multilateral cooperation, the leading sanctioner must coerce the other by means of issue linkage, side payments, or credible threats or promises. This view is consistent with the realist perspective in IR. A third type of strategic interaction is the classic prisoner's dilemma, in which the dominant strategy for each player is to not sanction, even though this is suboptimal for both. Martin calls this a "coadjustment game," because cooperation must be brought about through mutual policy adjustments.

The game theory analysis suggests a number of hypotheses that are tested in statistical estimation models, using data for 99 episodes of sanctions from 1945 to 1989. In addition to this aggregate analysis, microprocesses of sanctioning behavior are traced in four case studies.

A major empirical finding is that the more costly the sanctions are to the sender, the more likely they are to succeed in producing a cooperative multilateral effort. Self-imposed costs on a leading sanctioner enhance the credibility of that country in its efforts to build an international alliance. Another finding, supportive of the neoliberal-institutionalist school of IR, is that international institutions are crucial in producing cooperation because they facilitate issue linkages and credible commitments. A third finding is that states engage in bandwagon behavior: one state's decision to impose sanctions increases the probability that others will sanction, too. This bandwagon effect is enhanced considerably by the involvement of international institutions. Empirical support for "balancing" behavior—the opposite of bandwagon behavior—is much weaker. A final result is that, contrary to the hegemonic-stability thesis, the United States typically obtains less international cooperation than other countries in its sanctioning efforts, although the degree of cooperation elicited by the United States has increased over time.

This book is required reading for political scientists and economists who study economic sanctions, and it makes an important contribution to the IR literature on cooperation in general.

ANTON D. LOWENBERG

California State University
Northridge

OTHER BOOKS

ADLER, EMANUEL, ed. *The International Practice of Arms Control.* Pp. xiv, 287. Baltimore, MD: Johns Hopkins University Press, 1993. $42.50. Paperbound, $14.95.

ALEXANDER, ROBERT J. *The ABC Presidents: Conversations and Correspondence with the Presidents of Argentina, Brazil, and Chile.* Pp. xi, 321. Westport, CT: Greenwood Press, 1992. $45.00.

ALPERT, GEOFFREY and LORIE A. FRIDELL. *Police Vehicles and Firearms: Instruments of Deadly Force.* Pp. viii, 167. Prospect Heights, IL: Waveland Press, 1992. Paperbound, $9.95.

ATHENS, LONNIE H. *The Creation of Dangerous Violent Criminals.* Pp. x, 109. Champaign: University of Illinois Press, 1992. $22.95. Paperbound, $11.95.

ATTFIELD, ROBIN and BARRY WILKINS, eds. *International Justice and the Third World.* Pp. ix, 207. New York: Routledge, Chapman & Hall, 1992. $69.95. Paperbound, $16.95.

AYUBI, NAZIH. *Political Islam: Religion and Politics in the Arab World.* Pp. xi, 291. New York: Routledge, Chapman & Hall, 1991. $59.95.

BAKER, RICHARD W. and GARY R. HAWKE, eds. *Anzus Economics: Economic Trends and Relations among Australia, New Zealand, and the United States.* Pp. xii, 262. Westport, CT: Greenwood Press, 1992. $49.95.

BARRY, DONALD D., ed. *Toward the "Rule of Law" in Russia: Political and Legal Reform in the Transition Period.* Pp. xxv, 402. Armonk, NY: M. E. Sharpe, 1992. $90.00.

BATES, TIMOTHY. *Major Studies of Minority Business: A Bibliographic Review.* Pp. 143. Lanham, MD: Joint Center for Political Economic Studies, 1992. Distributed by University Press of America, Lanham, MD. $34.50.

BEN-DAVID, JOSEPH. *Centers of Learning: Britain, France, Germany, United States.* Pp. xviii, 208. New Brunswick, NJ: Transaction, 1992. Paperbound, $19.95.

BERSHADY, HAROLD J., ed. *Max Scheler: On Feeling, Knowing, and Valuing.* Pp. vii, 270. Chicago: University of Chicago Press, 1992. $41.00. Paperbound, $15.00.

BLISS, ROBERT M. *Revolution and Empire: English Politics and the American Colonies in the Seventeenth Century.* Pp. xi, 300. New York: St. Martin's Press, 1990. $79.95.

BOWMAN, GARY W. et al., eds. *Privatizing Correctional Institutions.* Pp. xi, 246. New Brunswick, NJ: Transaction, 1992. $34.95.

BROADBERRY, S. N. and N.F.R. CRAFTS, eds. *Britain in the International Economy 1870-1939.* Pp. xiv, 426. New York: Cambridge University Press, 1992. $64.95.

BROWN, WEIR M. *Bank Lending to Business Borrowers: Interest Rates and U.S. Monetary Policy.* Pp. xiii, 185. Boulder, CO: Westview Press, 1992. Paperbound, $34.95.

BUCHANAN, ALLEN. *Secession: The Morality of Political Divorce from Fort Sumter to Lithuania and Quebec.* Pp. xviii, 174. Boulder, CO: Westview Press, 1991. $38.50. Paperbound, $14.95.

CAMPBELL, JOAN, ed. *European Labor Unions.* Pp. xvii, 648. Westport, CT: Greenwood Press, 1992. $125.00.

CAMPO, JUAN EDUARDO. *The Other Sides of Paradise: Explorations into the Religious Meanings of Domestic Space in Islam.* Pp. xvi, 246. Columbia: University of South Carolina Press, 1991. $49.95.

CATANZARITI, JOHN, ed. *The Papers of Thomas Jefferson.* Vol. 25, *January 1793-May 1793.* Pp. xliii, 773. Princeton, NJ: Princeton University Press, 1993. $65.00.

CAVES, ROGER W. *Land Use Planning: The Ballot Box Revolution.* Pp. xiii,

247. Newbury Park, CA: Sage, 1991. $45.00. Paperbound, $19.95.

CHANDLER, DAVID P. *Brother Number One: A Political Biography of Pol Pot.* Pp. xiv, 254. Boulder, CO: Westview Press, 1992. $24.95.

COPETAS, A. CRAIG. *Bear Hunting with the Politburo: The Real Story of Doing Business in the New Russia.* Pp. 282. New York: Simon & Schuster, 1993. Paperbound, $11.00.

CRABB, CECIL V. and KEVIN V. MUL-CAHY. *American National Security: A Presidential Perspective.* Pp. xvi, 208. Pacific Grove, CA: Brooks/Cole, 1991. Paperbound, $17.75.

CROLY, HERBERT. *The Promise of American Life.* Pp. xxxviii, 468. New Brunswick, NJ: Transaction, 1992. Paperbound, $24.95.

CRUSH, JONATHAN et al. *South Africa's Labor Empire: A History of Black Migrancy to the Gold Mines.* Pp. xvi, 266. Boulder, CO: Westview Press, 1991. $39.95.

CULLEN, J. *The Orchid Book: A Guide to the Identification of Cultivated Orchid Species.* Pp. xxvi, 529. New York: Cambridge University Press, 1992. No price.

CUTHBERTSON, IAN M., ed. *Redefining the CSCE: Challenges and Opportunities in the New Europe.* Pp. xiii, 307. Boulder, CO: Westview Press, 1992. Paperbound, $28.85.

DANZIGER, SHELDON and PETER GOTTSCHALK, eds. *Uneven Tides: Rising Inequality in America.* Pp. x, 287. New York: Russell Sage Foundation, 1993. $29.95.

DERBYSHIRE, IAN. *Politics in China: From Mao to the Post-Deng Era.* Pp. 212. New York: Chambers Kingfisher Graham, 1992. Paperbound, $14.95.

DERBYSHIRE, IAN. *Politics in France: From Giscard to Mitterrand.* Pp. ix, 229. New York: Chambers Kingfisher Graham, 1992. Paperbound, $14.95.

DERBYSHIRE, IAN. *Politics in Germany: From Division to Unification.* Pp. 310. New York: Chambers Kingfisher Graham, 1992. Paperbound, $14.95.

DERBYSHIRE, J. DENIS and IAN DERBYSHIRE. *Spotlight on World Political Systems: An Introduction to Comparative Government.* Pp. xiii, 249. New York: Chambers Kingfisher Graham, 1992. Paperbound, $14.95.

ELLICKSON, ROBERT C. *Order without Law: How Neighbors Settle Disputes.* Pp. ix, 302. Cambridge, MA: Harvard University Press, 1991. $39.95.

FATTON, ROBERT, JR. *Predatory Rule: State and Civil Society in Africa.* Pp. viii, 165. Boulder, CO: Lynne Rienner, 1992. $30.00.

FERRARO, JOSEPH. *Freedom and Determination in History According to Marx and Engels.* Pp. 222. New York: Monthly Review Press, 1993. $38.00. Paperbound, $18.00.

FRANKLAND, E. GENE and DONALD SCHOONMAKER. *Between Protest and Power: The Green Party in Germany.* Pp. xiv, 257. Boulder, CO: Westview Press, 1992. $52.95. Paperbound, $18.95.

FULLER, GRAHAM E. *The Democracy Trap: Perils of the Post-Cold War World.* Pp. x, 285. New York: Dutton, 1992. $19.95.

GALLMAN, ROBERT E. and JOHN JOSEPH WALLIS, eds. *American Economic Growth and Standards of Living before the Civil War.* Pp. viii, 396. Chicago: University of Chicago Press, 1992. No price.

GEBHARDT, JURGEN. *Americanism: Revolutionary Order and Societal Self-Interpretation in the American Republic.* Pp. xi, 359. Baton Rouge: Louisiana State University Press, 1993. $45.00.

GOODMAN, LOUIS W. et al. *Political Parties and Democracy in Central America*. Pp. xiii, 407. Boulder, CO: Westview Press, 1992. $49.95. Paperbound, $17.95.

GOULD, LEWIS L. *The Presidency of Theodore Roosevelt*. Pp. xii, 355. Lawrence: University Press of Kansas, 1991. $29.95. Paperbound, $14.95.

HARIK, ILIYA and DENIS J. SULLI-VAN, eds. *Privatization and Liberalization in the Middle East*. Pp. vi, 242. Bloomington: Indiana University Press, 1992. $35.00. Paperbound, $14.95.

HEADLEE, SUE. *The Political Economy of the Family Farm: The Agrarian Roots of American Capitalism*. Pp. xii, 212. New York: Praeger, 1991. $42.95.

HERBST, JEFFREY. *U.S. Economic Policy toward Africa*. Pp. v, 82. New York: Council on Foreign Relations Press, 1993. Paperbound, $12.95.

HOWE, CAROLYN. *Political Ideology and Class Formation: A Study of the Middle Class*. Pp. xiv, 195. Westport, CT: Greenwood Press, 1992. $42.95.

HOYLES, MARTIN. *The Story of Gardening*. Pp. 313. Boulder, CO: Westview Press, 1992. $19.95.

HUMANA, CHARLES. *World Human Rights Guide*. 3d ed. Pp. xix, 393. New York: Oxford University Press, 1992. $35.00.

INGRAHAM, PATRICIA W. and DAVID H. ROSENBLOOM, eds. *The Promise and Paradox of Civil Service Reform*. Pp. x, 329. Pittsburgh, PA: University of Pittsburgh Press, 1992. $39.95. Paperbound, $18.95.

JACOBS, MARK D. *Screwing the System and Making It Work*. Pp. viii, 296. Chicago: University of Chicago Press, 1990. No price.

KAHN, PAUL W. *Legitimacy and History: Self-Government in American Constitutional Theory*. Pp. xi, 260. New Haven, CT: Yale University Press, 1993. $27.50.

KAMRAVA, MEHRAN. *Revolutionary Politics*. Pp. x, 164. New York: Praeger, 1992. $39.95.

KANTH, RAJANI. *Capitalism and Social Theory: The Science of Black Holes*. Pp. xxi, 227. Armonk, NY: M. E. Sharpe, 1992. $49.95. Paperbound, $19.95.

KATZ, MICHAEL B., ed. *The "Underclass" Debate: Views from History*. Pp. viii, 507. Princeton, NJ: Princeton University Press, 1993. $59.50. Paperbound, $16.95.

KENNAN, GEORGE F. *Around the Cragged Hill: A Personal and Political Philosophy*. Pp. 272. New York: Norton, 1993. $22.95.

KEREN, MICHAEL and GUR OFER, eds. *Trials of Transition: Economic Reform in the Former Communist Bloc*. Pp. xx, 308. Boulder, CO: Westview Press, 1992. $44.95. Paperbound, $17.95.

KOELBLE, THOMAS A. *The Left Unraveled: Social Democracy and the New Left Challenge*. Pp. xii, 162. Durham, NC: Duke University Press, 1991. $34.95.

KOVES, ANDRAS. *Central and East European Economies in Transition: The International Dimension*. Pp. xi, 150. Boulder, CO: Westview Press, 1992. $49.00. Paperbound, $17.95.

LAFEBER, WALTER. *Inevitable Revolutions: The United States in Central America*. 2d ed. Pp. xi, 452. New York: Norton, 1993. $22.95. Paperbound, $12.95.

LEMAY, J. A. LEO. *Did Pocahontas Save Captain John Smith?* Pp. xx, 144. Athens: University of Georgia Press, 1993. $22.50.

LEVIT, GEOFFREY M. *Democracies against Terror: The Western Response to State-Supported Terrorism*. Pp. xiv, 142. New York: Praeger, 1988. $32.95. Paperbound, $9.95.

LEVY, MARION J., JR. *Maternal Influence: The Search for Social Universals.* Pp. xxix, 255. New Brunswick, NJ: Transaction, 1992. Paperbound, $18.95.

LOEWENSTEIN, GEORGE and JON ELSTER, eds. *Choice over Time.* Pp. xxiv, 399. New York: Russell Sage Foundation, 1992. $39.95.

MACLEAN, ELIZABETH KIMBALL. *Joseph E. Davies: Envoy to the Soviets.* Pp. xii, 247. Westport, CT: Greenwood Press, 1992. $47.95.

MADDISON, ANGUS. *The Political Economy of Poverty, Equity, and Growth.* Pp. xiv, 248. New York: Oxford University Press, 1992. $27.95.

MARTIN, CURTIS H. and BRUCE STRONACH. *Politics East and West: A Comparison of Japanese and British Political Culture.* Pp. xvi, 335. Armonk, NY: M. E. Sharpe, 1992. $49.95. Paperbound, $16.95.

MASUGI, KEN, ed. *Interpreting Tocqueville's Democracy in America.* Pp. xxii, 526. Savage, MD: Rowman & Littlefield, 1991. $62.50. Paperbound, $24.95.

MERELMAN, RICHARD M., ed. *Language, Symbolism, and Politics.* Pp. vii, 310. Boulder, CO: Westview Press, 1992. $49.95.

MITCHELL, WILLIAM P. *Peasants on the Edge: Crop, Cult, and Crisis in the Andes.* Pp. x, 264. Austin: University of Texas Press, 1991. $30.00.

MONSMA, STEPHEN V. *Positive Neutrality: Letting Religious Freedom Ring.* Pp. xiv, 277. Westport, CT: Greenwood Press, 1992. $49.95.

MOOCK, JOYCE LEWINGER and ROBERT E. RHOADES, eds. *Diversity, Farmer Knowledge, and Sustainability.* Pp. xii, 278. Ithaca, NY: Cornell University Press, 1992. $49.95. Paperbound, $18.95.

MORRIS, CHRIS and JANET MORRIS. *The American Warrior.* Pp. xiv, 271. Stamford, CT: Longmeadow Press, 1992. $18.95.

MURPHY, JOHN W. and DENNIS L. PECK, eds. *Open Institutions: The Hope for Democracy.* Pp. viii, 201. Westport, CT: Greenwood Press, 1992. $49.95.

NAVIAS, MARTIN S. *Nuclear Weapons and British Strategic Planning 1955-1958.* Pp. 269. New York: Oxford University Press, 1991. $59.00.

NEUMAN, W. RUSSELL et al. *Common Knowledge: News and the Construction of Political Meaning.* Pp. xvii, 172. Chicago: University of Chicago Press, 1992. Paperbound, no price.

NEWMAN, SANDRA J. and ANN B. SCHNARE. *Beyond Bricks and Mortar: Reexamining the Purpose and Effects of Housing Assistance.* Pp. x, 149. Lanham, MD: Urban Institute Press, 1992. Distributed by University Press of America, Lanham, MD. $46.50. Paperbound, $18.50.

NUGENT, MARGARET LATUS, ed. *From Leninism to Freedom: The Challenges of Democratization.* Pp. x, 292. Boulder, CO: Westview Press, 1992. Paperbound, $39.95.

OBERSCHALL, ANTHONY. *Social Movements: Ideologies, Interests, and Identities.* Pp. x, 402. New Brunswick, NJ: Transaction, 1992. $39.95.

OSBORNE, DAVID and TED GAEBLER. *Reinventing Government: How the Entrepreneurial Spirit is Transforming the Public Sector.* Pp. xxii, 405. New York: Plume, 1993. Paperbound, $13.00.

PACELLE, RICHARD L., JR. *The Transformation of the Supreme Court's Agenda: From the New Deal to the Reagan Administration.* Pp. xv, 264. Boulder, CO: Westview Press, 1991. $39.95.

PHILLIPS, ANNE. *Engendering Democracy.* Pp. 183. University Park: Pennsylvania State University Press, 1991. $28.50. Paperbound, $13.95.

PLESTINA, DIJANA. *Regional Development in Communist Yugoslavia: Success, Failure, and Consequences.*

Pp. xxix, 223. Boulder, CO: Westview Press, 1992. $38.00.

QINGSHAN, TAN. *The Making of U.S. China Policy: From Normalization to the Post-Cold War Era.* Pp. xii, 178. Boulder, CO: Lynne Rienner, 1992. $32.00. Paperbound, $16.95.

RAAT, W. DIRK. *Mexico and the United States: Ambivalent Vistas.* Pp. xv, 277. Athens: University of Georgia Press, 1992. $45.00. Paperbound, $18.50.

SA'ADAH, ANNE. *The Shaping of Liberal Politics in Revolutionary France: A Comparative Perspective.* Pp. xiv, 248. Princeton, NJ: Princeton University Press, 1990. $32.50.

SCHALK, DAVID L. *War and the Ivory Tower: Algeria and Vietnam.* Pp. x, 258. New York: Oxford University Press, 1991. $24.95.

SEROKA, JIM and VUKASIN PAVLOVIC, eds. *The Tragedy of Yugoslavia: The Failure of Democratic Transformation.* Pp. xiii, 207. Armonk, NY: M. E. Sharpe, 1993. $39.95.

SHANNON, LYLE W. *Changing Patterns of Delinquency and Crime: A Longitudinal Study in Racine.* Pp. xi, 174. Boulder, CO: Westview Press, 1991. Paperbound, $27.50.

SLAPIKOFF, SAUL A. *Consider and Hear Me: Voices from Palestine and Israel.* Pp. xii, 263. Philadelphia: Temple University Press, 1993. $34.95. Paperbound, $16.95.

SMITH, BRIAN H. *More than Altruism: The Politics of Private Foreign Aid.* Pp. xxi, 352. Princeton, NJ: Princeton University Press, 1990. $37.50.

SMITH, DALE L. and JAMES LEE RAY, eds. *The 1992 Project and the Future of Integration in Europe.* Pp. xv, 236. Armonk, NY: M. E. Sharpe, 1992. $45.00. Paperbound, $17.50.

SNOWBALL, DAVID. *Continuity and Change in the Rhetoric of the Moral Majority.* Pp. xiv, 181. New York: Praeger, 1991. $39.95.

STEDMAN, STEPHEN JOHN, ed. *Botswana: The Political Economy of Democratic Development.* Pp. ix, 214. Boulder, CO: Lynne Rienner, 1993. $35.00.

STREET, JOHN. *Politics and Technology.* Pp. viii, 212. New York: Guilford Press, 1992. $40.00. Paperbound, $14.95.

TAVUCHIS, NICHOLAS. *Mea Culpa: A Sociology of Apology and Reconciliation.* Pp. ix, 165. Stanford, CA: Stanford University Press, 1991. $29.50.

TAYLOR, BRON RAYMOND. *Affirmative Action at Work: Law, Politics, and Ethics.* Pp. xvii, 251. Pittsburgh, PA: University of Pittsburgh Press, 1991. $29.95. Paperbound, $14.95.

TORDOFF, WILLIAM. *Government and Politics in Africa.* 2d ed. Pp. xvii, 340. Bloomington: Indiana University Press, 1993. $35.00. Paperbound, $14.95.

TULCHIN, JOSEPH S., ed. *Venezuela in the Wake of Radical Reform.* Pp. viii, 183. Boulder, CO: Lynne Rienner, 1993. Paperbound, $9.95.

TYACK, DAVID and ELISABETH HANSOT. *Learning Together: A History of Coeducation in American Public Schools.* Pp. x, 369. New York: Russell Sage Foundation, 1992. Paperbound, $14.95.

VAN SCHENDEL, WILLEM. *Three Deltas: Accumulation and Poverty in Rural Burma, Bengal and South India.* Pp. 344. Newbury Park, CA: Sage, 1991. $35.00.

VAUGHAN, MEGAN. *Curing Their Ills: Colonial Power and African Illness.* Pp. xii, 224. Stanford, CA: Stanford University Press, 1991. $37.50. Paperbound, $12.95.

INDEX

SOCIAL JUSTICE

On Resistance, Rights, and Justice

Vol. 19, No. 3

This issue explores the interplay between ascendant political movements and the institutionalization of their demands for justice once a new society is constructed. Violations of human rights are viewed internationally and domestically, with emphasis on the balance between political rights on the one hand and social and economic rights on the other.

Social Justice
P.O. Box 40601
San Francisco, CA 94140

Individual Copies: $12
1-year subscription: $30 (4 issues)
Institutions: $75 per year
Add $4.00 for mailing outside the U.S.

Is This What Your 16-Year-Old Daughter Looked Like The Last Time You Bought Insurance?

Yes, it really has been that long. A lot of things have changed since then. The size of your family. Maybe your job. And more than likely, the amount and types of insurance coverage you need. That's why it's important to have coverage that can easily adapt to the way your life changes—AAPSS Group Insurance Program.

We Understand You.

Finding an insurance program that's right for you isn't easy. But as a member of AAPSS, you don't have to go through the difficult task of looking for the right plans—we've done that work for you. What's more, the program is constantly being evaluated to better meet the needs of our members.

We're Flexible.

Updating your insurance doesn't have to be a hassle. With our plans, as your needs change, so can your coverage.

Insurance through your association is designed to grow with you—it even moves with you when you change jobs.

We're Affordable.

We offer members the additional benefit of reasonable rates, negotiated using our group purchasing power. Call 1 800 424-9883 (in Washington, DC, (202) 457-6820) between 8:30 a.m. and 5:30 p.m. Eastern Time for more information about these insurance plans offered through AAPSS:

Term Life • Excess Major Medical • In-Hospital • High-Limit Accident • Medicare Supplement

AAPSS Insurance

Designed for the way you live today. And tomorrow.

"When this project was initially conceived, the editors were struck by the extent to which contemporary comparative political scientists had ignored these developments. No article even remotely touching on the topics of courts, judges, or constitutions, for example, had ever appeared in the leading fora of the field, Comparative Politics *and* Comparative Political Studies.*"* — Martin Shapiro and Alec Stone,
Guest Editors

THE NEW CONSTITUTIONAL POLITICS OF EUROPE

Edited by Martin Shapiro, *UC Berkeley* and Alec Stone, *UC Irvine*

Long considered a North American anomaly, constitutional judicial review is today a global phenomenon. Since 1945, Japan, India, the Philippines, Turkey, and more than a dozen polities in Western Europe and Latin America have established or reestablished constitutional courts with review powers, that is, the power to declare legislative enactments and administrative rules invalid on the grounds that they violate constitutional norms. The post-regimes in the Czech Republic, Hungary, Poland, Slovakia, and Russia will likely provide for the same.

This Special Issue of **Comparative Political Studies** focuses on the politics of constitutional review in Western Europe. European courts are striking down laws and administrative actions. European governments, parliaments, and administrators interact differently as a result of this judicial activity. The language, the style, and the outcomes of European policy processes are now different from what they would have been in the absence of constitutional review.

With this volume, **Comparative Political Studies** contributes to a general rediscovery of courts through comparative studies and evaluates the impact of European courts on their institutional and policymaking environments.

Comparative Political Studies
Volume 26, Number 4 / January 1994 / (203104)
Single issue price: Individual $15 / Institution $37

 SAGE PUBLICATIONS, INC • **2455 Teller Road** • **Thousand Oaks, CA 91320**